Light in the Far East

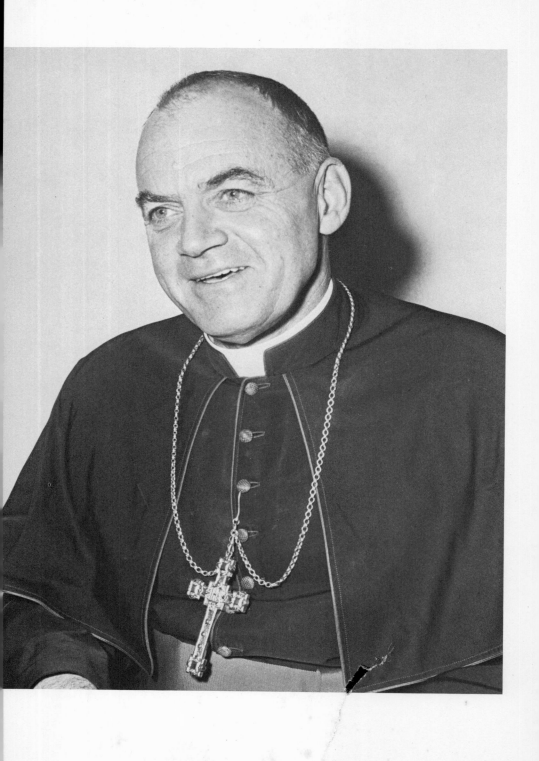

LIGHT IN THE FAR EAST

Archbishop Harold Henry's Forty-Two Years in Korea

EDWARD FISCHER

WITH A PREFACE BY ARCHBISHOP FULTON J. SHEEN

A CROSSROAD BOOK

The Seabury Press / New York

The Seabury Press
815 Second Avenue
New York, N.Y. 10017

Printed in the United States of America

Library of Congress Cataloging In Publication Data

Fischer, Edward.   Light in the Far East.

"A Crossroad book."
1. Henry, Harold, 1909–   2. Missions—Korea. I. Title.
BV3462.H38F57   266'.2'0924 [B]   76–22466
ISBN 0–8164–0307–4

To the benefactors

who made possible

Harold Henry's work

in Korea

this book is dedicated

CONTENTS

PREFACE

THE pendulum of life for most men swings in a narrow orbit. Only few have been arrested and imprisoned by the Japanese for no other crime than that of being an American, and at another moment of life have been a chaplain under General Patton in the muck and mud of the Battle of the Bulge.

How many have moved spiritually, like Paul, from a point of hate on the road to Damascus to a love of Christ in a Roman prison, unless it be the hero of this book who, as a boy, deliberately walked on the opposite side of the street when passing a Catholic church in Northfield, Minnesota; then as a young man entered that same church to celebrate his first solemn Mass as a priest?

How many in their lives have deprecated building—Harold Henry said that there are three ways to tempt a priest: liquor, women, and the construction of a church where one hopes to find final rest—and at the same time built forty-six churches, one hundred chapels, a hospital, three clinics, a major seminary, a retreat house, nine high schools, a kindergarten, and many leper colonies?

Who in a lifetime has had the experience of being expelled from a country by the Japanese in an old ship bound for Africa, being trailed by an American submarine to prevent sabotage?

Who could ever find a more fitting climax to the life of a man who founded a leper colony—where he led over 300 of the sick every day to make a Holy Hour before the Eucharistic Lord—than his own death before the Blessed Sacrament, the vestibule of heaven?

This book is the story of a missionary whose life explains why the Resurrected life kept the imprint of nails: to manifest to the world a stooping love, a bending love, a kenotic love.

† Fulton J. Sheen
Titular Archbishop of Newport

Light in the Far East

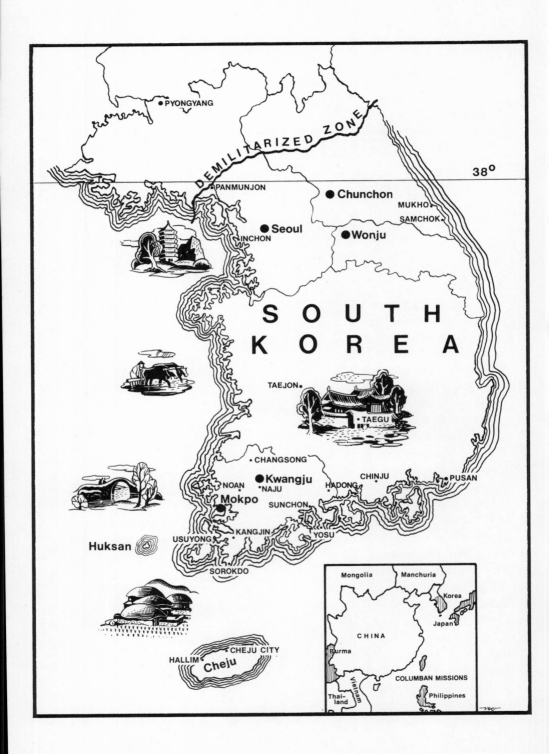

PYONGYANG

DEMILITARIZED ZONE

38°

PANMUNJON

● Chunchon

MUKHO

SAMCHOK

● Seoul

INCHON

● Wonju

S O U T H

K O R E A

TAEJON

● TAEGU

● CHANGSONG

● Kwangju

CHINJU

● PUSAN

NOAN

HADONG

● NAJU

● Mokpo

SUNCHON

Huksan

USUYONG

KANGJIN

YOSU

SOROKDO

● CHEJU CITY

HALLIM

Cheju

Mongolia   Manchuria

Korea

CHINA

Japan

Burma

COLUMBAN MISSIONS

Thai-
land

Vietnam

Philippines

CHAPTER

I

The Lure of China

WHILE a Japanese guard lolled outside the door, a young American priest in the crowded cell stared into the cold Korean night and dreamt of home. He recalled how he had been baptized while wearing a baseball uniform. He could still hear the tremulous piano in his father's movie house, as William S. Hart rode off into the sunset. And there was his father coming down the street in the town's first automobile, and the little girl next door running into the house yelling, "He's driving a buggy without a horse!"

Now, at thirty-two, Harold Henry was old enough to realize that the life he had taken for granted as ordinary was not so ordinary after all. He wondered if other unusual years lay ahead, or did the Japanese have different plans. He would have felt more at ease had he foreseen the long series of surprises stretching well into the future.

Harold Henry's life suggests that there is truth in the Greek philosopher's observation: Your character is your fate. At the core of Harold Henry's character was his instant response to any problem: "No sweat!" Fate, as though trying to test his attitude, and determined to break it down, confronted him with problem after problem, a recurring motif in his life.

Even as a boy he lived larger than life, leaping over improbabilities as though they were not there. Surely no future archbishop ever became a Catholic in a more improbable way.

When Harold was born, July 11, 1909, in Northfield, Minnesota, his father, Frank Henry, and his mother, the former Minerva Suess, were both Protestants. The baby was baptized in the Moravian Church but had the experience of several religions in his early years.

"We moved around quite a bit when I was young," Archbishop Henry explained. "We lived in various small towns in southern Minnesota, but my parents always found a church and insisted that we children attend Sunday school. I attended all kinds of services—Methodist, Episcopal, Presbyterian, Lutheran, Baptist, and others."

Minerva Suess Henry died suddenly when Harold was ten, Mary, seven, and Robert, four. The three children lived with relatives until a year later when Frank married a widow, a Catholic with three grown daughters.

His father changed occupations so often that Harold attended seven public schools in the six years from 1915 until 1921. His stepsister Isabel said he ought to quit flitting from school to school and settle down at St. Stephen's, a parochial school in Minneapolis. She made the idea attractive by saying that he could play football. Years later Archbishop Henry observed that Isabel must have had her fingers crossed because he found no football there, but only a great deal of religion for which he was unprepared.

He entered St. Stephen's on condition that he would not have to become a Catholic. Recalling that time, he said: "I believed that Catholic priests had sinister powers and could put the 'double wammie' on me. In Northfield I used to cross the street when passing St. Dominic's, the very church where I eventually said my first Solemn Mass."

He wasn't asked to join the Church at St. Stephen's, but he did have to study religion along with the other children. On the first day of school Sister Mary gave him a catechism and said that if he wanted to catch up with the class he should memorize the Our Father, the Hail Mary, and the Apostles' Creed. The Our Father posed no problem for a Protestant boy, but the Hail Mary and the Apostles' Creed kept him up until two in the morning. The next day he recited the prayers proudly, proving he had overcome what had seemed an impossible task the previous afternoon. Sister Mary was so impressed she gave him several more prayers to memorize.

On that day St. Stephen's was not his favorite place, but he remembered it with some affection seventeen years later, when he responded to a gift of eighty dollars that the pupils of St. Stephen's had sent to help his Korean parish.

Why did young Harold Henry become a Catholic? What was the turning point? The archbishop said: "It came a few months after I entered St. Stephen's. One morning Father Ellerbusch was explaining about Our Lord in the Blessed Sacrament. That hit me hard because I had been led to understand that Catholics did not believe in Our Lord, only in the Blessed Virgin Mary. When the thought struck me that I had been wrongly informed, I decided to find out about the Catholic Church for myself. I studied the Baltimore Catechism and Bible history during recess. Although we were supposed to be outside running off energy, Sister Mary looked the other way when I stayed inside to read."

Harold was ready to make his First Communion in May, but first he had to be baptized. On Friday morning, May 12, 1922, Sister Mary told the boy he should go over to church during the lunch hour so that Father Gaughan might baptize him. She ignored the fact that Harold was wearing a baseball uniform and spikes, for she knew as well as he did that St. Stephen's was playing a game that afternoon. Harold thoughtfully removed his spikes in the vestibule before entering the church, little realizing how much coming events cast their shadows before. As a priest, he would, out of deference to a custom, remove his shoes before entering any Korean house, even his own rectory. Also in his future were the forty-six churches he would build, their vestibules filled with a clutter of shoes.

"At the end of the ceremony," the archbishop recalled, "Father Gaughan said, 'I hope you win that ball game this afternoon.' We lost. Two days later I loomed up at the communion rail, a twelve-year-old among all of those third-graders."

At that time Harold began reading a mission magazine which his stepsister Priscilla subscribed to. It was called *The Far East* and was published by the Columban Fathers.

The magazine carried a series of articles by Father Edward Galvin from Han Yang, China, stories that would cause a stir in the blood of a boy ready for adventure. Father John Dawson also wrote from Han Yang telling about feeling his way through the strange but fascinating intricacies of language, streets, and people: "It is a new world and not an easy one to describe. Indeed it is so new that I sometimes pinch myself to make sure I have not actually left the old earth on which I was born and lived until now. One seems to be under the spell of some modern Aladdin and his wonderful lamp. I suppose the feeling will wear off in time."

And the pictures! Pagodas, rickshaws, pagan idols, terraced rice fields, sampans. Not all of the pictures were glamorous. Those of lepers gave Harold pause. He certainly never thought that some day six leper colonies would be under his spiritual direction, one of them named after him, and another the largest in the world. The very grimness of the photographs of the maimed enticed the boy to read the accompanying stories.

He was moved by the article about Sister St. John the Baptist who gave her life nursing lepers. The article said: "She is tall, slender, fair, and blue-eyed. After a moment you perceive the marks leprosy has already left on her face and figure. The feet are badly swollen and have lost all feeling; the ears are changing their shape, and the hands are stiff and shiny. A general indication of extreme anemia is visible, but the voice of the sufferer is still soft and sweet, not yet having acquired the raucous tones of the leper. The gaze is calm and direct."

Sister St. John the Baptist expects no cure, according to the writer. She says she feels a weakness to the very depths, the same symptoms Father Dupuy felt when he contracted the disease. She is thankful, though, that she still has no running sores.

An article about the difficulty of the Chinese language must have given Harold pause; his own report cards were not covered with constellations of gold stars. In telling of the many dialects, Father Edward O'Doherty was somewhat consoling when he wrote that in Eastern Hupeh, the province in which the Columban Fathers worked, Mandarin was the official language and the one the missionary studied. "As well as learning the best Chinese he has the satisfaction of knowing that he can be understood by practically three hundred million people out of a total of four hundred million."

The Far East magazine inspired Harold's interest in the priesthood. He was forever quoting it to his father and describing the exciting lives the missionaries led. No doubt he saw it all as a great adventure. And although Frank Henry wanted his son to follow in his footsteps as a master mechanic, he couldn't help but notice the boy's growing interest in missionary work. So at breakfast one morning in August 1922, three months after Harold had been baptized, Frank Henry pointed to a notice in *The Far East* that said the Columban Fathers would accept at their new preparatory seminary at Omaha any bright boy who had finished the seventh grade. Harold, never one to dally, got off a letter before lunch.

A reply came from Father Paul Waldron by return mail. Enclosed was a lengthy questionnaire. Among the ordinary questions were scattered a few exotic ones that must have quickened the pulse of the small-town boy: Have you ever taken part in a duel? Have you ever abused the sacred species? Have you ever been a judge and passed the sentence of death? Have you ever committed voluntary homicide? Wow! This was living larger than life!

A few items in the questionnaire did slow down Harold. He had to explain that he had no confirmation certificate, having been baptized only three months ago. And that part about the parents' marriage—his parents had been married outside the Catholic Church. The item that slowed him down most, though, was the one asking for a letter of recommendation. He knew that the letter should rightly come from his pastor, but then there was that matter of playing hooky from school. In the spring he had skipped classes to see the Minneapolis Millers play St. Paul in the season's opener. The pastor had been furious. As the mechanics used to say around Frank Henry's auto shop, "He raised hell and slid a block under it."

All his life Harold Henry had as a rule of thumb that when you have a problem you go to the top man. But here was a time to make an exception. He detoured around the pastor and sought out the assistant, Father William Murphy. But Father Murphy begged off, saying that since he didn't know Harold well enough perhaps Sister Mary should write. The boy's heart sank because Sister Mary had agreed with the pastor when he said in vigorous language that playing hooky was not acceptable conduct at St. Stephen's.

There was nothing to do, however, but take a chance on Sister Mary. She came through by writing to the seminary that Harold was "a very good boy." By return mail came the suggestion that since Harold had not been confirmed, he should finish the eighth grade, get confirmed, and reapply the following year. No mention was made of the parents' marriage, although that may have been the main reason for the suggested delay. Later, unknown to the boy, the marriage was the subject of an exchange of letters heavy with the Latin prose of canon lawyers.

No sooner had Harold opened the letter suggesting the delay of a year than Father Murphy arrived at his front door. It was mid-afternoon on Friday, August 25, 1922. He had just received a telegram saying that if Harold could be in Omaha, 350 miles away, by ten o'clock Sunday morning, he could be confirmed and enter the seminary right away. Harold Henry almost surely said, "No sweat," if the expression was in use by then. Less than forty-eight hours later he was confirmed by Archbishop Harty in the private chapel of the episcopal residence in Omaha along with a dozen Mexican children.

When Harold began studying with the Columbans, he knew scarcely anything about them. Since the society was only four years old there was not a great deal to know. On the opening day of school, Father Paul Waldron, the assistant to the superior, Father McCarthy, gathered into the small chapel the first students in the school's history and told them about the organization they had become a part of.

The society, named in honor of St. Columban, an Irish missionary monk, was founded in 1918 by Fathers Edward Galvin and John Blowick at Maynooth, the celebrated seminary not far from Dublin. The idea for the society began to grow in China where Father Galvin, working under French priests, felt compelled to form an organization in his native Ireland dedicated to bringing the Christian Gospel to the Chinese. When he returned home, he and Father Blowick, then a brilliant young theologian, went through two years of discouragement and red tape before the society became a reality.

Three months after entering the seminary at Omaha, young Harold

Henry resumed his practice of going to the man at the top. He wrote a letter
to Father Blowick, the first superior general. Father Blowick, in turn, wrote
from Ireland to Father Waldron: "I have a letter from one of your young
students, named Harold Henry, in which he makes a curious remark that
this was his first Christmas in the Catholic Church. The thing struck me as
very peculiar, and I would like you to get into the matter to see whether he
has been converted from Protestantism . . . and let me know the result of
your inquiries. It is possible that he meant something altogether different,
but I would like to be sure."

Father Waldron assured Father Blowick that Harold Henry spoke the
truth when he said that he had been baptized, confirmed, and had started
studying for the priesthood all within three months. "Now as to his standing
and the impression he has made, I may say without exaggeration that he is
the model boy of all the youngsters, and a good pattern for his elders. He is a
remarkable child for his years, displaying a piety and devotion far beyond
what one would expect in one of his age—not an effusive piety but one solid
and serious. Whether that lasts is, of course, something no one can tell. But
he is certainly having an influence for good on the house. In ability, he is
somewhat above average, and in application first class. Healthy, normal . . ."

The accuracy of Father Waldron's favorable judgment could be tested only
by time. It so turned out that of the seven boys who began studying for the
priesthood in Harold's class that year at St. Columban's only Harold Henry
would eventually reach the major seminary. It wasn't that he never considered dropping out. Years later he was to say, "Those days were times of trial
and discouragement. On two or three occasions I had my bag packed, ready
to leave. But I had sense enough to listen to advice which I often repeat to
seminarians. I was advised never to make a decision when discouraged, to
stick it out, to think it over, and to pray. The moments of trial and discouragement would pass. The old soldier, St. Ignatius, said never to make any
decisions in desolation or in jubilation—in desolation you don't see things
clearly and in jubilation you promise too much."

However, the offbeatness of the boy's case kept haunting Father Blowick.
A year later he wanted to be reassured again, and this time Father Waldron
wrote: "Harold is a boy of unusual sanctity and character. This has been observed in him almost from the first. Though he is only fourteen, he has impressed all in the house, faculty and students, in this matter. He is not in any
sense either abnormal or supernormal or a psychic phenomenon, but he is
one of the clearest examples of great graces given and corresponded with that
I have ever seen in a young soul."

Father Blowick was what is called "a stickler," and so a year later when Harold Henry moved on to St. Columban's Preparatory Seminary at Silver Creek, New York, he asked Father M. J. O'Dwyer, the newly elected superior general, to look into the case that kept haunting him. Father O'Dwyer was a noted scholar and had been one of Ireland's great athletes. If the scholar in him was not impressed with Harold Henry, the athlete in him just had to be. Father O'Dwyer reported that the director, rector, and priests at the seminary all gave good accounts of Harold Henry. He said that the boy impressed him favorably. "He has a fine appearance, is well set up and, according to accounts, is a good student."

The next summer, Harold wrote to Father O'Dwyer, telling him how much the students enjoyed life at Long View Cottage, the seminarians' vacation place at Clear Lake, Iowa. He described the boat, the roughness of the lake, and the old Ford that "if it does anything it does its duty," meaning that it took the students a mile and a half to Mass each morning. Harold praised the people of the parish who gave the students pastry, jam, and pickles. He spoke with enthusiasm of a priest from Mason City who, before leaving for Ireland, promised that the boys would receive a ham every two weeks. Harold enclosed photographs of the May altar and the Holy Thursday altar, two he had helped decorate. At Christmas he sent "presents from the tree" to Fathers O'Dwyer, Blowick, and Galvin. He also enclosed photographs of himself and his classmates.

In his letters to the men at the top, Harold mentioned sports from time to time, but he couldn't stir up much enthusiasm for them at either Omaha or Silver Creek. Years later as an archbishop he recalled the lack of athletes among the priests and students. "They weren't very good at sports. They played 'for the honor and glory of God,' which didn't improve the game any."

Even fifty years later, priests recalled Harold Henry's athletic ability. He retained through life the look of an athlete, the tight-knit body, the easy movements. But it was not just physical; it had something to do with leadership and with courage, characteristics that cropped up from time to time under trying circumstances.

Since nothing in Harold Henry's life followed the beaten path for long, the time had come in his seminary career for the unusual to happen once again, and so it did. When he had finished his work at Silver Creek in June of 1926, he was told that nobody had any idea of what would happen to him next. Since he was the only one left in his class, the seminary could ill afford to develop a program in philosophy for just one student.

In recalling those times, the archbishop said, "While I knew there were

difficulties in the early days, I found out later that the Columban Fathers
were on the verge of financial disaster. Actually on many occasions they did
not have the cash to buy groceries for the students and their credit rating was
so poor that they could not buy on credit."

Harold returned to Minneapolis wondering what would happen next. His
father had died a year earlier, and so he felt at loose ends. But he had the optimism that Cardinal Cushing was to speak of at his consecration as a bishop:
"The missionary work of the Church is always done in a supernatural spirit
of divine optimism. Catholicism is a religion of optimism. It never broods on
the past or fears the present. It always looks to the future. Missionaries are
the heralds of a supernatural spirit of optimism."

On the Feast of the Assumption, August 15, the telephone rang and the
operator asked for Mr. Henry. Never having been called Mr. Henry before,
the boy said that Frank Henry had died a year earlier. The operator said the
call was for Mr. *Harold* Henry, and while the boy listened in astonishment,
he was told he was to go to Ireland to spend a year at St. Senan's College in
County Clare.

CHAPTER

2

Ireland was an Adventure

WHEN the Minnesota boy first caught sight of St. Senan's he really felt he was living larger than life. The college, formerly a fine old mansion, was located on an estate that stretched along the River Shannon at a place called Cahiracon, one of the beauty spots of Ireland.

The experience of study in Ireland started out just as offbeat as everything else in Harold Henry's life. "When I arrived," the Archbishop recalled, "I shocked the staff and students by sporting a snazzy pinstripe suit and a multicolored tweed coat and hat. All the seminarians were completely in black. I'm sure the rector thought I was an impostor, what with those clothes and lacking the documents I was supposed to bring with me. I showed him my passport and dropped a few names of some Columban priests, but he kept pursing his lips and tapping together the tips of his fingers. When he was more or less convinced that I was no impostor, he ransacked the house until he found a black suit, cassock, and coat, all equally ill-fitting. He told me to give my clothes to a beggar who frequented the seminary grounds. Then I looked more like a beggar than the man who received my new clothes."

The year of novitiate began with a thirty-day spiritual retreat. In his opening conference, Father Timothy Harris, the retreat master, said, "You will find scales in the library. Weigh yourself today. Weigh yourself again at the close of the retreat. If you lose weight, while it is not an infallible sign, you probably made a good retreat. If you gain weight, while it is not an infallible sign, you probably made a poor retreat."

Judging from statistics Harold Henry's retreat was a disaster. He loved

Irish tea—so strong and black you could trot a mouse across it, as they say over there—but that didn't cause the problem; it was the brown, crusty soda bread and the rich, creamy butter spread thick on top of it that caused Harold to gain twenty pounds during the thirty-day retreat. Later he would discard the weight, not in pursuit of asceticism but in pursuit of sports.

The proper use of creature comforts was the subject of one of Father Harris's sermons. He urged as a guiding principle St. Ignatius's admonition: "If you have the good things of life, enjoy them and thank God for them. If you don't have them, don't complain." Harold Henry would quote that often in the next fifty years.

At breakfast, the morning after the sermon on the proper use of creature comforts, the soft-boiled eggs seemed barely to have touched warm water. The eggs at St. Senan's were repulsive to begin with; the chickens ate the wild garlic growing around the college grounds and so flavored their products that it was best if one thought of something else while eating them. The boys left the breakfast table with the barely boiled eggs lying untouched in the cups.

During the sermon an hour later Father Harris said, "We prepared those eggs that way this morning on purpose. I wanted to see what you had learned about the proper use of creature comforts. Not much. I can't say I am surprised, but I am disappointed." Then he told them how, in the days of the classical Chinese society, when someone asked, "How do you do?" the answer was not the mindless, "Very well, thank you!" but the thoughtful, "I am trying to remedy my grave defects, but so far without success." Father Harris urged the boys to at least make a try at remedying their grave defects.

Father Harris was a major influence in Harold Henry's life. The severe priest was full of such maxims as "It is not *when* you die but *how* you die that counts." These struck deep into the impressionable boy's psyche and became a permanent part of his outlook on life. Father Harris shared Paul Claudel's opinion that "Youth is not made for pleasure but for heroism." He used to admonish, "Be like the Jesuits; work hard and die young." Long afterward Archbishop Henry said wryly, "After all that talk about wearing out instead of rusting out, he went ahead and lived to be nearly ninety."

After completing his year at St. Senan's, Harold went to St. Columban's College in County Galway to major in philosophy. The college was located on an old estate called Dalgan Park; 250 wooded acres with a sluggish river lined with drooping willows and tall ferns. In the Georgian manor house were classrooms and faculty quarters; British war-surplus barracks housed the seminarians. When any student spoke of the draughts in the barracks or the snails in the spinach, the set reply was, "Ah, sure a missionary isn't supposed to be comfortable."

How uncomfortable a life a missionary might lead had been more than hinted at when the seminary was dedicated on a June afternoon in 1918. Thomas O'Dea, the Bishop of Galway, said, "You won't be any good at all, you know, until some of you are knocked on the head out there in China. You will want a martyr's room here in Dalgan." That day the society numbered twenty-two priests; well before its fiftieth anniversary it would number almost that many martyrs, nineteen to be exact.

No sooner was Harold Henry settled into one of the barracks than he began to correspond with another man at the top, Father McCarthy, in Omaha, the superior of Columbans in the United States. It was natural that the boy who loved action should be drawn toward the middle-aged priest, known among his confreres as a go-getter with unbounded energy and ideas galore. Father McCarthy did things with flair and a touch of sentimentality, a style that the youthful Henry approved of. He put into his letters to Father McCarthy all of the chatty details he would have written to his family if he had one. In his first letter, written five years before sailing to the Orient, China was on his mind: "Before closing I want to assure you that I am very happy. Of course I feel blue at times, but it is good preparation for China. Both priests and students are exceedingly nice to me."

This feeling of uneasiness, this whistling-in-the-dark attitude is reflected in the next letter: "I am glad to assure you that I am as happy now as I was before, if not happier. Both priests and students see that the 'Yank' enjoys himself—particularly Father Harris. No doubt I find a few things hard, but as John McFadden says, 'It's all in the game.' At first there seemed to be a wall between myself and the students, but it is gradually crumbling."

As time passed the letters became more upbeat. In January 1928, he wrote that he was on holiday in County Mayo because Father John McFadden had invited him to visit relatives. "I am in with the old Irish country people and, needless to say, I am enjoying the experience. They certainly feel as though they can't do enough for a priest or a clerical student. I have been on the go visiting about. Every place Father John and myself go there is a royal welcome. I generally have about three chicken dinners a day. Thank God we have no visiting today. I have a chance to recuperate."

Father John McFadden took Harold to visit two uncles and two aunts who lived in a whitewashed cottage with thatched roof halfway up a hill. Picturesque it was, but comfortable it wasn't, for there was no running water. The aunts had to carry heavy buckets from a spring at the foot of the hill. Father

John discovered an artesian well atop the hill and so he took a few of the
pound notes tucked away behind the picture frames and bought some pipe
and a sink. All during the digging and the pipe-laying, Uncle Michael kept
objecting, "John, we'll be the laughing stock of the neighborhood with water
coming into the house." When John went away the uncle moved the sink outside, but would bring it back into the house whenever he heard that his
nephew planned to visit.

Sports, of course, always found a way into his letters to Father McCarthy:
"I had a very enjoyable holiday. There was only one factor which had a
dampening effect on my happiness: namely, the Irish climate. This summer
was the worst since I have come over.

"I entered a couple of golf competitions at Kilkee, qualified for one, but
then was knocked out by Dr. O'Neil of Maynooth. Charley O'Brien and
myself are getting to be proper 'swanks,' associating with Maynooth profes-
sors. I also had the good fortune to go trout fishing with Dr. Mulcahy a few
times. He didn't think much of my trout fishing as I just started this summer."

Years later Archbishop Henry said that if he had not gone to Ireland he
probably would never have reached the priesthood. At the preparatory
seminaries in Omaha and Silver Creek the sports programs that he needed to
keep up his morale just didn't exist. But in Ireland he found rugby and
gloried in it. He brought to the game a technique he learned in American
football, running with knees high and spinning. His colleagues from Dalgan
days still speak of the speed and aggressiveness that caused so many injuries
that the college authorities warned him that he must tone down or he would
be banned from the playing field. During vacations he went to Wales with a
fellow student who had relatives there, and he played for the Welsh Rugby
Union under the name of Ivor Thomas. "I found the Welsh miners tougher
than I was!" he recalled years later. "They'd kick you in the ribs when the
referee wasn't looking. The student who took me to Wales died when a rib
punctured his lung."

Against college rules, Harold made an appointment to see a dentist on a
Saturday afternoon in Galway. When he asked Father McGrath for permission to go to town the Dean said, "Don't you know it's a rule of this college
that no one leaves the campus on Saturday or Sunday?"

"Yes, Father, I know."

"Then why in God's name did you make the appointment!"

"It's like this, Father, Galway College plays Ballinasloe tomorrow. We
play Ballinasloe in two weeks."

"That's a valid reason," said the Dean. "Report to me as soon as you get back."

Although cigarette smoking was not allowed in those days—only pipes were legal in the seminary—Father McGrath waited for Harold's return with a full pack. As the young athlete recalled the game play by play, the dean urged cigarette after cigarette on him, all the while drumming with his fingers on the desk top and repeating, "Yes, yes, and then what!"

Harold repeated, "John Howe, he's the one to stop."

"Ah, yes, John Howe. We must remember that name."

The seminarians beat Ballinasloe by three touchdowns. The student who had gone to the dentist got two of them.

Incidentally, the two star athletes, Harold Henry and John Howe, talked about that game forty years later. It was in Bhamo, Burma where Bishop Henry had come to attend Bishop Howe's consecration.

As time went on Harold's letters to Father McCarthy contained less about sports and more about reading. In June of 1929 he told of the books he had read lately: *Paradise Lost, Letters of St. Jerome,* Belloc's *French Revolution,* Chesterton's *Everlasting Man, A Tale of Two Cities,* and *The Merchant of Venice.*

Of the 108 students at the college, those who impressed Harold Henry most were the ones who had been "in the world," as he said. He stood in awe of Frank Woods, Charlie O'Brien, Tom Powers and Ambrose Gallagher, for they knew how things were "out there." Frank Woods was a bartender before studying for the priesthood. Charlie O'Brien had been a stock broker in Chicago and Kansas City. Tom Powers was a taxi driver in New York. And Ambrose Gallagher, an awesome figure in Harold Henry's eyes, had prospected for gold, had trapped furs in Alaska, and had been a lumberjack and a logger. And—Glory be!—he had played on the Mount Angel basketball team. All four of these men became involved in Harold Henry's life in the years ahead.

The nearer Harold Henry advanced toward the priesthood the darker life became for Columbans in China. Things went from bad to worse in 1929. The Communists were claiming that religion was a foreigner's trick, a device used to enslave men in an imperialistic system. Many Catholics abandoned their faith and people were afraid to be seen talking to a priest.

In July of 1929 the seminary was shocked by the news that Father Timothy Leonard had been chopped to death by a band of young Communist bandits in Nangfeng. Harold's sense of adventure was tempered with twinges of uneasiness as he listened to some of the priests tell of the night in Dublin when a group of young missionaries were discussing the possibility of martyrdom. Father Leonard, a robust man given to great roars of laughter, had said, "Oh, what of that! What is it, after all, but a bad quarter of an hour? And think of the reward!"

In November Bishop Galvin wrote a letter to the seminary expressing an attitude toward difficulties, one that Harold Henry would eventually adopt: "Missionaries in general are quite discouraged. Some of them are entirely fed up, but then there are men who would never give up and who keep hoping. China is a dark place at present for mission work. Personally, I am not discouraged. I feel that we must look at the whole business with the eyes of faith, try to see God working it out in his own way and keep right on. A simple creed, but it is hard to get some men to see it."

To add to the discouragement, 1930 began with the most severe cold China had known in sixty years. Bishop Galvin couldn't write for weeks because his bottle of ink was frozen solid. After the thaw, his first sentence was one that would make an excellent opening for a short story: "North of Yo Kow every mother's son seems to be a bandit."

Shortly after Easter the seminary was filled with the kind of talk that thrilled Harold Henry. It was about how Bishop Galvin had smuggled five Columban nuns out of the mission compound for a twelve-mile run to freedom through Communist lines. The bishop wrote, "It was a terrible pace. I was glad that the sisters who followed me were young Irish girls to whom brisk walking presented little difficulty."

In that same mission compound on that same day Fathers Patrick Laffan and James Linehan were captured by Communists and held for ransom for seven months. Several times the two priests smuggled out messages urging Bishop Galvin to refuse to pay the ransom. The bishop tried to comply with their wishes but eventually, when he could stand the strain no longer, he sent his houseboy through the lines with $5,000. The boy returned with the two priests, who were thin, scarred, and sick from the treatment they received.

While negotiations were still in progress for the release of Fathers Laffan and Linehan, the Communists captured Father Cornelius Tierney, who at fifty-nine was the oldest Columban priest at the time. In the beginning, his captors seemed more intent on beating and humiliating him than on seeking ransom.

Bishop Galvin wrote back to Ireland: "Life has been an agony here during all these terrible months, and, at the present moment, it is as dark as it could be. Father Tierney is still a captive. God knows how it will all end. We need faith and courage. Only fifty miles from here a young Chinese priest has been murdered by the Communists. They stripped him naked and beat him terribly. They blinded him with lime and then, tying a rope around his neck, they slowly strangled him to death."

Father Cornelius Tierney died in captivity on February 28, 1931. Harold Henry was deeply impressed by the charity reflected in a letter written at the time by Father William McGoldrick: "God rest him in his lonely grave out there among the bandits. He won't forget us or his poor mission at Kienchang. And he won't forget his captors, either. When his prayers bring some of those same captors into Heaven, I know he'll have a warm and cordial welcome for them."

In the summer of 1931, about the time Harold Henry was getting ready to leave Ireland and return to Omaha, things were getting worse in China. Father Hugh Sands was captured and held for a ransom of $17,000. The great floods came about this time and wrought such destruction that even the tough-minded Bishop Galvin was unprepared to face all of that avalanche of despair. He wrote: "I have never encountered such desperate people as the people who are camping out here on the hillside. Hunger has made them desperate. I am honestly afraid to go out. Every time I do they catch on to my clothes. They hold on for dear life until I promise them something. I cannot feed everyone. We are now feeding 900—a drop in the ocean. It is estimated that there are thirty million homeless in the Yangtze Valley and most of them have absolutely nothing. I never knew what 'nothing' meant until I came to China. Poverty is hard, but hunger is terrible. And the Communists? My God, what demons they are! Robbing and killing right and left. They have taken the boats from the people and what little they were able to save from the flood. There is no money anywhere. It is a hard country. Every single one of our missions has been attacked and looted. No one has escaped."

Father Sands smuggled notes out of prison and some of them reached Bishop Galvin. In one he said that he was crowded in with sixty-six other prisoners, all of whom were held for ransom, and that the place was squalid, filthy, infested with vermin and rats. There were two buckets in the room and these were the toilets. In one smuggled note was a sentence Harold Henry often thought of later when undergoing similar hardships: "Nothing dries more quickly than a tear."

Bishop Galvin sent $1,500 for the release of Father Sands. When the money arrived, the Columban priest pointed to a Franciscan, Father Lazzeri, old and seriously ill, and said, "Let him go instead." That's what the Communists did, and Father Sands was not released for another six months.

Things got so bad that for the one and only time in his life Bishop Galvin seemed ready to give up on China. He wrote to Father McCarthy in Omaha:

"The vicariate is in a frightful state. No priest can put his foot in the greater part of Mien Yang, and the northern country is almost as bad. It is a frightful time and I do not know where I am standing. I think the society ought to look for some other field in which to work. Flesh and blood can't stand the strain that we are under here. Our hospital bills for this year have been fearfully high. At one time there were as many as ten in the hospital together, and there is always someone there."

That sentence, "I think the society ought to look for some other field in which to work," probably changed the direction of Harold Henry's life. Of course he wouldn't realize it for years to come because, as he came to understand later, hardly anyone ever recognizes the shadow that a coming event casts before it.

Harold Henry was dismayed when he learned that in the middle of all these discouraging events Father Patrick Cleary sailed to China as ecclesiastical superior of Nancheng. Father Cleary had been a brilliant professor at Maynooth before joining the original band of Columbans. He had been an equally brilliant rector and professor at Dalgan where young Henry came to admire him. The seminarian couldn't understand why this scholarly, sensitive young priest should be sent to replace the martyred Father Tierney. Father Cleary didn't seem to have the tough fiber and aggressiveness needed for such an assignment. But as a priest who knew Father Cleary better than Harold Henry knew him said, "He has more the look of a poet than of a fighter, but watch out!" How right his observation turned out to be! The Japanese, a dozen years later, found out how tough Father Cleary could be when they faced him in a fight over General Doolittle's wounded pilots. More of that later.

CHAPTER
3

Where in the World
Is Korea?

HAROLD HENRY returned to the United States in the summer of 1931 to study theology at the new major seminary that the Columbans had opened in Omaha. He left Ireland with some twinges of regret. He has always been thankful that he studied in Ireland because most of the Columbans he met in the missions were Irish and it was good that he could reminisce with them about things back home.

In Omaha, Harold found that Father John McFadden was the new rector, the same Father McFadden who had taken him to visit relatives in Ireland. The happy reunion soon became a disappointment. Father McFadden, with his scientific mind, his concern for the letter of the law, and his asceticism, was too straightlaced for the freewheeling Harold Henry.

Father McFadden's had been a delayed vocation. In his youth he was considered something of a scientific marvel. Before entering the seminary he had helped develop an automatic signal system for the railroad, and had gone on the Carnegie Expedition, in a metal-free sailing ship, to study variations of the compass in various approaches to the North Pole.

As an example of his severity, Harold Henry often recalled the bitter winter night, the kind Omaha specializes in, when he went to the rector's room to find him huddled in his overcoat with the radiator turned off. The priest explained that he preferred a cold room as it made for a clearer head, and he offered Harold a bathrobe against the chill. In those days seminarians were not supposed to read newspapers. So Father McFadden folded a newspaper with great care so that none of it would be exposed except the advertisement announcing a concert of the Vienna Boys' Choir that he wanted to show Harold. He was keeping the letter of the law—seminarians are not to read newspapers; ergo, Harold Henry must not get one glimpse of the news.

Friction between Father McFadden and Harold Henry developed from time to time. As ordination approached Harold went to the rector's room to ask that his sister Mary and his brother Bob be invited to the ordination. The rector said absolutely not because the other two men to be ordained, both from Ireland, would have no relatives present and so Harold couldn't either.

Later, Father McFadden was sent to Buenos Aires to serve as a port chaplain for sailors. Down on the wharf, against a warehouse wall, he used to set up an altar, a simple, homemade affair, a hinged table with four rods supporting it. Stubs of candles in water glasses flickered in the breeze, and the ribbons that marked the place in the missal were weighted with three heavy iron washers to keep the pages from blowing about. The breeze was filled with the sounds and smells of wharves all over the world. Around the altar knelt rough men from many ports, and in the middle stood John McFadden, his vestments flapping in the wind.

In time sailors from all over the world began to speak of Father McFadden with high regard. They recalled how he would search through a drunken sailor's pockets for his identification card, and then throw the fellow over his shoulder and carry him to his ship just to be sure he didn't miss the sailing. The severity had melted quite a bit.

Since no major event in Harold Henry's life happened according to the book, when the time approached for ordination his case once more required special handling. Permission had to be requested from Rome so that he might be ordained six months before the canonical age. With permission granted, he and John Quinn and Thomas Connolly were ordained on the morning of December 21, 1932, in the chapel at St. Columban's in Omaha. Archbishop Joseph Francis Rummel of Omaha, and later of New Orleans, performed the ordination rite. Monsignor Nicholas Wegner, until recently the director of Boy's Town, was master of ceremonies. No ordination was ever simpler.

Father Henry's first Solemn Mass was scheduled to be said on Christmas Day in St. Dominic's in Northfield. However, Father Francis Lang wanted the young priest to say his first public Mass in the Church of the Annunciation in Minneapolis on the day before Christmas.

In Omaha, Father Henry boarded the Chicago-Northwestern to ride the

350 miles over the same route he had ridden ten years earlier when he hurried from Minneapolis to Omaha to be confirmed. This time, because of a blizzard, the train moved much slower. Instead of reaching Minneapolis at eight he did not arrive until nearly noon, but Father Lang kept the parishioners waiting in the church until the Mass could begin.

That afternoon the young priest drove Father Lang to Northfield, about forty miles over icy roads. When the car went into a spin, the elderly Father Lang showed concern. The cocky twenty-three-year-old said, "What's the matter, Father, aren't you in the state of grace?" In later life the archbishop cringed when he remembered the brashness of his youth.

Many of the young priest's Protestant relatives attended the service and came forward for his blessing at the first Solemn Mass in St. Dominic's. The archbishop recalled, "I can still see Uncle Arne Winger. He looked like he was going to faint. I whispered, 'Don't worry. This won't do you any harm.' and he said, 'Thanks for saying that.' "

After three weeks at home, the young Columban returned to Omaha to complete his studies. In June he was sent to Silver Creek to help with some work at the seminary; and from there to Bristol, Rhode Island, to help Father William Kelly establish a new novitiate. He kept hoping he would get some vacation. After all, he had spent ten years in the seminary and would soon leave on a slow boat to China for another ten years. That three weeks at Christmas didn't seem enough. But Father McCarthy said that was all the vacation there would be.

The archbishop said forty years later, "I accepted it. I had taken the oath of obedience and that was that. If that happened today a priest might call a press conference, leave the Church, and write a book."

When he received his appointment to go to the Columban mission in China, he read the letter over and over. Every now and then he would say, "China," aloud; it was the most beautiful word in the world. A group of Sisters of Loretto from Kentucky were scheduled to sail for China from Seattle on September 15, 1933, fifteen days before he was scheduled to sail, and he was told that he should go along to say Mass for them.

First he went to say goodbye to his brother Bob, who was then at the Columban minor seminary in Silver Creek. The two brothers had little chance to get to know each other. When Bob had written saying he wanted to become a priest, Harold suggested Maryknoll. The reply was, "No, the Columbans are a new society; you'll be a big shot some day and then you'll take care of me." Sixteen years later when Bob left for the missions in the Philippines, Father Harold wrote to friends, "I'm proud of that kid; didn't think he had it in him. But I hardly know him." Both were pleased that their sister, Mary, had followed them into the Church and that their father had been baptized on his death bed.

While riding through the Rockies on the *Olympian*, Harold wrote a farewell letter to Father McCarthy. It was filled with breathless expectation of adventures in China. He closed by saying, "How soon will I be escorting you up the Yangtze River? If your wish to see China ever comes true, I shall be delighted to welcome you and be your interpreter."

His breathless expectations were justified because all of a sudden favorable news was coming from China. The floods had subsided, the villages were rebuilt, and the bandits were less aggressive for the time being. It was a lull between two storms.

The missionaries were enjoying a wave of conversions that exceeded their best and highest hopes. A few sentences from a letter written by Father Timothy Leahy will give a suggestion of what was happening: "I went out with the expectation that conversions would be slow. The people came to me. They asked for catechists. I foolishly promised that if they passed their catechism exam to the teacher's satisfaction they could come down in the off-season, after the rice planting, to my mission and spend six weeks of intensive study prior to being baptized. That was toward the end of the year and I thought no more about it."

Father Leahy happened to look out toward the hills one morning early in 1933, and saw the whole horizon in motion. Rolling toward him was every kind of conveyance—wheelbarrows, carts, rickshaws—with cooking utensils piled on them and human beings pulling and pushing.

"It took well nigh miraculous organization to house and take care of the horde that descended upon me. We had to rent a number of neighboring houses. In my house, in the church, in the school, everywhere, there were boarders. And from morning to night there was the buzz of catechism questions and answers, prayers, and everything else that goes toward making a thorough Catholic. The buzz never ceased. As the Chinese chant their morning prayers, you can imagine what this upcountry philharmonic sounded like."

When Father Henry arrived in Seattle with all of this promised excitement in mind, he decided to visit the Maryknoll Fathers. They had had a great deal of experience in China; perhaps they could give some advice on what to do and what not to do in the Orient.

When an old brother came to the door at the Maryknoll house, Father Henry introduced himself as a Columban on the way to China. The brother didn't even unlatch the screen door, but disappeared for a few minutes. This puzzled the young priest, for Maryknoll priests have a reputation of being great hosts. The brother returned and, without any show of warmth, led Father Henry into a parlor where two priests served him coffee. The priests kept asking him questions until they were satisfied that he really was a Columban. Then they told him why they had treated him with such suspicion. A year earlier a priest had come to the door introducing himself as a Columban en route to the Orient. They gave him a key to the house, took him sightseeing, and provided tickets for the opera. Later they learned he was a Maryknoll priest playing a joke on them and they were in no mood to be fooled again.

En route to China the ship stopped at Kobe in Japan. Father Henry was standing at the rail of the *President Jefferson* enjoying his first sight of an oriental port when the ship's purser brought him a letter that had arrived earlier. When he opened it the bottom fell out from under all his high hopes and bright plans. He was not to go to China after all. Go to Korea, the letter directed, the Columbans are opening a mission there.

Father Henry turned to the woman standing next to him at the rail and asked, "Where in the world is Korea?"

CHAPTER
4

Troubles in Taegu

AT DAWN, Father Henry and seven of his classmates fresh from Ireland shivered in a damp wind on a ferry crossing from Japan to Korea. With them was Father Owen MacPolin, an old China hand. All agreed that this was an auspicious day to make a beginning—it was the feast of Christ the King, in October of 1933—and yet Father Henry kept saying to himself that this is only Korea. His heart was on the way to China.

The letter aboard ship had so lowered his *kibun* (mood) that he wondered how long the dejection would last. The Koreans say that when the *kibun* is high you walk on the mountain tops, but when it is low you crawl in the valleys. Since mood is so important in life, the feeling is that anything raising it is good and anything lowering it is not good.

Rain was beating down that chilly Sunday morning when the Columbans boarded the train in Pusan. They looked out on barren, soggy fields and felt as miserable and forlorn as the view from the window. They saw mushroom-shaped mud huts thatched with rice straw and huddled together, some hanging dangerously at the edge of flooded rice fields. Were these the homes of their parishioners?

The lone bright spot of the trip was an ancient Korean gentleman, a *yung-kam*, in white baggy trousers fastened at the ankles, sitting tailor-fashion on the upholstered seat with his white stockinged feet crossed neatly under him, smoking placidly a long-stemmed pipe. He wore the long stringy beard that Koreans take pride in, and the black horsehair hat, varnished stiff, that was something of a stovepipe.

Harold Henry didn't know at the time that Korea and his native Minnesota were the same size, some 85,000 square miles. A big difference, though, is that Korea has about ten times as many people. Only about one fifth of the land is worth farming, because the country is mainly mountains of such formidable shape that the French missionaries described them as "a sea in a heavy gale." Years later when the Archbishop flew across them he realized how apt the description was; they look as though an angry, lashing sea had suddenly congealed. Father Henry learned in time that each mountainside and valley had its own weather conditions, and so crops were planted to take advantage of the various weathers. He learned too that winters were colder and summers hotter than most places with the same latitude. But on that first morning in Korea all the young priest knew about the landscape was that the view from the train between Pusan and Taegu was dreary, and that the weather inside the coach was a damp cold that penetrated the marrow of the soul.

Father MacPolin, the first Columban superior in Korea, could see that the Yank, Harold Henry, was not his usual effervescent self. The Irish lads seemed a little let down, too, and well they might. They also had talked and dreamed about China for years. Huddled in their black overcoats, their teeth chattering with the cold and the excitement, were Fathers Patrick Monahan, T. D. Ryan, Patrick Dawson, Daniel McMenamin, Gerard Marinan, Thomas Neligan, and Brian Geraghty.

They were entering a country that, 150 years after the introduction of Christianity, numbered perhaps a hundred thousand Catholics. It would have been consoling if they could have foreseen that most of them would live to see a Korea in which a million shared their faith.

Of the nine Columbans on the train only Father MacPolin knew very much about the unusual way Catholicism had reached Korea. It had been introduced by one man, a layman, in the latter part of the eighteenth century. Korea was then known as the Hermit Kingdom, meaning no one was welcome to leave and no one was welcome to enter, with one exception—an official party traveled to Peking each year to pay tribute to the emperor of China.

On one such trip a Portuguese Franciscan in China gave a Korean official some religious books written in Chinese. Back in Korea scholars read the books and decided that here was a religion worth considering. One of the scholars accompanying the delegation in 1783 was baptized by the Portuguese priest, and returned home as a lay apostle. When the first priest, Father James Chu, a Chinese, arrived in Korea eleven years later he found 4,000 baptized Catholics.

Since the Korean government was against all foreign influences, it attempted to stamp out Catholicism, a foreign influence. Father Chu was put to death in 1801, and all through the nineteenth century persecution followed persecution.

As the train approached Taegu, Father MacPolin reminded the missionaries that the official name for this country was Chosun. Somebody said, "We have come to serve God's Chosun people." The pun has been repeated through the years, but on that morning nobody laughed. Father MacPolin explained that Chosun means "Land of the morning calm." Somebody laughed then, as the wind lashed rain against the window.

At the Taegu railroad station, Father Henry studied the signs. The lettering reminded him of the marks chickens' feet made in the mud on the farms he had visited in Ireland. The sound of little children calling to each other made him feel stupid; after all these years of study in a dozen schools, he was now in a position where children understood what was going on better than he did.

Just then Father Germain Mousset, with the kind of luxurious beard French missionaries featured in those days, hurried down the platform to meet the disheveled, uneasy Columbans. After a warm greeting, Father Mousset called two taxis to have the new priests delivered to their destination. It was at this point that Harold Henry realized he was indeed a stranger in a strange land, for the conversation between the priest and the taxi drivers sounded like fragmented cacophony.

Fortunately, he did not know then that linguists find Korean one of the most difficult languages in the world for occidentals to master. His disappointment at not being in China was enough of a burden to carry that first day. Later, one of that group of pioneering Columbans, Father Gerard Marinan, would write: "Korean is not what you would call a difficult language. Nothing so simple. Latin was difficult and so was Greek. Korean is in a class by itself."

At last the cab drivers took off as though they knew where they were going, displaying the self-assurance that Koreans show, especially when they are not sure of what to do next. Even in those opening minutes the young priest was startled by a standard of living and dying greatly in contrast with the conditions in Minnesota. On that hectic, labyrinthine ride he took his first step toward becoming a heavy smoker. He often said that he did not turn into a chain smoker out of a craving for cigarettes, but as a way of deadening the sense of smell. While lurching through the streets of Taegu he became aware of the odor of decay, poverty, antiquity, and human excrement that sometimes hangs heavy on Asiatic air, especially in those days before the government made an effort to enforce health standards.

As an additional enrichment to the Far Eastern atmosphere, Korea offers *kimchi*. On that first day, Father Henry didn't know the ingredients of *kimchi*, but he soon learned that it is a mixture of pickled turnips, cabbage, peppers, and garlic, which is kept fermenting in earthen jars, filled in the autumn and drawn on for every meal until summer. *Kimchi* has a penetrating flavor and an equally penetrating odor that clings to the clothes and persists in the nostrils. Father Henry soon learned that *kimchi* makes hearing confessions more of a penance for the priest than for the penitent, who comes bearing "a breath you could light your pipe on." As one Irish missionary said, "It took the shellac off the confessional screen."

As the taxis swerved through Taegu, the Columbans noticed long-dead, desiccated fish hanging in bundles gathering flies in street stalls. From houses drifted the smell of a malodorous soup made from those fish. Father Henry lit another cigarette.

The taxis lurched to a halt at a compound marked "Catholic Mission." Two clean-cut young priests approached. Father Henry, mistaking them for French missionaries, reached for his best Latin, of which he was none too proud, yet he felt sure it was better than his meager French. One priest answered in Oxford English, "You must be looking for the French Catholic compound. This is the Anglican one." The priests got back into the taxis, bracing themselves for another uncertain ride.

The taxi drivers gave the Columbans a good introduction to the sights and sounds of Taegu before they finally located St. Justin Major Seminary, operated by the Paris Foreign Mission Society. The eight Irishmen and one American found the French priests gracious hosts.

Many of them had come to Korea in the 1890s and had never been home since. Their commitment to the missions was for life. The same Father Germain Mousset who greeted the Columbans would be sent to Japan by the United States Army at the start of the Korean War in 1950. He went unwillingly and upon arriving in Tokyo searched out the United States Military Civilian Affairs Section to ask permission to return to Korea. When told there were no facilities for civilians at army installations, he said he wanted to go back anyway. Asked if he had a valid reason for going back he said simply, "I live there." He unfolded his passport, a document the size of a diploma, the ink faded and the paper brown with age. It had been issued in 1897, more than a half century earlier. When the United States Army officer saw it, he said, "I guess you really do live there," and sent Father Mousset, by then a bishop, back to Korea immediately.

When the Columbans arrived at St. Justin's, the Korean seminarians circled them with a barrage of questions in Latin. Father Henry felt a further letdown at realizing his shortcomings in the language. He could answer, yes and no, and not much more.

He told himself to try to see some bright side to this new life; it must be there somewhere if he could just find it—the kind of advice Father Harris used to give at St. Senan's. The search for optimism suffered a fatal blow at lunch. Blood sausage and a ripe cheese that smelled like a hot afternoon in an oriental slum sent him hurrying from the table fearing he would vomit right there in front of everybody.

He went to bed in the cold dormitory that night embarrassed, disappointed, and homesick. Five years earlier he had written to Father McCarthy, "Of course I feel blue at times but it is good preparation for China." It hadn't been enough of a preparation for Korea. With a lump in his throat and burning eyelids he wondered if he could ever feel greater despair.

Language lessons began the next morning. The teacher, Youn Chan Do, removed his shoes at the classroom door and greeted each student with a profound bow. Every day the rubric was the same. Sparkling with great good cheer, the professor would attack the blackboard, filling it with Korean script and Chinese characters. He also knew Japanese well. But he knew not a word of English.

Father Henry, who was remembered by his fellow students at the seminary in Ireland for his ability to take thorough and rapid notes, just didn't know where to begin. The professor, sensing there was a problem, would try to communicate through pantomime. He would grab a book, clutch it to his chest, run across the room, throw it down, pick it up, and come back smiling. The students, out of politeness, would smile and nod, and the professor would pass on to the next demonstration.

The gymnastics that he put himself through to explain the honorifics would have been laughable had not the situation been so depressing. For example, all the parts of one verb with all of its honorifics add up to several hundred words. The ending of a verb changes depending on the social status of the speaker and the social status of the person spoken to and the social status of the person spoken about. Imagine trying to demonstrate the subtlety of expressions used when an oldest son speaks to his grandfather about a stray dog. As one of those Columbans admitted years later, "We still murder the honorifics."

To compound the confusion, at that time Chinese characters and a Korean alphabet were both in use. A move was on to use pure Korean, but the spelling of many Korean words was undergoing a change. Father Henry's *kibun* sank still lower, if possible, when told that since the Japanese were ruling Korea, the missionaries would need to understand Japanese also. He little knew how much he would be speaking Japanese when dealing with the omnipresent Thought Control Police.

He was really puzzled when told that a Korean, a Chinese, and a Japanese might read the same newspaper with ease, but then find it impossible to discuss what they had read. The answer is that the characters printed on a page present information to their minds, but the sounds they make repeating that information vary greatly one from another.

All of this had him repeating what he had said in the dormitory the night before: If this is mission work, let me out! All of those articles in *The Far East* had not prepared him for this.

By the end of the first class, Harold Henry knew that studying Korean day after day could be a droning monotony that would demand his best courage. It would put his attitude of "no sweat" to a test it had never been put to before. By lunchtime he realized that any language of the Far East is exceedingly foreign to Western tongues and ears. A Westerner studying French, Spanish, or Italian, or even the classic Greek and Latin, finds many words familiar. And they seem to fit the tongue somehow. But in an Eastern language every step is truly foreign.

Harold Henry knew that this would also be a test of his humility. At age twenty-four he had been in school for nearly twenty years and he was getting tired of the smell of the lamp. He was ready for action. He wanted to get out and use some of the things he had learned. But he realized that as a Korean missionary the most painful words he would have to say are, "Chosun-mal-morumnida." (I don't understand Korean.)

Each Columban found it an exercise in humility to leave the little world of the seminary compound and wander alone through the tangle of Taegu. Each returned with tales of embarrassment, and while the stories made everybody laugh they also made each young priest less willing to take his chances outside the walls.

One newly arrived priest in search of a church stopped a Korean to seek directions. The priest blessed himself, folded his hands with an excess of piety, rolled his eyes heavenward, and said, "Ding-dong, ding-dong." The Korean led him to the corner and pointed to a steeple silhouetted against the horizon.

Those frustrating days in language class so appalled Father Henry that he resolved to urge better language-training at every opportunity. As he rose in the scheme of things in Korea he worked for better and better language schools, especially after he had taken a Berlitz course in French, right after World War II, and saw the possibilities of such a system.

Today the language courses are a far cry from those sorry efforts in 1933. New missionaries go to the Myongdo Institute, run by the Franciscan Fathers, and to Yonsei University, under Presbyterian direction, both in Seoul. Koreans jokingly refer to the institute as "the foreigner's kindergarten," because the alphabet, writing, and correct speech are kindergarten subjects. The course consists of six forty-minute sessions a day, five days a week, for two years. After a year at an institute, Columbans do a year of pastoral work and then return for the second year. They find that the pastoral year helps consolidate what was learned in the first year.

In the spring of 1934, after only six months of ineffective language study at St. Justin's in Taegu, the young Columbans said goodbye to the French missionaries and the Korean seminarians. They left the familiar seminary compound with some regret, feeling unprepared for the hectic life outside the gate. With uneasiness they took a train to the province of Cholla Nam Do in the southwest, the territory assigned to the Columban Fathers. That assignment, made in Rome a year earlier, had changed the direction of Harold Henry's life from China to southwest Korea.

CHAPTER

5

The Curate of Noan

MONSIGNOR OWEN MacPOLIN, the first Columban superior in Korea, assigned Father Henry to assist Father John Pak at Noan. Father Pak met the American at the railroad station at Naju and they set off by a steaming Model T taxi which stopped often to take on water. A mile from the church the priests got out and walked because the path became too narrow for the Ford.

More than forty years later Archbishop Henry recalled that at this point something nice finally happened to him in Korea. It was like the sun coming out from behind a dark cloud: "Suddenly, near the compound, I felt like the potentate of Baghdad. Several hundred Catholics and many of their pagan neighbors were there to welcome me. And what a warm welcome! Father Pak insisted I give a speech, but the only thing I could summon were butterflies in the stomach. He told me to talk in Latin and he would translate into Korean. What I said and what he said I said didn't match too well. He took my banal Minnesota sentiments, poured oriental courtesy over them, and tacked on enough honorifics to sink a ship."

In short order Father Henry realized he would learn little Korean from his pastor, a born orator of Ciceronian stamp, who held forth in Latin at breakfast, lunch, and dinner and during all spare times in between. What Father Henry hadn't yet learned about life is that hardships so often turn into advantages: all of that Latin would stand him in good stead thirty years later sitting in St. Peter's basilica during the Second Vatican Council.

When it became evident even to Father Pak that his new curate was avoiding all conversation with the parishioners, he hired a Korean boy, Lorenzo Ri, to help with language lessons for an hour each evening. What really hurried the progress, though, was Father Pak's illness. When Father Henry heard that his pastor must leave for a few months of recuperation, he was of a mind to take off, too. He had to keep reminding himself never to make a decision while feeling depressed.

Up until this point he dared not hear confessions, but now the duty was thrust upon him. He had to make all the decisions in the parish, and, even more frightening, he had to make the autumn visits to every mission station to examine Catholics in their knowledge of the catechism.

On each visit to a mission station the young priest could feel sure that when he stepped from the train or bus at least twenty parishioners would be standing there waiting for him. He liked their greetings, "Are you in peace?" or "Have you slept in peace?" The distance to the house where the services were held was usually about five miles; the parishioners walked along feeling it would be a flaw in courtesy to permit the *sin-bu-nim* to walk alone.

He so much wanted to call each parishioner by name, but soon learned that each had several names. Koreans believe that the name given at birth will influence a child's destiny and so they give such names as Gentle Heart, Prosperous Old Age, Many Talents, Increased Happiness, Spring Fragrance, and Bright Jade. Soon after getting this "fate name" the child gets a nickname, often uncomplimentary. This is a carry-over from the Chinese belief that spirits try to infect the best loved child; so the parents try to fool the spirit with such names as Stupid Dog, Bed Bug, Poor Potato. In school there is a book name, later a business or professional name, at marriage another name, and, if baptized, a Christian name. This great diversity of given names is in contrast with the sameness of family names: a survey showed five and a half million Koreans are named Kim; four and a half million, Yi; two and a half million, Pak; one million, Choi; and one million, Chang.

Harold Henry had three names during his forty-two years in Korea. At first he was Hyun Sin-bu-nim. Hyun is the Koreanization of his own name, and *sin-bu-nim* means father. As bishop, he was Hyun Joo-kyo, a master of religion; as archbishop, he was Hyun Dae-Joo-Kyo, a big master of religion.

In these early contacts with the parishioners he learned many things that nobody had taught him in school. For example, when a Korean says, "I have come to work," he usually means I am ready to go to confession, a code that carries over from the days of persecution. He also learned that when asking directions, never put the question in such a way that a yes answer is possible.

If you say, "Is this the road to Kwangju," the answer will be yes, even if it isn't. So the question should be, "Where is this road going?"

As the young priest walked along with his parishioners he was aware of the many devil posts at the edge of the road. These symbols of shamanism, standing always in pairs, were constructed to appease evil spirits. The posts, with the faces of demons carved on them, were usually painted red, with hats and eyebrows blue. As the priest grew older, the posts grew fewer until today only a few are found decaying along the paths approaching remote villages.

During those walks from the railroad station Father Henry practiced his Korean on the children. One day he said to a boy, "Do you really understand my Korean?" The boy bowed. "You speak Korean very well," he said, "but it is difficult to understand."

When Father Pak returned, a parishioner told him that his assistant's Korean had so improved, but that he was using so many words derived from the Chinese that the women could not understand his sermons—a great tribute for any speaker in Korea.

Language is the first thing a stranger in a strange land is aware of, and food is next. Father Henry had expected a language problem, although not all that much, but as for food he hadn't given it a thought. He soon began to give it thought at Father Pak's table because it was there that his digestive problems began. Here again was a case of a hardship turning, in time, to an advantage: Five years later digestive problems would send him to the Philippines for treatment and there he would make new friends, who would, in turn, introduce him to other friends. Altogether they brought great changes into his life. Such turning of hardships into advantages led him to see, in time, the wisdom of the Korean proverb, "Trouble is the seed of joy."

Digestive problems began with Peter, the cook. A woman cooked Father Pak's food, but the pastor hired Peter to cook Western style for Father Henry. At the first meal it was evident that Peter had not the slightest idea of what Western food was like. Father Henry, no chef himself, tried to teach him the fundamentals. Since Peter had a genius for making food appear repulsive, the young priest stressed aesthetics first.

One day—Glory be!—Peter served a dish of fish, potatoes, and cabbage in such an attractive manner that it deserved to be photographed for the jacket of a cookbook. But the taste! To show appreciation for the great visual improvement Father Henry tried to force himself to eat it. Finally he pushed the plate aside and said, "I can't eat this. What did you do with it?" Peter said, "You Americans don't like the hot, spicy food we like in Korea. So I put sugar on everything." For the rest of his life Archbishop Henry avoided sugar, even in his coffee.

Since the cookhouse was thirty yards from the dining room, the soft-boiled eggs were usually cold when they reached their destination. Father Henry suggested to Peter that he carry the eggs across the yard in a bowl of hot water. Peter put hot water in a bowl, an egg cup in the hot water, and the egg atop the cup so that it rode a full inch above the water line. As the Archbishop remembered it, he was very pleased with himself.

One day, when Monsignor MacPolin made the mistake of asking Father Henry how he felt, he said, "My stomach is killing me. Peter will be the death of me. Father Pak won't fire him because he says he is a good and holy man." "As Aristotle would say," the monsignor observed, "holiness in a cook is a purely accidental quality."

Father Henry's problems with Korean food continued. Later, as an archbishop, he said, "The best piece of advice the seminary gave its future missionaries was, 'When in the Orient, peel everything!' "

Learning to eat with chopsticks was just one more frustration. It was especially disturbing when spectators, standing around the table, focused attention on the diner's every uncertain move. Somewhere the young priest had heard of the Korean proverb, "One eye finds more truth than two ears," and he wondered what truth those curious eyes were finding. He had also heard that Koreans called occidentals, *Yang-ko*, "big noses," and that added to the uneasiness whenever he was the center of concentrated attention.

Father Henry, although only twenty-four, was beginning to realize the truth of the old Chinese saying that although a man's life does not fill a hundred years it has in it enough cares to fill a thousand. It was clear to him now that of all the vocations he might have followed, he had selected the most care-ridden. He realized that the difficulties of language and food were minor in that they would disappear; the real problems would be lasting.

One of the real problems was to stop seeing his parishioners as ciphers, as foreigners, all with the same unfamiliar look about them. The Korean race is characterized by high cheek bones, noses flattened at the bridge, Mongoloid eye folds, straight dark brown hair, stockiness, and medium height. To Harold Henry they all tended to look alike. He did not see them as individuals in the way he saw Minnesotans. He kept telling himself that each was an individual and as different from the rest as were his neighbors in Northfield.

The hardest thing of all would be to achieve what a French missionary at the seminary in Taegu had told Father Henry he must try to achieve, *adaptation totale*. He must cease being a stranger in a strange land and try to see life as Koreans see it, to react and feel as they do. He knew he would never be able to bring this off completely because he looked at life through a template formed long ago in Greece and Rome, formed by a Judaeo-Christian culture and an Anglo-Saxon heritage. The Korean template was formed by Buddhism, Confucianism, Shamanism, with Chinese, Japanese, and, of recent date, American influences.

Father Henry decided that the best way to begin seeing things through Korean eyes would be to attend social functions, birthday parties, weddings, and festivals. Right off he learned that there are two big birthday celebrations in a Korean's life, the first and the sixty-first.

The first birthday is more than a milestone, it is a formal introduction to family and friends. The climax of the ceremony, and a ceremony it is, comes when the baby is placed in front of a table on which are displayed symbols of trades and professions—a writing brush, pieces of thread, coins, a hammer, a flute. Tradition says that the child's future career can be guessed by observing the thing he grabs first.

When a Korean reaches his sixty-first birthday, *hwankap* as it is called, he has completed the Chinese (or Lunar) cycle of sixty years. He has reached the fullness of his years and is supposed to retire to seek serenity. When young Father Henry entered into the festivities of a *hwankap*, shortly after coming to Noan, he never dreamed that his own *hwankap* celebration would be one of the biggest in modern times.

Father Henry stood in awe at the lavishness of the first Korean marriage he attended. The parents spend so freely on such events that sometimes they destroy themselves financially. All marriages in those days used to be arranged, not for the benefit of the boy and girl but of their families, but that is going out now. "I was shocked," the archbishop recalled, "to see so many sad-looking brides. No bride ever smiled on her wedding day, and sometimes after the ceremony she would lean against a tree and cry. As a young priest I didn't realize she was putting on an act. She is expected to do that to indicate that she is not really happy to be getting away from her parents, after all."

Young Father Henry had heard of the Lunar New Year celebration, but he had no idea of how social and solemn it was. There in remote Noan he saw Koreans celebrating a feast he had hoped to see celebrated in China. That disappointment was still there.

New Year's Day is a family holiday. Just before the fifteen-day feast, all who can travel go to their home towns so that the master of the household might perform the ceremony with all relatives on hand. Thankfulness for things received is the motif for the last ceremony of the old year and the first of the new. This is followed by the "making-up feast," a time when all quarrels are to be forgotten so that harmony might reign. The special dish at this meal is *ttok-kuk*, rice-cake soup. After the ceremony the children make deep bows and offer older relatives some coins strung on a strong red string; these are known as "the coins that crush the years."

In Noan Father Henry learned the omens to watch for on New Year's Day. If the wind blows from the southeast, the harvest will be good. If clouds fill the sky, food will be scarce. When the cat washes it's face, guests are on the way. When the eyelids quiver, some friend is confessing his sins. If the candle flickers, wealth is in the offing.

Father Henry was intrigued by the "Feast of the Excited Insects," on March 5, and was told that this was the time of year that insects and other underground animals bestir themselves from a winter's sleep.

Sure enough, two underground creatures that he had come to dislike, the snake and the centipede, were beginning their activities. In his long hikes to the mission stations, he had learned to watch for both along the faint trails. Korean snakes range from big fellows four or five feet long and as thick as a man's wrist, on down to eighteen inches and the thickness of a finger. The big ones are harmless but the little ones can be deadly. One of the little fellows, an adder, lived beneath the stone that served as a step at the bedroom door; every time Father Henry went outside, the adder slithered off into the tangle a few feet away where he lay and watched.

He found the centipedes more annoying than the snakes; they were more difficult to see. When fully grown, a centipede is only six inches long and no thicker than a worm. It has a black body, a red head with strong pincers in the mouth and a multiplicity of red legs each armed with a stinger.

The centipede can go almost anywhere, pass through little chinks in doors, floors, or walls. It can climb up a chair or table, march across the ceiling, and drop on your bed or your head. Father Henry learned early that if you come in contact with a centipede you are in for two days of fierce pain.

He noticed that the games Korean children play are very seasonal. He was especially impressed with one they play on September 25th, the anniversary of a military victory. The children join hands and dance in a circle singing, slowly at first, just the words *Kang Gang Suwollae* (the mighty waters are coming). By degrees they quicken the pace until it sounds like an alarm, a perfect example of onomatopoeia. At first one can hear the water murmuring on the shore, but at the frightening crescendo one feels the great waves smashing on the beach. After a rest the children commence all over again.

The song recalls an event of 600 years ago. When an invading army threatened to land, the Korean warriors hid themselves and had the women dance on the shore and the surrounding hills. They gave the signal of the approaching enemy by singing *Kang Gang Suwollae*. The ruse worked; the invaders landed and the Korean warriors cut them down as soon as they touched the shore.

At the birthday celebrations, weddings, and feasts Father Henry began to see how important the Confucian system of "correct relations" is to the Korean. An awareness of superior-inferior status is the basis of all relationships, even personal ones. It extends to husband-wife, father-son, older brother-younger brother. This awareness is reflected in just how profound is the bow and just how glowing is the honorific.

Meanwhile, Father Henry was developing a relationship he had not been prepared for. His relationship with the Thought Control Police was one that grew more uneasy with the years and would eventually send him to prison.

One evening shortly after Father Henry had arrived in Noan a policeman came to the rectory. Father Pak invited him in as though expecting the visit. The policeman had not come to visit Father Pak; he was there to question the American.

Usually oriental courtesy requires that a conversation open with vague observations and glittering generalities. The policeman though, got right to the point and began questioning Father Henry about his life history.

"Why are you asking these things?" the priest wanted to know.

"For the records."

The next question the policeman asked was, "Did you ever meet a policeman in the United States?"

"Several times," said Father Henry. "But he didn't ask questions like this. If he had I would have told him to mind his own business."

After the policeman had gone, Father Pak explained to Father Henry that ever since 1910, when Korea had become a colony of Japan, police interrogation was part of a Korean's way of life. He warned the American to be nice to those fellows or they would make life miserable for him. During the next nine years he would often recall Father Pak's words.

Thought Control detectives, plain clothesmen all, visited Father Henry twice a week. They were suspicious of "dangerous thoughts" and so they always asked his thoughts on various matters. If he said he had no thoughts on a certain subject, the next question was, "I know that you do not think about it, but if you did think about it, what would you think?"

One time when the young priest was hearing confessions in a mission station, a policeman asked an old lady what the American was up to. To impress him she said that the *sin-bu-nim* was listening to what people had done wrong, and that even though threatened by death he would never reveal what he had heard. This got the policeman so excited that he said he must sit in the confessional next to the American. Although Father Henry was able to scotch this plan, the policeman was so disturbed that he kept sucking on his teeth in the Japanese manner for the rest of the day.

The Japanese police always associated confessions with espionage. What else but state secrets would a Korean whisper to a foreigner through a screen of plaited rushes?

Forty years later Archbishop Henry recalled those days with displeasure: "Whenever we took a bus or a train the ubiquitous policeman asked for our name card, destination, purpose of travel, and time of return. During the trip a plainclothesman would sit and talk, picking our brains. On arrival another policeman would ask the same questions asked at the start of the trip. Shortly after arriving at a rectory to visit a priest you could bet that two detectives would drop by to talk an hour or two. This was maddening, for they were such dull fellows. On the return trip we ran the same gauntlet, and upon reaching home we were asked what we had discussed during the visit. This meant that during the visit the guest and the host had to decide on what answers they would give, because the slightest conflict in answers would drive the Thought Control Police right up the wall.

"I'll never forget one time a couple of priests visited me from China. They said that in China when you went visiting you were always asked how many bandits you had met on the road. In Korea the question is how many policemen had you encountered on the way."

Father Henry knew that all his answers were being kept in the local police station, but he had no idea of how fat his file was becoming.

CHAPTER
6

The Orange-Crate
Church in Naju

ONE APRIL DAY in 1935, Father Pak told Father Henry that the two
of them had been asked to go to Naju to talk with Father Owen MacPolin,
the superior of Columbans in Korea. With this news the young curate began
to fear that his days in Noan were numbered.

Suddenly his two small rooms, each eight feet square, became quite dear
to him. They were nothing to look at and, in their cramped severity, they
bore the air of sadness so often found in the cheerless quarters of missionaries. The iron bed and straw mattress, the first in Noan, had caused as
much comment as had his father's first car in Northfield. The Koreans never
tired of coming by to marvel, for they slept on the floor with a block of wood
for a pillow, and were surprised to find that anyone slept any other way.

It had been an uneasy year, and yet he would be sorry to leave. He would
even miss the adder under the great stone just outside the door. One thing he
would not miss, though, was that big bell ringing outside his bedroom window at four o'clock each morning. Father Pak went to bed before dark and
arose before dawn to say Mass at four-thirty, and he insisted that Father
Henry say his at five. Somehow Father Pak had picked up the idea from the
French missionaries that to be holy one must rise very early. Perhaps he had
heard the French superior general say, "I ask our missionaries what time they
arise. If they are up and about by four-thirty, I need not worry about them;

the rest of their spiritual life is in good order." Father Henry, however, had picked up the idea from the Irish that it is best to let the day get a slight head start.

Father MacPolin brought with him to Naju Father Thomas Quinlan, who would in time become a survivor of the "Death March" in 1950. Before coming to Korea he had dickered with the Chinese bandits over the amount of ransom the Columbans would pay for Fathers Laffan and Lenihan. Since Fathers MacPolin and Quinlan were "old China hands," Harold Henry regarded them with a certain awe.

When Father Pak and his young assistant arrived from Noan, the first thing the Columban superior said to Father Henry was, "We've decided that the Columbans will establish their first Korean Parish in Naju. I'd like you to be the first pastor."

Father Henry's heart skipped a few beats. To be asked to start the first Columban parish in Korea was an honor, but at Naju, of all places! It was a sorry, smelly town—rundown, backward, disheveled. And the people had a bad reputation—tough and stubborn and difficult to deal with.

It had been the capital of a province until, at the time the Japanese took over, somebody assassinated the governor. So, out of spite, the Japanese moved the capital to Kwangju. It was also in Naju, in March 1919, that the student riots against the Japanese had started at the railroad station and spread across Korea. From then on the Japanese made sure that nothing nice happened to Naju; the official attitude was "let it lie there rotting in the sun."

After breaking the news, Father MacPolin went on to tell how Naju had been started as a mission station in a remarkable manner. It had to be started in a remarkable manner if Harold Henry was to become a part of it, for nothing in his life ran along ordinary lines.

It began one day, Father MacPolin said, when the police siren blew the signal for high noon. Mr. Augustine Ri, a merchant in Naju, paused, made the sign of the cross, and started to say the Angelus. When he had finished, a lady came to him to ask if he were a Catholic, because she and her husband, the bank manager, were. They had just been transferred to Naju and wondered where the nearest church might be. When Mr. Augustine Ri told Father Pak of the incident, the pastor of Noan decided to assign a woman catechist to Naju, and began going there himself at regular intervals to say Mass. And now, two years later, Naju was about to get a church, a rectory, and even a school.

The four priests—two Irishmen, one American and one Korean—tramped back and fourth across the building site speaking in Latin. Father Quinlan said that the church ought to stand just about here, but Father Pak said, no, no *"propter pontem."* No matter what Father Quinlan said, Father Pak disagreed, *"propter pontem."* In annoyance Father Quinlan said in English, "Where is that crazy bridge he keeps talking about? I don't see it, do you?" Father Henry felt pleased to be able to explain that Koreans cannot pronounce "f" or "v" and that Father Pak was really saying that the church should not stand on that exact spot, *"propter fontem"* because of the well and not *"propter pontem,"* because of the bridge.

The church was finally built, avoiding the well, of orange-crate lumber. It wasn't exactly a cathedral, its young pastor had to admit, but after all there were only seventeen Catholics within walking distance.

Father Pak told Father Henry that if he wanted to develop his parish he ought to attract the interest of the *yungkams*, for they were the most respected people in the land. A *yungkam* is a man who seeks to become the Confucian ideal man, *sin-sa*, a gentleman. He pursues learning and seeks serenity; he moves slowly with measured tread through town and village, perfectly at ease and always careful of his conduct. He tries to inculcate the Confucian observation that "the gentleman makes demands on himself; the inferior man makes demands on others," believing that through such example he can still have influence in life.

The young priest sent a message to some old men deep in the mountains saying that a *sin-bu* would be visiting their village. *Sin-bu* means priest, but, depending on the Chinese characters used, it can also mean bride. So when Father Henry arrived and introduced himself as Henry *Sin-Bu* there was great puzzlement among the sages. Finally, they admitted that they had expected a beautiful young bride to come visit them. Despite their disappointment, they treated the priest with the deep courtesy a *yungkam* prides himself in. The old men said that Henry *Sin-Bu* was the first Westerner they had ever seen, and, according to Korean custom, inquired of his age. He asked them to guess. After a long earnest conversation, scarcely any of which the priest understood, an old man with a long, stringy, white beard and a black stovepipe hat, said in all seriousness, "We estimate you to be about seventy-five years old." When the young priest showed suprise, the old man explained, "You misunderstand. We speak not of your age in years. We speak of your age in wisdom and experience. You have the wisdom and experience of a man of seventy-five."

Forty years later the archbishop was to recall, "Since I was only twenty-five at the time, I came down from the mountain walking on cloud nine."

Harold Henry rarely walked on cloud nine during his first few years as a pastor. He was painfully aware that there he was in an area of half a million people and had only seventeen parishioners in his Naju church and only 150

scattered throughout the mission stations. He seemed to be making no head-
way. He tried repeating to himself something heard in the seminary: "In
God's plan some sow and others reap." But he still wanted to see a little of the
harvest. Right now! He was young and eager and had been getting ready for
this since that August afternoon in 1922 when Father Murphy came to the
house to say the Columbans had accepted him. That was thirteen years ago!

Father Henry needed to keep reminding himself of something Father Galvin had said, "We are not here to convert China, we are here to do God's
will." He had to keep repeating that he was in Naju to do God's will, and that
if he happened to convert some Koreans along the way, well and good; but
first he must be concerned with God's will. Deep down inside he had a
strong sense of vocation, the push of destiny. He kept telling himself that following the push was victory enough, no matter what the statistics showed.
Some time in his life he had said, Yes, and, having said it, felt sure that God
gives his grace in proportion to the job he wants done. If Harold Henry
hadn't believed that, he would have shaken the dust of sorry Naju from his
sandals and sought refuge in a parish in the States.

He often thought of that pastor in Minneapolis who couldn't understand
why anyone would want to be a missionary. The old priest used to say to the
newly ordained Father Henry, "There is China enough at home!" Maybe he
is right, maybe there is Korea enough at home. There is a shortage of priests
in the States. . . . Yes, but . . .

As he stumbled across rocky trails, there was no hint of a harvest. Like all
missionaries he took seriously the command, "Going therefore teach ye all
nations." But what, O Lord, if the nations aren't listening? A sentence in
Scripture used to give him pause: "Master, the whole night through we have
toiled and have taken nothing, but at thy word I will lower the net."

He could have walked on cloud nine had he known that eventually he
would see the little orange-crate church in Naju divided into eight parishes
serving fourteen thousand Catholics. The little mission station of Yeong
Kwang would develop into a church with more than a thousand parishioners.
Remote Ham Pyeong would grow into a flourishing parish of over 3,300.
After a dark night he would lower the net and find it filled.

Although conversions were few that first year, there was no lack of conversations at the rectory. All day and half the night visitors came saying they
had just dropped by for a *nollo*—to kill time. Father Henry found he could
stand about four hours of such aimless visiting and then every nerve in his
body started screaming for deliverance. If someone came on official business,
the time-wasting visitors gathered to listen to the conversation. When they
became bored, they took books from the shelf, leafed through them, and re-

placed them upside down—always upside down. If the priest tried taking a nap, the visitors leaned in the bedroom window saying they had just dropped by for a chat.

During meals, five or six Koreans stood around the table watching their pastor eat. They refused to sit down, but just stood and stared and tried to be helpful—passing plates that were within easy reach, putting the sugar he didn't want into his coffee, always proffering things with both hands in the polite oriental manner. They said that no one of importance should eat unattended. In time he began to enjoy these services; he no longer propped a book up beside his plate and gulped his food. Perhaps this would be a cure for the indigestion that had started with the blood sausage back in Taegu.

One day, during one of those interminable conversations, Father Henry said something and the visitor replied, "That is not what you told John Kim six months ago." At that instant the missionary realized that anything he said to anyone in that room was soon repeated all over town. Here was a way of getting the word around! This was not wasting time; this was a method of evangelization. He realized the truth of the Korean proverb, "A word has no feet, but it travels a thousand miles."

Yet this isn't how he thought it would be. He had always pictured missionaries preaching to the multitudes. But here he was in a shabby little room in a mangy town talking to a few Koreans who smelled to high heaven of *kimchi*. He realized that one of his main weaknesses was that he was a perfectionist. He rebelled against the reality of an imperfect world—imperfect at least when seen close up, but perfect as an overall plan.

Archbishop Henry said that the only thing that helped him keep his sanity during his first years as pastor of Naju was the school he started. In a red-clay building that came with the church grounds, he began a class in catechism. Before the children could read the catechism, they had to learn to read Korean, and so he began with the alphabet.

He had a feeling things were going too well and, sure enough, one day there came two unwelcome visitors—the chief of police of Naju and the head of the Thought Control Department. Upon entering the compound and hearing the children droning the Korean alphabet, they turned and left immediately to decide what action whould be taken against the *sin-bu*.

The next morning Father Henry had to report to the police station to explain why he had started a school without permission. He explained that it was not really a proper school, that he taught the alphabet merely to help the students read the catechism. The officials kept repeating, "There is a blackboard on the wall; therefore, it is a school." They made a concession, though, saying that the *sin-bu* could have a *kang-sup-so*, an institute for short courses, providing he reapplied for a permit every six months, a discouraging tangle of red tape.

The law allowed only sixty students for each grade, and so, with four grades, the enrollment was always 240. Since twice that many usually applied, it was necessary to give entrance exams to hold down the number. On the day the results of the examinations were published, Father Henry would go away for a week to escape the parents sitting on his doorstep imploring him to take children who had not passed the exam. He realized his school was popular, not because of the religion he taught but because only three out of ten Korean children could get into school in those days. The Japanese seemed to have a policy of keeping their colonials ignorant.

It would have been encouraging for the young pastor had he foreseen all the good results that would come from that dilapidated red-clay school. He got some hint of what it had meant to the children when, in 1958, as Bishop of Kwangju, he was invited to Naju for an "alumni reunion." He learned that three of those children grew up to be admirals in the Korean Navy, many became successful businessmen, civic leaders, and teachers. At the reunion, the school historian reported that of the 1,300 children who had completed the fourth grade, nearly a thousand had entered the Catholic Church later in life.

About the time of the reunion a young man, with his family of five and six of his neighbors, called on Father Patrick Brandon, a pastor in Kwangju City, saying they all wanted to be received into the Church. The young man said that while attending the Naju school he had been too poor to afford the fees and that Father Henry had told him to come to him personally to collect the money so that the boy might hand it to the teacher without embarrassment. The young man also said that at least two-thirds of the children were too poor to afford lunch and that the *sin-bu-nim* used to buy about 400 rice cakes for those who brought no food with them. In gratitude for this charity, the young man had been saying the prayers he had learned in school twenty years earlier.

A short time after the reunion Bishop Henry was in Seoul for an official government function. A man introduced himself as a member of the Korean Parliament and said that he used to play tennis on the court Father Henry had scraped out on the school grounds a quarter century earlier. He said that from what he had heard about the Church from Father Henry and from having seen the Church in action he decided that when free to do so he would become a Catholic. He didn't feel free while serving as a city official under the Japanese; any hint of an interest in the Church would have scored against him. After World War II he went to a parish in Seoul, received instruction and was baptized.

Even while still in Naju the young pastor saw enough results to feel encouragement. After two years the parish had grown from 17 to 100. Since the little orange-crate church was now inadequate, plans were started for a new one, but where the money would come from was still a mystery. At that time Bishop Cushing, later the Cardinal, was director of the Propagation of Faith in Boston. He sent the Columban Fathers $2,500 for a new church. Since Naju was the first parish the Columbans had established in Korea, and since it had now outgrown its church, it got the money. Shabby, disheveled Naju—the town of scurrying rats and rank sewage—celebrated the dedication of a new church on October 7, 1937.

Father Henry not only had a new church, he had three fast-growing mission stations, *kong-sos*, as they are called. He enjoyed visiting those smaller places; it appealed to his sense of adventure. Besides, it helped him to know the people better for he had to live with them while on the road; and he soon learned the truth of something Father Neligan was to observe: "There is more faith in the *kong-sos* than in the town. There is also more insect life."

The young priest would pack his Mass kit and other needs on the back of a bicycle and take off down a road of ruts and boulders. People would stop him to ask what he was selling. It seems that years before a Russian had covered the same territory on a bicycle loaded with cloth for sale.

At the mission station he would go to an ordinary Korean house built of wood and mud and thatched with rice straw, just like the houses seen from the train window on that dreary Sunday morning he and the Irish priests had traveled from Pusan to Taegu. The floor was raised a foot from the ground and consisted of granite slabs about two inches thick, the joints sealed with mud, and the whole covered with thick, oiled paper securely glued down. Since Koreans wear no shoes indoors, the tread of their stockinged feet wore the oiled paper as smooth as silk. To give heat in bitter winter, a fire sent fumes through a series of long tunnels beneath the floor keeping the surface warm where the Koreans sat and slept.

The catechist, who represented the missionary at the *kong-sos*, usually served the dinner. He placed before Father Henry a table scarcely a foot high and displayed on top of it an array of brass bowls filled with soup, seaweed, rice, fish, and eggs. Instead of tea or coffee, the beverage was usually the hot water in which the rice had been boiled. Next to all of this he placed a pair of brass chopsticks and a flat brass spoon. Having arranged this in a spirit of ritual, the catechist stood back, tucked his hands in his sleeves, bowed deeply, and uttered the polite Korean equivalent of "Get going!"

To sit at the tiny table without sprawling was a problem for all occidentals. Father Henry marveled at how even the tallest and stoutest Korean could gracefully fold his legs under and contentedly rock back and forth. He found that it helped some if he could squat on his heels near a wall, leaning back for support.

Of course some of the parishioners, the pillars of the church, sat around and watched the young priest eat. He was not expected to speak during the meal, for Koreans feel one should focus full attention on the food. Father Pak had told him that as a compliment to his host he should make noise while eating, and that the highest accolade would be a resounding belch at the close of the final course. For the sake of good public relations, Father Henry tried to make noise, but his early Minnesota training that stressed soundless swallowing kept getting in the way.

The young priest came to cherish these quiet minutes at the table, not so much because of the food but because they were the only ones free from hurry. From the time he wheeled his bicycle up to the out-station until he mounted again it was a case of go, go, go.

First he would hear confessions and say Mass. Then came the slow process of examining the catechumens, those who were studying prayers and doctrine, usually a six-month program, for admission into the Church. Sometimes there were baptisms to perform. And there was always the pesky matter of keeping records of baptisms, deaths, marriages, emigrants, and immigrants. In between he visited the sick to make sure they received the sacraments. At night the Catholics crowded into his room for an *iya ki,* a long session of talking, talking, talking. That is when he got to know every person in the parish.

Often there would be a delegation. Father Henry came to dread the sight of a delegation, not so much that it usually brought a problem, but that it took so long to get around to saying what it had come to say. He was always impatient to hear the worst, and at first he tried delving to the bottom without delay. Soon he learned that this was not the Korean way. And so, with much profound bowing all around, he would ask the visitors to be seated and would begin to chat pleasantly about the weather, crops, and market, which in Korea as elsewhere form the stock-in-trade of ordinary conversation.

The members of the delegation did not easily tire of such commonplaces. They made it sound as though their only concern was the delay of the rainy season, but Father Henry knew that deep in their hearts was a single thought and that, in time, they would allow it to surface. He found it frustrating to sit there knowing that he could not hurry along the ritual by so much as a minute. Often he would think of the tombstone somewhere in an Asiatic cemetery: "Here lies he who tried to rush the East."

Presently the conversation might take a religious turn. The old persecutions might be recalled and anecdotes of martyrs long dead retold. This could lead to a lengthy discussion on the growth of the Church in Korea. Now they were beginning to come out into the open and Father Henry could foresee the next step, but he dared not let on lest he drive the conversation back into the shadows.

Finally the delegation would say what it had come to say: we need a church, or a school, or a cemetery. This would lead to a lengthy discussion on the inconvenience of the present arrangement, both for the priest and the people. Added to this would be the fact that if the number of Catholics continued to increase, the situation would become impossible. The matter was one that demanded immediate attention.

Now it was Father Henry's turn. He could not answer yes or no as befit his character. To gain their respect he must reach the answer over a route as circuitous as the one they had taken in bringing their request. This he could never get used to.

As an archbishop, Harold Henry received letters imbued with the spirit of delegations. Page after page were filled with such purple prose as "Now that spring is here and snow is melting in the mountains and blossoms delight the valleys. . . . Knowing how honorable and faithful have been the ways in which you have brought new light into dark corners of Korea. . . ." The archbishop let his eye flit across the first few pages "like the flight of a joyful bird on a bright summer morning" and come to rest on a paragraph on the last page which began, *"Darumi anira"* (It is nothing else but this). Then followed the heart of the matter. He made his decision on the request stated in that final paragraph, and couched his answer with a touch of purple prose reminiscent of those long hours he squatted on his heels listening to delegations in mission stations years ago.

The better the young pastor came to know the people in the Naju area, the more he realized they were hungry for religion. He realized that Korea really had no religion. Of course there were some Christians, but they were only a tiny fraction of the population. Buddhism was practically dead in Korea; the temples had become museums, and ill-kept museums at that.

Confucianism, imported from China more than a thousand years ago, lay at the root of Korean society. But Confucianism is not a religion; it is a code of social behavior describing the duties between man and man, and especially between father and son. Its only religious implications are in the ancestor worship inherited from the Chinese culture in which it was formed. While Confucius taught no creed, he did say, "He who does not recognize a Divine Law cannot be a superior man."

Father Henry found that the religion he came across most often was shamanism, the worship of spirits inhabiting sun, moon, earth, mountains, rivers, trees. It is Korea's oldest religion and its influence is often encountered. Time and again the young priest came upon cases where illness or family misfortune were attributed to the power of hostile spirits. Sorcerers were engaged to placate such spirits with drums and incantations.

Sometimes he found a blending of Confucianism and shamanism. For example, the care with which the site for a grave is chosen is a meeting of Confucian ancestor worship with the animist's fear of spirits. If the ancestral spirit is at peace, things go well for the family; but if the spirit is restless in a poor grave site, an avalanche of misfortune might follow.

Father Henry had enough sensitivity—*nunchi* the Koreans call it—to feel the difference between villages of old Catholics and those of new. Catholics in the old out-stations are descendants of the martyrs of the last century. In times of persecution their ancestors fled from the cities to the mountains. Long periods of oppression made them suspicious of their neighbors, suspicious even of new converts. They are, however, steeped in a Christian tradition and faithful to their Church in a solid way. While the new Catholics show more enthusiasm for their faith and are far more zealous in its growth, still, in times of stress they are less dependable.

The young missionary is usually more impressed with the new Catholics. He sees a hundred catechumens preparing for baptism in a village where there had never been a Catholic before; he sees a young convert bringing twenty of his friends into the fold. And then he sees a hundred old Catholics who, between them, cannot persuade more than two or three to enter. He does not realize the peculiar difficulty of spreading the faith in an old station. In a completely pagan village there are always some people groping for something to believe, when suddenly a new doctrine flashes before them in all its splendor—free from all the blemishes of the men who profess it. Many of the well-disposed grasp at it, thinking that it will automatically overcome all their flaws and cure all their defects. In long-established missions, however, the non-Catholic sees not only the doctrine but the imperfections of those who follow it and, accordingly, puts less faith in the power of the doctrine.

A little experience teaches the young missionary to have more respect for the old Catholics. He finds few problems among them; the few converts they do bring in will be quickly absorbed and in a few years will be scarcely distinguishable from the old Catholics themselves. In the new missions, however, every new Catholic is a problem in himself; the youth who brought his twenty friends may himself lapse. There is no Catholic tradition in the place and mere theoretical knowledge cannot make up for it.

CHAPTER
7

Thought Control Pressure

B<small>Y EARLY</small> 1939 Father Henry was feeling ever-increasing Japanese pressure. Here was another case of coming events casting their shadows before them. He wrote to Father Patrick O'Connor, a Columban in the States: "They wanted us to sing the national anthem in the church and bow to the East (to the Emperor) before Mass every Sunday. We objected, and for once they gave in. The people were becoming very discontented being forced to go to the railroad station every time a soldier passed through. My school kids walked to the station as often as five times a day. The people could get no work done, so the authorities eased off."

Each Columban had a collection of anecdotes about the Japanese police that he traded with other Columbans at their rare meetings. One of these had to do with a letter that one Korean seminarian wrote to another during the holidays. In it he went into great length describing his feelings about Thomas Aquinas.

The letter was inspected at the local police barracks and caused great puzzlement. A policeman called on two Columbans to ask, "Have you heard about this man, this Thomas Aquinas?" watching closely their reactions.

They admitted having heard the name.

"What is his occupation?"

He wrote some books, the priests said, barely keeping a straight face.

"What is his address?"

That did it! They could no longer keep up the act.

Another suspicious policeman visited a Columban who had just entertained some of his Irish classmates.

"Why did they come here?"

"To celebrate their national Feast Day."

The word "national" caused the policeman to make a hissing sound that indicated suspicion.

The priest hastened to add that the Feast Day of Ireland is Saint Patrick's Day. The policeman took out his notebook and sat with pencil poised wondering how to spell Saint Patrick. The priest spelled it as phonetically as he could, "Sung Pa-triku."

A group of priests were to meet for a spiritual retreat, but when the retreat master took sick he sent a wire to each of them: "Retreat called off." The word "retreat" caused consternation among the Japanese police. One of them hurried to Father Henry and said, "We have read of the Crusades. Are you in Korea to organize a Crusade, and for what purpose?"

With each passing month Father Henry found that he gave less time to his converts and more time to the police. As the pressure grew he felt sure that Japan was preparing for war with the United States. He was not sure whether the Thought Control Police in Naju really considered him a spy, but no matter, they had to keep fattening his dossier to impress their superiors in Kwangju, Seoul, and Tokyo.

They seemed to go out of their way to create incidents just to have something to report. One such incident began when a man came from Ham Pyeng to visit Father Henry. He said he had moved from Taegu and, not knowing where to find a priest, had married in a civil ceremony. Now he wanted to be married in the church. He had been instructing his wife and about a hundred neighbors who gathered each Sunday in his yard for a prayer service. Almost immediately the young pastor biked to Ham Pyeong and, finding the wife well-instructed, baptized her and performed the wedding ceremony. He also found the neighbors well-instructed. In a short time these catechumens grew in number to three hundred. All this the Thought Control Department had under surveillance but hid its displeasure for the time being.

Seeing this rapid increase in conversions in Ham Pyeong, Monsignor Mac-Polin, the Prefect Apostolic of Kwangju—which means he had a bishop's jurisdiction without a bishop's orders—decided the town should have a *kong-so*. The Columbans made a down payment on a piece of property, but before the settlement was completed the owner said he had changed his mind. The same thing happened with a second piece of property. Father Henry gave one of his parishioners the money to buy property in his own name; after all was signed and sealed, he "donated" it to the Church. On hearing this the police flew into a rage. They arrested all the men coming to the mission station and tried to dissuade them from having anything to do with its pastor.

In retrospect Archbishop Henry said, "This seemed to strengthen the people in their faith. Or maybe they found it just one more way to protest against Japanese domination. Anyway I stopped going to Ham Pyeong so that the police would stop their harassment. I told my parishioners to come to church in Naju in small groups, not more than fifteen at a time. This worked for a short time."

On Christmas Eve of 1940 the Catholics from Ham Pyeong and those from the several mission stations converged on the church of Naju for Midnight Mass. To amuse themselves, early in the evening various groups danced, sang songs, and performed skits. The young pastor was so busy hearing confessions that he missed the entertainment and so knew little of what had gone on.

On Christmas afternoon a detective from the Thought Control Department came to the rectory to ask the name of the song that three girls from the mission station at Seok Jung Ri had sung the night before. Father Henry said he hadn't heard the song but imagined it must have been a hymn. The detective said, no, no, it was a song forbidden by the Japanese government. Father Henry doubted that this could be so because the children were scarcely ten years old. The detective said just forget about it, everything will be all right.

But evidently everything wasn't all right because a few days later a young man came rushing into the rectory so upset and out of breath that he could hardly report that the three girls were in a nearby jail. He said the police threatened to keep the girls from attending the Catholic church unless they revealed who had taught them the song. Lucia, the impudent one, said that the only way they could stop her from going to church was to kill her. After a week the police released the children from jail. They never learned that it was Lucia's father, the catechist, who had taught them the objectionable words: "The flower of freedom will bloom in Korea once again."

The flower of freedom bloomed less and less for Father Henry. A detective came to see him in July 1941 to say that from now on the priest would have daily twenty-four-hour "protection." Father Henry felt sure now that Japan, in preparing for war with the United States, wanted to make sure that every American was in easy grasp the instant hostilities began. His uninvited house guest intimated as much when he said, "Do not worry, if and when war comes I will be here to protect you."

Every visitor, on leaving the rectory, had to recount everything that had been said and Father Henry had to retell the conversation while the detective made copious notes. Nothing seemed too insignificant for the police to ponder. Without doubt the local Thought Control Department was under heavy pressure from above to provide more and more details.

The archbishop recalled that the Korean policeman assigned to protect him, Patrolman Pak, was an honorable gentleman. "He used to tell me not to worry, and that he would send in many reports but none unfavorable. And I don't think he sent any unfavorable ones. We have met from time to time through the years and our meetings are always cordial."

To increase the inconvenience, Japanese authorities in Naju told Father Henry that they were freezing his money—all of thirty dollars—in the bank. He was allowed to withdraw twenty yen a month, about five dollars. The bank manager, a Japanese, said this was a lot of foolishness, and he obtained permission to give the priest all of the money.

Each month Monsignor MacPolin's secretary came from Mokpo to Naju to help Father Henry with his financial problems—money for the salaries of the catechist and the cook, and for food. The pastor never ate so well before or since; the Koreans, Catholic and non-Catholic, brought chickens, eggs, vegetables, and delicacies. They did it partly out of pity for him and partly in protest of Japanese rule. "It was during this time," said the archbishop thirty-five years later, "that I realized why the Koreans are called the Irish of the East: They have a deep faith, a sense of humor, and are usually against any government that tries to tell them what to do."

The restriction that made Father Henry most uneasy was the one forbidding him to cross the city limits of Naju without permission from higher headquarters. He knew that higher headquarters meant Seoul and felt that if he asked permission it would either be refused outright or long in coming. This gave him a trapped feeling.

He had tried to achieve what the French missionaries called *adaptation totale* and had succeeded to some extent. After eight years, he no longer felt such a stranger in a strange land. He could look at Koreans now without being aware of the high cheek bones, noses flattened at the bridge, and Mongoloid eye folds. They could talk to him without focusing attention on the size of his feet or the length of his nose, and they no longer asked how he liked Korea or commented on his mastery of the language.

And still there was that need to get away from time to time, to be with other Columbans. He was hungry to hear English spoken and to talk about the green hills of Ireland, the cold winters of Omaha, the World Series, and the Notre Dame football season. This hunger, he knew now, would lessen with the years, but one can't come to the East as late as age twenty-four and shake off the West in all ways.

So on December first he asked permission to visit his fellow Columbans in Mokpo. He believed that by the time the request went through the tangle of red tape in Seoul he would, at best, get permission shortly after the first of the year. To his surprise the request was approved within a few days.

This brought up a problem. If he left immediately he would be away on December 8, a holy day in the calendar of the Church. He disliked that. And yet if he went now he would be back in plenty of time to make preparations for Christmas. He still remembered how crowded the compound was last Christmas Eve, and all the singing and dancing and other activities that caused the police to scurry about trying not to miss anything.

He felt a great push to go and to go right away. And so he and his police escort boarded the train for Mokpo. From time to time during the forty-five-mile trip he thought of December 8 and felt guilty about it. He didn't know, of course, that December 8, 1941, would be a big day in history, and the day his own little world would come tumbling down.

CHAPTER
8

Life in Korean Jails

A MAGAZINE WRITER once described Harold Henry as having "a soldierly look and something of the air of concentrated, swiftly directed vitality often seen in all-conference quarterbacks." The soldierly look and vitality were evident that cold December morning as he climbed the steep hill from the Mokpo railroad station to the Columban headquarters. He was on his way to visit another priest with a soldierly look, Monsignor Owen MacPolin, who retained the military bearing that had fitted him so well when serving as chaplain with the British forces in Europe during World War I.

Monsignor MacPolin's headquarters were in Mokpo even though he was Prefect Apostolic of Kwangju, fifty-two miles away. He chose this unusual arrangement because there were 700 Catholics in Mokpo and only 70 in Kwangju. Also he was taking the advice of an old French missionary, Bishop Florian Demange, who told him to get as far away as he could gracefully get from the Japanese officials in Kwangju.

As Father Henry approached the new headquarters he thought of how substantial and dramatic it looked sitting near the crest of a steep hill. The three-story brick building with its thick walls and ample beams had been completed by a Chinese contractor three years earlier, in 1938, at a cost of $8,000, which gives some idea of how far a dollar went in Korea in those days. Fortunately it was well-constructed, because it was destined to bear a great deal of abuse, especially during World War II and the Korean War. The first dramatic event would happen just inside the front door, within a few days, and Father Henry would play a leading role.

Not until he got inside the headquarters did the young pastor of Naju realize how hungry he was to speak English and to hear it spoken. From the first minute, he thoroughly enjoyed his winter holiday and readily fell into the routine of the establishment. Part of the routine was that each evening he would follow Monsignor MacPolin and Father Joseph O'Brien up the stairs to the monsignor's office where the three of them would listen to the news. Father O'Brien, pastor of the tiny Japanese church next door, acted as translator; the broadcasts, even though they came from the Mokpo radio station, were in Japanese.

On the Monday night, December 8, the announcer exploded onto the air in a frenzy. Monsignor MacPolin and Father Henry looked toward Father O'Brien. A shadow seemed to fall across his face. He seemed reluctant to start the translation. The voice on the air grew more angry with each sentence. It screamed with such violence that Father Henry wondered if Father O'Brien could understand what was being said. Maybe that was why he wasn't speaking. At last Father O'Brien said in a dry, flat voice, with all life gone out of it, "They bombed Pearl Harbor." (Although it was still December 7th in the United States, it was already the 8th in the Far East because of the International Date Line.)

Father O'Brien began to translate, "The United States fleet has been destroyed. . . . The American imperialists have committed untold crimes against the Japanese. . . . The imperialists have long interfered with the prosperity of the Far East."

As the voice ranted on, Father Henry said, "They'll come for me soon. They won't bother the two of you. You are Irish. They believe I'm a spy."

"What makes you think so?" asked the monsignor.

"They've often asked me at which bank in the United States the money was deposited—the money I got from the government for spying. I don't think the Japanese in Naju believe that, but the higher-ups do."

"We'll stand by you," said Monsignor MacPolin.

At that moment there was a loud banging on the front door. It had to be loud for the sound to reach all the way to the second story back of that substantial brick building. As Father Henry started down the stairs, the newscast was coming to an end. It only took them fifteen minutes, he said to himself.

Several Korean policemen led by a Japanese officer burst into the house and pinned Father Henry against the wall in the hallway. They shouted excitably, "Where are the other priests?" He said they were upstairs and offered to go after them. The officer ordered him to stay where he was and sent three of the patrolmen to the second floor. The rest began a search of the house. Soon three policemen were dispatched to the rectory of the church up the hill to arrest Fathers Patrick Monaghan and Harry Gillen.

The five Columbans were marched down the steep hill, herded into the Mokpo police station, and lined up in front of Chief Morinaga. The chief started to give a speech in English but by the middle of the first sentence it was evident he was not up to it, and so he continued in Japanese while a Korean acted as translator. The chief's speech turned into a tirade. Again and again, he returned to the theme that Americans had tried to destroy the Japanese and now they themselves must be destroyed. At the end of each statement he would ask, "What do you think of that?"

Suddenly Chief Morinaga sounded sad, "Americans must be punished and yet we must protect you. That is our duty. You must stay here. The accommodations are not of the best. What do you think of that?"

The monsignor answered the rhetorical question, "If it's all the same with you I'd rather go back to the house and take my chances."

"Do you want to die!" screamed the chief of police, pointing toward the street. Outside a crowd chanted for the death of all Americans. Mokpo was thirty percent Japanese and a good many of them had rushed to the police station to start a demonstration the minute the newscast had ended.

"Most of us are Irish," said the monsignor.

"But they cannot tell you from Americans," yelled the Chief.

"But we are neutral."

"Yes, you are neutral," admitted Chief Morinaga, "but you are neutral on the wrong side."

The chief brought the discussion to a sudden end by ordering the priests to remove their shoes and belts and empty their pockets. A policeman handed each a large brown paper bag and told him to print his name on it. Every item was listed as it was placed into the bag, and after the bag was sealed each prisoner was told to sign the list approving its accuracy.

The five Columbans were herded into a *yu-chi-chang*, an investigation cell. Father Henry saw that if he stretched out his arms he could touch both sides, so it was about six feet wide and perhaps nine feet long. This would be a tight fit for five large men and a oval wooden box that served as a toilet. Yet these accommodations were luxurious compared with those in some of the other small cells into which twice as many Koreans were crowded.

The guard at the door stressed no talking, no matter what. No talking! Never! Since they were not allowed to talk, and the hour was late and the cell was dark, the five priests experimented to see if it was possible for all of them to lie down at the same time. After some stumbling about, and some bumps and bruises, they found that if each lay on his side and didn't shift or turn, they could fit. The monsignor had always believed that on any expedition the leader should carry the heaviest burden, and now he lived that belief by being the one to sleep with his head tight against the oval wooden box.

They awakened in the cold, grey December dawn, stiff, aching, and nauseous, and they began to realize how serious their situation was. They soon learned that when the guard said no talking he meant it, and that they would not be given a chance to wash or shave or leave the cell for even a minute. Of course nobody had any cigarettes and there was nothing to read. Another rule that the guard enforced was no stretching out on the floor during the day; either stand or squat on the haunches oriental style, but no sprawling.

The one bright spot in their dark lives was the monsignor's cook. He asked the chief if he might prepare food for the prisoners, and, to everyone's surprise, was told to go ahead. The parishioners gave the cook food, and the meals he prepared from it were the only things the priests had to look forward to all day long.

The worst thing about the enforced silence was that it accentuated the sounds of torture from down the hall. Father O'Brien, who bore nothing but bad news, said that the Japanese police claimed to solve every crime and this is how they did it; they tortured someone until he admitted to the crime, guilty or not.

With each thud and scream and groan, Father Henry suffered a double agony, one for the victim down the hall and one out of fear that at any moment he would be given like treatment. As the only American in the cell, the only official enemy, he would surely be the first to be put to torture.

He desperately wanted to walk through that door. As he was wishing that most intensely the guard unlocked it and pointed at him. Suddenly the inside of that crowded, stinking cell seemed more attractive than the outside. Would it be torture or execution?

He whispered to Father O'Brien standing at the door, "Quick, give me general absolution," and dropped down on one knee. The young Irishman made the sign of the cross and said, "*Absolvo te, ab omnibus peccatis tuis, in nomine patris et filii et spiritus sancti.*"

Father Henry was led to Chief Morinaga's office and there stood Horse Feedbag, the policeman from Naju. Father Henry never thought he would be pleased to see him, for he had been a thorn in his side, but at least his was a face from back home. Horse Feedbag was the nickname given by the Koreans to the Thought Control policeman because of the way he used to nose around trying to sniff out the last grain of information the way a horse sniffs around inside a feedbag searching to find the last speck of grain.

The chief handed Father Henry the sealed paper bag containing his belongings and asked him to sign a receipt. "I am sending you to Naju. That is where you came from; that is where you should be interrogated. This officer will protect you. What do you think of that?"

Father Henry thought it seemed like an improvement, but he didn't say so. The word "interrogation" had a sinister sound.

He and Horse Feedbag walked out into the Mokpo street and the world looked wonderful. He was disheveled, unwashed, unshaven, but as he walked along working the stiffness from his body and drawing in one deep breath after another, even the smell of open sewers seemed delightful. Tiny flakes of snow were falling, and it was near Christmas, and he was going back to Naju. As they approached the railroad station, Horse Feedbag stopped at a kiosk, pointed to the cigarettes and suggested, "You'd better buy some." My, thought Father Henry, it is easy to love your enemies when they treat you like this!

On the hour and a half trip to Naju, Father Henry flinched each time Horse Feedbag used the word "interrogation." The clean, well-dressed policeman sat up straight on the upholstered seat; the dirty, disheveled priest slumped beside him. One was up, the other down. Years later the tables would be turned. Horse Feedbag, despised by his fellow Koreans and down on his luck, would lurch into the rectory reeking of drink and say that he had tried three times to make this call but could not do it until thoroughly drunk. After the visit he would go out and hang himself.

At the door of the Naju police station Horse Feedbag spoke one sentence that Father Henry clung to during the days of interrogation. He put his hand gently on the young priest's arm and said in the darkness, "Just tell the truth and everything will be all right." This suggested that Father Henry's dossier, which the policeman knew well, contained no damaging evidence.

Inside the jail, the cold seemed more penetrating than that outside. Father Henry did not expect to be pleased by what he found inside the cell, but as the thick wooden door swung open there stood Father Tom Kane, a young Columban from Chicago, now pastor of Noan. Both priests were delighted to see each other. Father Henry looked around the cell; it was twelve feet square, had a thirteen-watt bulb, and only Father Kane to share all of that space. This was palatial!

Father Henry signed the police record at ten o'clock at night, and at dawn the priests were still talking. Father Kane found it amusing that his superior, Monsignor MacPolin, slept with his head against the oval wooden box. The horrors of the Mokpo cell were beginning to fade enough for Father Henry to find certain things amusing, too.

Father Kane said he had refused to eat the jail food. It was a seaweed soup of such sorry quality that even the cheapest restaurant in Korea would have thrown it out. Much to his surprise the Japanese chief of police had said that Dominic, Father Henry's cook, could bring food. Father Henry exclaimed that this was really a red-letter day: first he was released from that Mokpo cell, then Horse Feedbag did two nice things for a change—allowing him to buy cigarettes and giving some consoling advice—then Father Kane was waiting in the cell, and now this good news about Dominic!

At nine o'clock the next morning the interrogations began. Chief Honda of the Thought Control Department plopped Father Henry's dossier on the desk. What a fat volume of documents it was! Detectives sat on each side of the chief with their backs to a window. That left the priest facing into the light, and in the morning the sun was in his eyes much of the time. Word by word, line by line, the chief moved with dogged thoroughness through Father Henry's eight years in Korea.

The radio caused the prisoner some trouble. It had been a real companion during those long evenings in the Naju rectory. He had listened without fail to the English language newscasts from Shanghai each night and then set his alarm for 2 A.M. to hear the newscast from New Delhi. Over that static-prone radio Father Henry followed the Sino-Japanese war from the day it started, July 7, 1937, at the Marco Polo Bridge. On September 16, 1938, he heard Dr. V. K. Wellington Koo report to the League of Nations that one million Chinese had been killed during the first year of fighting. He paid special attention to the news from the Columban mission areas, and for the first time he wondered if Providence had not spared him by sending him to Korea instead of to China.

While Hitler and Mussolini moved from triumph to triumph, he heard Chamberlain speak of "peace in our time," not realizing that within five years he himself would be playing a role in that unhappy pageant. He followed the war in Spain, and learned of Franco's victory, little dreaming that in twelve years he would learn through personal experience that civil wars are the most cruel of all.

The little radio brought him the news on February 10, 1939, that Pope Pius XI was dead. On March second he learned that Eugenio Cardinal Pacelli was now Pius XII. He wondered if the new pope would be mission-minded or, now that the times were out of joint, more concerned with the established Church.

Perhaps the radio itself would have been easy enough to explain away when discovered by his Japanese captors, but the map beneath it caused a problem. The detectives had found a National Geographic map of Asia tucked under the radio. The word "under" is the one the interrogators stressed, and paused to suck breath through their teeth each time they said it. Had the map been out in the open it may not have bothered them too much, but to have it hidden *under* the radio, surely that is the work of a spy. To explain to them that it was there because the housekeeper put it there, that it was part of his compulsion to have everything neat and tidy and squared off—to explain that was just a waste of breath.

The locked metal safe in the rectory was another object of suspicion. Father Henry explained the combination time and again, and each time the detectives returned to the jail to report that the prisoner must be lying because they could not open it. So, under cover of darkness they took the prisoner to the rectory. Within seconds the iron door swung wide and the detectives pushed the prisoner aside as though he might try to destroy the damaging evidence. Inside they found a little money, some records of births, deaths, marriages, and baptisms, and a deed to a piece of property.

The deed aroused suspicion. It was a deed to someone else's property. Surely to hold a deed to someone else's property hints at skulduggery. Both parties must be investigated.

The prisoner explained that his laundress, the poorest of the poor, was trying to raise a son; she needed a house to live in. He bought one for her and offered her the deed, but she said, no, he should put it in the safe so that nothing would happen to it.

The Japanese could not imagine anyone giving the deed to her house to someone else. Surely the prisoner must be holding it as a kind of ransom to be sure she keeps supplying him with the kind of information a spy needs. The detectives hurried off to interrogate the laundress. The prisoner could imagine the confusion of that confrontation and thought it would be laughable were it not pathetic.

In a final effort to get the prisoner to reveal himself as a spy, two detectives entered his cell at two o'clock one morning. Although the prisoner slept on a cold floor in an icy cell with only a blanket pulled over himself, he was able to sleep well after a day of interrogation. A detective shook him awake and said hurriedly, "We have just run out of invisible ink. We need it to send a message. It is very important. Please help us. We know you have some hidden in your house. Tell us where to find it. We won't hold it against you."

The sleepy prisoner said, "Invisible ink? How can you see it if it is invisible?"

The detectives sucked air through their teeth and let the prisoner go back to sleep.

Harold Henry remembered with gratitude a Korean policeman who said, "Today they will ask what you think of Hitler. Don't speak favorably of him. The Japanese don't like him; they don't trust him. Just say he has a strong army, but cannot be trusted completely." When making this response the prisoner could see by the look on the interrogators' faces that it was the perfect answer.

The interrogations went from nine in the morning to five at night for six days, and then on the twenty-third and twenty-fourth of December they went from nine in the morning until eleven at night. It was late on Christmas Eve when Chief Honda completed the last page in the dossier and wearily tied up the binding.

Watching that final gesture, Harold Henry felt like Father Henry again; suddenly he was free from the mentality of the prisoner. He went back to his cell walking tall. Hardly had the heavy wooden door closed behind him than the church bell, that big one he had ordered from France, began to ring for midnight services. It seemed to ring louder and longer than usual as though Dominic, riding the rope, was trying to wish the pastor a merry Christmas. Father Henry knew that his parishioners were gathering and that the catechist, Matthew Kim, would conduct the service of prayers and hymns.

Father Henry and Father Kane wished each other a Merry Christmas, said the rosary together, and talked far into the night. They felt sure Father Kane's interrogation would start on the morrow.

And so it did. Since he had been in Korea for not much more than a year, his dossier was rather lean. And also his facility with the language was lean. So the chief of Thought Control asked Father Henry to act as interpreter. After two days of interrogation, the chief admitted that the only thing he had against Father Kane was that he was an American from Chicago. The word Chicago seemed to evoke sinister feelings in the Japanese, as it did in many Americans in those days, less than a decade since the bootleggers' gang wars.

After the interrogations were over Father Henry was fingerprinted. He had heard that if you are fingerprinted it means you are to be brought to trial. He knew that if brought to trial his chances of being executed or at least sentenced to a long prison term were excellent. Since Father Kane was not fingerprinted, it seemed certain that something special was in store for the Naju pastor. He awakened each morning of Christmas week wondering if this was the day.

One day before New Year's Eve, Chief Honda said to him, "Because you have done so much good for poor people we are treating you better than we treat other prisoners." He said he would bring the priests' razors and soap and toothbrushes from their homes and then take them to his house for a bath.

Once Father Henry heard the good news he could scarcely wait for the chief to keep his promise. He became more aware than ever of the itch of his beard, of the bitter taste in his mouth, and of the fleas and lice that demanded so much of his attention by day and night.

Late at night Chief Honda took the two priests to his home for a Japanese bath. The two Americans didn't know that the Japanese soap themselves thoroughly and then rinse off the soap so that they are quite clean before they step into the large steaming tub. The Americans plunged directly into the tub leaving it looking as murky as the Mississippi at flood time. Father Henry noticed that Chief Honda seemed appalled at the barbaric bathing habits of his guests. Before returning the priests to jail, however, the chief had his wife serve them port and sandwiches.

During Christmas week the chief allowed his two priest prisoners to sit in his office while his daughters served them, in an elegant oriental manner, fragrant tea and beautifully wrought sandwiches.

Near midnight on New Year's Eve, the chief of police had the priests brought to his office. He told them he regretted being the one who must keep them confined because he was sure they had come to Korea for a good purpose and no doubt had helped the people.

Then he led the prisoners to the large waiting room where a party was in progress. All the policemen, both in the Criminal Department and in the Thought Control Department, were pouring rice wine and toasting each other freely. When the chief entered with the two priests, the festivities quieted. The chief poured three glasses of rice wine, he handed one to each prisoner, lifted his own, and paused until every policeman in the room had lifted his. Then he looked his prisoners in the eye and said, "To our guests!"

The toast was scarcely made before the noisy clock on the waiting room wall struck twelve. An hour later the two prisoners returned to their cell feeling that with a start like this 1942 couldn't be all bad.

Such optimism died almost as fast as the effects of the rice wine wore off. The new year began with a parade of dreary days. Looking back the interrogations seemed a godsend; at least they gave direction to the day. Now each day was as much alike as the marks scratched on the cell wall to make sure no day was lost track of.

The priests very much wanted their breviaries to say the daily office, that would have taken up more than an hour each day, but it is a tradition in oriental jails to allow no reading matter. The prisoner is expected to spend his waking hours contemplating the wrong he has done to the state and society. So they recited in common all the prayers they knew by heart and let it go at that.

The body needed care, too. The chemistry of youth was not enough. Exercise was needed. For a program in exercise he could not have drawn a better cell mate. Tom Kane was a rangy athlete. So the two priests spent long sessions putting each other through all the routines they knew and making up a few as they went along. It not only passed the time but made them feel they were preparing for the future. If and when they were released from the cell, they would bring fitness to whatever new life waited outside.

Dominic continued to send in larger meals than men ought to eat when confined to a cell twelve-foot square. The cook went around among his friends at the market and all contributed something—a chicken, a fish, a dozen eggs, a basket of potatoes, cabbages and carrots, and even jars of *kimchi*, the last thing people living in close quarters ought to eat. Later Dominic would pay a price for his faithfulness.

Some of the children in the parish asked Dominic to let them deliver the meals. This touched their pastor's heart because he knew how they had grown up fearing the police and that for them to walk through the jail door took an act of courage. While one boy handed the desk sergeant the tray of food and others gathered around to block his vision, the smallest boy would hurry to the cell door and toss cigarettes, matches and candy through the window near the top.

They did not fool the desk sergeant too long. He said to Father Henry, "Don't tell anybody this—I don't like the Japanese any better than you do—but you ought to tell those boys not to do what they are doing. They'll get in trouble."

The next time the little boy hurried to the cell door to deliver the contraband, his pastor told him he must stop it. Why? Because the police would put him in jail. The boy said, "If jail is good enough for you, it is good enough for me."

CHAPTER
9

Good News at Last

THE BEST NEWS that Fathers Henry and Kane had in the Naju jail came from the Japanese provincial chief of police. He said, "I'll make a prediction. You will be in internment, and after a few months you will be returned to the United States." The priests wanted to believe him but were afraid to; they didn't feel up to facing another disappointment. They quoted his words to each other often, sometimes seeing them as reasonable, but more often condemning them as sheer nonsense. They didn't know he had heard that the Japanese, through the Swiss, had requested an exchange of civilian prisoners.

In early February, two months after Pearl Harbor, the chief of police had the two priests brought to his office. He said they were being released from the Naju jail and their first thought, of course, was that they were being sent to the States. The bottom dropped out of that brief hope when he said they were going to Kwangju for further internment.

On the train ride to Kwangju, under guard, they wondered what this new internment would be like. Would it be more of the barbarous crowding of the Mokpo cell? More long hours of interrogation? If given a choice they would have stayed in Naju jail for it offered a way of life that they could come to terms with. They felt depressed at the thought of losing Dominic and his wonderful meals.

But hardly had they arrived in Kwangju than there was Dominic. The cook showed up all smiles at the old parish rectory where the two Americans were interned with fourteen other Columbans, all Irish, except for one Australian.

One of the things that brightened their lives in their new quarters was the word received from a judge of the courts through Dominic that General Doolittle's planes had bombed Tokyo. He insisted that they not let the Japanese know that they had heard of the raid.

No sooner had Father Henry rejoiced at the news than seven policemen came to the rectory and sat him in a chair facing a window filled with glaring sunlight. They asked if he had heard any startling news and he answered with a question, "Is the war over?" They said, no, that Tokyo had been bombed but that only schools and hospitals had been destroyed. What did he think of that?

Father Henry said that Americans wouldn't bomb schools and hospitals unless gun emplacements were in or near them. At this the seven policemen sucked air through their teeth and mumbled among themselves.

The chief interrogator said, "You must know where those planes came from."

The statement so startled the priest that he showed surprise. The reaction was misinterpreted by the police. They made a buzzing sound, like swarming bees. At last they had hit the mark!

Father Henry learned in the Naju jail that when being interrogated by the Japanese never say, "I don't know." Make up an answer and the more definite the better. To stall for time he asked, "Were they big planes?"

This caused another conference filled with the buzzing of many bees and the sounds of air drawn rapidly through the teeth. Evidently they knew no details of the raid, but they did not feel free to admit it. So the chief of the team said, yes, the planes were big.

Father Henry said, "Well, if they were large they couldn't have come from an aircraft carrier, now could they?" This sent the Japanese into another buzzing conference that he was thankful for as it gave him time to think. He had seen some propaganda films that said something about Vladivostok; that from there any place in Japan could be bombed within an hour. When the name popped into his mind he said with great conviction, "Those planes could only have come from Vladivostok!"

The seven policemen, full of buzzing and hissing sounds, hurried from the room. They were off to report to their superiors the valuable piece of intelligence that they had wrung from the American.

Life in the old rectory was not too bad. Certainly it did not lack in good conversation. As for good food, there was some lack. Dominic had to buy it now and all he had for money were IOUs written by Monsignor MacPolin saying that after the war he would repay in rice the value of the food donated now. After the war, when money was scarce, Father Henry made it a special point of repaying all of these debts.

Since the wooden fence around the church compound was not guarded at night, the priests had a chance to do a certain amount of pastoral work. The Catholic Koreans used to remove sections of the fence each morning before the rooster crowed to come into the compound to attend Mass at 4:30. Heavy with sleep and cloudy of brain, Father Henry used to look at them and say to himself, they are as bad as Father Pak; they actually prefer these early Masses. He little dreamed that as an archbishop he would see the day when Koreans would prefer evening Masses.

The Irish priests continued to protest their internment, harping on the theme that they were neutrals. The Japanese continued to remind them that they were neutral on the wrong side. However, all of a sudden in early March, the Irish were told they could return to their parishes. The Korean priests, who had been in jail for a brief time because of their contact with the Western priests, were already back to work.

All of the Korean priests were back except Father Thaddeus Ri, who had been sentenced to serve two years in prison. It all revolved around an observation he had made on a post card to Father Thomas Cusack, a Columban in a parish twenty-five miles away. Father Ri had commented on seeing many military horses on the streets of Yosu, and this, the Japanese said, was giving away a military secret.

Dominic, the cook, would soon become a prisoner, too. The Japanese seemed to have second thoughts about the way he had been giving aid and comfort to the enemy and so they sent him to Manchuria to work in the coal mines. After the war he returned to Mokpo suffering from malnutrition; the man who had fed others so well seemed on the point of death. Monsignor MacPolin took one look at him and hurried him to the United States military medics who brought him back to health.

Monsignor MacPolin resumed his work as Prefect Apostolic of Kwangju in March of 1942, but his problems with the Japanese were far from ended. The Japanese military officials urged him to resign so that a Japanese bishop might succeed him. He said that since he had not appointed himself to the position to start with he could not absent himself from it without approval of the Vatican. The Japanese persisted. Finally he wrote a letter to Rome, by way of the apostolic delegate in Tokyo, asking to be relieved of the post. Rome accepted the resignation and appointed Bishop Wakida, a delightful Japanese gentleman, to fill his post.

Of the nine Columbans who had arrived in Korea on that dreary Sunday morning in October of 1933, seven were arrested by the Japanese. The two no longer working in Korea were Father Gerard Marinan, back home in Ireland for medical care, and Father Daniel McMenamin who had died in Kwangju hospital of intestinal tuberculosis four years to the day before Pearl Harbor.

Of the remaining seven, Monsignor MacPolin, and Fathers Patrick Monahan and Harold Henry were detained in Kwangju; Thomas Neligan and Brian Geraghty were under house arrest in Chun Chon, the newly established diocese in the northeast. The roughest time of all, because it was of the longest duration, was suffered by Fathers Patrick Dawson and T. D. Ryan in Cheju, an island off the southern coast of Korea.

Radio broadcasts giving information about the Japanese to the American military came from the island. The Japanese took for granted that the messages were being sent by three foreigners, Fathers Dawson and Ryan and their fellow Columban, Father Austin Sweeney, who came to Korea shortly after the original nine had begun work there. They imprisoned the three priests, but the messages went on. Next they arrested the male Catholics. The messages continued. Then they arrested the female Catholics. The messages did not cease. In searching for the transmitter, the Japanese tore walls and ceilings out of churches and rectories, but messages kept filling the air. The spy, captured and executed a few weeks before the end of the war, was a Japanese.

Father Dawson was sentenced to five years of hard labor and was still in prison when the war ended, August 15, 1945. Fathers Ryan and Sweeney, sentenced to two years in prison, were required to knit socks for the Japanese army. By knitting lumps into toes and heels they sabotaged the war effort in their own small way.

After the Irish Columbans were released from house arrest in Kwangju in the spring of 1942, the two Americans, Fathers Henry and Kane, and the Australian, Father Kevin Mangan, were kept confined to the rectory. In theory they were three "enemies," but also they had the best chance of going home if the chief of provincial police had any reason for the prediction he had made.

Finally, in late May several Japanese officials came to the Kwangju rectory to say that the three Columbans were to be exchanged for Japanese prisoners in the United States. American civilians in Japanese territories not conquered by Japan during the war were eligible for exchange; those in recently conquered territories such as Hong Kong, Malaysia, and the Philippines were not eligible.

Father Henry was escorted back to Naju to pick up a few personal belongings and to make an inventory of things that had to be left behind. When he came out of the rectory, the children were in the school yard standing very quietly. He looked at the Japanese guard and the guard nodded. Father Henry started to talk to the children but after a few sentences broke down. The children were crying, too. It was then he realized that he had come a longer way than he had supposed over the rocky road toward *adaptation totale.*

Fathers Henry, Kane, and Mangan were escorted by train to the docks at Pusan where they met several Maryknoll priests and sisters. And there was Father Pat Brennan, a Columban from Chicago! The two American priests just off the train from Kwangju threw their arms around "Pere" Brennan. Nobody could foresee that in time he would join the Korean martyrs, and that Harold Henry would be given the awesome task of filling his shoes.

On June first, as the Japanese ship sailed from Pusan, Father Henry remembered that dreary Sunday dawn nearly nine years ago when he had first seen the shoreline of Korea. His own future seemed even more uncertain now. Certainly the futures of Korea and of the world were more uncertain. And yet he was happy.

CHAPTER

10

Home on the *Gripsholm*

NOBODY SPIT. Nobody shouted expletives. It was unbelievably ordinary." Thirty-three years later that is how Archbishop Henry remembered that afternoon in June 1942 when Japanese police paraded him and his fellow prisoners through the streets of Kobe. The Japanese explained that they wanted the Americans to see how peaceful Japan was even in war.

"During the march we passed the Seamen's Institute where American civilians from Guam and Wake Island were housed. They were hanging out of windows, waving, apparently in good spirits. A Capuchin monk, his beard flowing in the wind, shinnied up a flagpole and shouted, 'See you in 1945!' There in 1942 he guessed the year the war would end."

The Japanese reception was downright effusive in Yokohama, where the prisoners were brought to board ship. The officials staged a traditional dockside send-off with streamers curling through the air and a band playing "Aloha."

Father Henry found he had more spring in his step than he had known for a long time as he went up the gangplank of the *Asama Maru*. The Japanese ship was scheduled to take the prisoners to Lourenço Marques in Portuguese East Africa. There the Japanese civilian prisoners would move from the *Gripsholm* to the *Asama Maru* and the Americans would board the Swedish ship for the long trip to New York.

All these well-laid plans seemed to come to a sudden halt when, ten minutes from the pier, the *Asama Maru* dropped anchor in the harbor. Day after day it floated there and nothing happened, except that rumors bred and hatched and thrived and multiplied among the prisoners. The most persistent rumor was that the Japanese had given the *Asama Maru* the unpleasant assignment of being a sitting duck. It was just waiting, rumor had it, for an American submarine to come along and blow it out of the water, so that the Japanese could say isn't it too bad that the Americans even destroy their own people.

After about a week, quite suddenly, the motors began to turn at two o'clock in the morning. Everybody awakened and hurried to the deck. They began to laugh at all those rumors that now seemed so dead and silly. Imagine a United States submarine in Yokohama Bay!

Four years later, shopping in a church goods store in St. Paul, Father Henry learned that an American submarine was, in fact, quite near. He met a sailor who, upon hearing that the chaplain had been a part of the prisoner exchange said, "So you were on that ship anchored in Yokohama Bay—the one with the big white crosses on the sides. It kept the lights burning all night. We watched you every minute. We followed you from Yokohama Bay to the Indian Ocean just to make sure you weren't scuttled."

Archbishop Henry remembered the trip on the *Asama Maru* the way one remembers a nightmare, frightening, but haunting in its surrealism. "Most of us just had the clothes on our backs. I slept in the prow where there were four-tier bunks. We nearly suffocated in the Indian Ocean. We were allowed water for drinking and washing for half an hour in the morning and half an hour in the evening. Because of numbers, we were given two meals a day. We were hungry all the time." After that he no longer agreed with a sentiment expressed by the patron of his society, Saint Columban, who exclaimed, "What joy to sail the crested sea!"

The *Gripsholm* was waiting at Lourenço Marques and once again life took a turn for the better. As the *Asama Maru* moved toward the Swedish ship to dock stern to stern, somebody on the *Gripsholm* yelled, "How is the food on that ship?" And back came the answer, "It's lousy!" Immediately, Swedish sailors began tossing the Americans Eskimo pies, Hershey bars, and fresh fruit. The Japanese crew, especially the waiters who had been so surly, looked with annoyance at this shower of manna from heaven.

A row of freight cars pulled up parallel with the docked ships. The Japanese were sent down one side of the cars and the Americans down the other so that in the smooth exchange the prisoners scarcely saw each other. Up the gangplank marched 900 Americans from the *Asama Maru* and 600 from the *Conte Verdi,* an Italian vessel seized in Shanghai at the start of the war. This formed a passenger list that totaled about 900 Protestant missionaries, 150 priests, about 200 nuns and a couple of hundred diplomatic personnel.

As the Americans reached the top of the gangplank, each beheld a vision—a smorgasbord laid out on tables that ran the length of the promenade deck. Although dirty and grimy, the newly freed fell upon the smorgasbord, annihilating it and three thousand bottles of beer and several hundred bottles of liquor.

And—Glory be!—each passenger was assigned to a stateroom with only one roommate. Since the assignments were alphabetical, Father Harold Henry shared a cabin with Father Michael Henry, a Maryknoll priest.

Father Henry found life aboard the *Gripsholm* of luxury-liner quality. The service was superb, all facilities worked, and the amenities were well kept. Having lived a rough-hewn life for the past nine years, this took some getting used to. He awakened each morning wondering where he was. Upon realizing that he was sleeping between clean sheets and could have whatever he wanted for breakfast, he would jump out of bed and look through the porthole to enjoy the sight of the world. For him the days unfolded as one long amazement interrupted by only two events—a burning ship and two mysterious colonels.

A ball of fire glowed against the sky at dusk one evening. A tanker torpedoed by a submarine was white hot, for it had been burning three days. The *Gripsholm* circled for several hours searching for survivors, but none could be found. Of course that started rumors. If a sub was in the vicinity, would it hesitate to torpedo the *Gripsholm?* Opinions on that question were equally divided.

Unknown to the passengers, two United States Army colonels in mufti boarded the ship in Rio de Janeiro. A couple of days after they had come aboard a steward tapped Father Henry on the shoulder, interrupting a bridge game he had been steeped in since breakfast. He was wanted on D deck, well below the water line.

Two Coast Guardsmen stood watch outside the cabin. Inside sat the two colonels in full uniform. They said right out that since Father Henry knew Korea, the people, and the terrain, it was his patriotic duty to join the Army as chaplain. Henry said he would gladly join but that in his work, as in theirs, he could not make such a major decision without consent of his superiors. He assured them, though, that after being on the water about two and a half months, if he joined anything it would *not* be the Navy. The colonels were supersalesmen enough to get him to sign a statement saying that if his superiors gave their permission he would join the army.

As the *Gripsholm* moved up the Hudson the passengers began edging toward the gangplank. A Coast Guard cutter came alongside and a squad of Marines boarded to pass out leaflets stating that the country was at war—

surprise!—and that nobody could leave the ship until questioned by the FBI, Army and Navy Intelligence, and the State Department. This might take a week.

The interviews were to be held in alphabetical order, which meant that of the three Columbans, Father Brennan would get away the first or second day but Fathers Henry and Kane would cool their heels while looking at the Colgate sign that loomed on the Jersey shore.

"I pulled a few strings, I was always good at that," Archbishop Henry said later. "All three of us were interviewed on the second day. My brother Bob and Father Pat O'Connor, a correspondent for the Catholic News Service, met us at the pier. We all went off to see Bishop Cushing in Boston. The first thing he said was, 'Now that you are back the first thing you need is something really American,' and he went out for hot dogs and beer. He asked how much we paid the United States Government to bring us home. We said five hundred dollars each. He wrote a check for $1,500 and said, 'Give that to your superior, Father Waldron. Maybe then you'll be more welcome.' "

Three days later, Father Paul Waldron, the Columban superior in the United States, came to St. Paul and said to Father Henry, "You are a hero. You and Tom Kane and Pat Brennan. Arrange for a series of talks for the missions. Forget that stuff about humility we taught you in the seminary." He recalled the oft-quoted remark of fellow Columban Richard Ranagan, "There is no use in a fellow being humble if he doesn't show it."

Just before Christmas of 1942, a year after he had been taken from the Mokpo to the Naju jail, he began giving talks in the Boston area. But it felt all wrong. The lecture circuit was too mild. There was a war on, and he had an itch to be a chaplain.

On one of his quick trips to the Columban headquarters in Omaha, several navy officers made an appointment to meet him in the Blackstone Hotel. They interviewed him from 10:30 in the morning until 8:30 at night with twenty minutes free for a sandwich. As Archbishop Henry remembers, "They told me that I was essential to the war effort. They almost convinced me that the war wouldn't be won unless I joined the navy."

Father Waldron said no, the Columbans would not release him. But then Bishop Cushing influenced a change in that decision. One day, talking with Father Ambrose Gallagher, the bishop growled, "What's wrong with that Harold Henry? Here he is chasing the almighty dollar. That'll ruin a good missionary! Why doesn't he become a chaplain? The military is the greatest mission field in the world today."

"He wants to be a chaplain," Father Ambrose said, "but Father Waldron won't let him."

Bishop Cushing reached for the telephone and talked to the Columban superior in Omaha. A few minutes later he made another call, this time to Bristol, Rhode Island, and said, "Harold, you're in the army now! When can you join?"

Even as Father Henry stammered to express his surprise and appreciation, the name that flashed into his mind was Rowland. It had become habitual in the past four years that whenever he had a problem he thought of Chester and Marie Rowland, the way some young men think of their parents, for that is what they had become to him.

He had met them through Father Ed Martin, a colorful character he had become friends with in the Philippines. On the military base at Fort William McKinley, Father Martin lived across the street from Captain Rowland, his petite wife, two teenage boys, and a six-year-old girl. A relationship grew between Father Henry and the Rowlands that flourished through the years. They kept in close touch through correspondence, and the Rowlands became a "family" for Father Henry.

While the bishop was still expressing his best wishes for his new assignment, the young priest was thinking about something Marie Rowland had written in a recent letter: Colonel Rowland was organizing the 1103rd Engineer Combat Group and was still without a Catholic chaplain. Father Henry got in contact with the colonel, who asked General William Arnold, the chief of chaplains, to assign the young Columban to his outfit, and the deed was done. After attending Chaplain's School at Harvard, Chaplain Henry was told to report to Fort Devens, Massachusetts, on August 10, 1943.

CHAPTER

I I

A Hero in Europe

MORE THAN thirty years later the archbishop remembered the day well. "When I got off the train there was Colonel Rowland to meet me. This was an unusual sight, a colonel coming to the railroad station to greet a lieutenant. I met my co-chaplain and senior, Captain Lundblad, of the Missouri Synod Lutherans. He was a man of great faith and high ideals and gave the best sermons based on scholasticism that I ever heard. I used to take notes."

Again there arose the problem of adaptation. It seemed that Harold Henry was always being asked to adapt to somebody else's world: as a Protestant boy he had to adapt to a Catholic school; as an American student he had to adapt to an Irish seminary; as a Catholic priest he had to adapt to pagan Korea; as a free American he had to adapt to the confines of a Japanese prison cell. And now he had to adapt to the military and find some rapport with soldiers.

Colonel Rowland gave him good advice: in training, try to do everything the GIs do. That suited the young chaplain just fine because the athlete inside him was forever clamoring to be free. It pleased him that on twenty-five-mile hikes a battalion commander used to put him at the head of one of the columns.

On one such hike, the troops spent the night in the White Mountains. On awaking in the morning, Father Henry saw a snake slither from under his bedroll. He jumped up, pulled back the roll and saw another snake. He told the story at breakfast, and the next morning he awakened to find that the GIs

As a military chaplain in Europe Harold Henry was decorated for bravery.

had scattered beer cans all around his tent. As soon as he came out they began to point to the cans and say, "Chaplain, you still seeing snakes?" He knew he was accepted.

Of course Harold Henry, the idealist, the perfectionist, the romantic, had to learn the lesson all over again that people will let you down. To him each GI was a knight in shining armor and he was there to help in the search for the Holy Grail. The disillusionment set in early.

Two days after he had joined the combat engineers he was told that Charley Kane wanted to see him in the stockade. So he hurried over. Charley, a master mechanic, had lost his sergeant's stripes for going AWOL. As the story unfolded the new chaplain could almost hear tremulous music in the background, the kind the piano played in his father's movie house when someone in the movie was deeply wronged. The military police at the stockade said they had heard Charley's story again and again, and no doubt he was a victim of sinister forces.

The young chaplain hurried back to his unit with the air of a crusader determined to right a wrong. He went straight to the transportation officer, not knowing that transportation officers have the reputation for being harder than rear axles. He spoke with such eloquence that the transportation officer actually listened, and he said he would look into the matter. He not only got Charlie out of the stockade, he even gave him a two-day pass to visit in Bayonne, N.J. Charlie left Friday evening and was supposed to stand reveille Monday morning, but as far as Charley was concerned Monday never dawned.

That's when the new chaplain learned about transportation officers. As his Korean parishioners would say, his *kibun* was soon dragging, not because he was called a "goddam do-gooder" but because any mistakes he made reflected on Colonel Rowland's judgment. Right then he realized that there are disadvantages in having a commanding officer who is practically your father.

A few weeks later came the Jewish holidays, and again the new chaplain learned that some GIs would take advantage of him as readily as some of the Koreans had. Since there was no Jewish chaplain in Fort Dix, the post commander issued orders that any soldier who professed the Jewish faith could get leave to go home for the holiday services. Provided their homes were less than 500 miles away, all they needed to do was get a recommendation from the chaplain.

Right off several soldiers from Brooklyn came in and the chaplain gave them permissions. They were followed by Carver Washington, a black, asking for a Jewish holiday pass. The chaplain paused, sent up a quick mental prayer for guidance, and decided to give him the benefit of the doubt.

Next came a sandy-haired Pfc with the brogue on his tongue and the map of Killarney on his face. He, too, wanted to go home for Yom Kippur.

"What's your name?"

"Patrick Murphy."

"Get the hell out of here," growled the chaplain.

"Now Father don't be getting mad at me," said the Pfc. "You can't blame me for trying, now can you?"

By this time Chaplain Henry was of a mood to admire a soldier on a three-day pass who sent back a telegram that read: "Grandmother did not die. Wife is not sick. I do not have the flu. Request extension of two days just because I am having a good time."

The commanding officer replied: "Because of your honesty, extension granted."

Chaplain Henry was about to have leave problems of his own. For a fleeting moment he toyed with the idea of going AWOL. It had to do with a certain date.

The date, December 18, 1943, had a red circle around it in his mind for a long time. Even in Korea he used to make plans with that date in mind. That was the day he wanted to be in Buffalo for his brother's ordination. He often looked forward to the occasion during harsh hours on the range and dreary cross-country marches.

On December 16 the blow fell. Suddenly his unit was transferred to Camp Kilmer, an overseas staging area. He knew that to get permission to leave a staging area would take all of the string-pulling skill he possessed. Colonel Rowland felt like a heel in saying there was nothing he could do about it. Chaplain Henry remembered that letters written from Korea often mentioned December 18, 1943.

At nine in the morning of December 18, the hour the ordination ceremony was to begin, Father Henry went to the post chapel and poured out his heart to a Methodist chaplain, a lieutenant colonel. The chaplain listened with sympathy and said, yes, he thought something could be done. The two chaplains hurried off to see the Ground Force General who agreed to let Father Henry go if the Service Force General saw fit. The two chaplains then hurried to see the Service Force General who asked a sergeant when the unit was to ship overseas and got the secret information that it would be in about a week. The general gave Father Henry some forms and told him to have his commanding officer sign them. Colonel Rowland signed them before they were even filled in. In his staff car the Methodist chaplain rushed the Catholic chaplain to the station in New Brunswick, New Jersey, to catch a train to New York.

Since the unit had been on the move and its pay had not caught up with it, Father Henry had only two dollars left after buying his plane ticket for Buffalo. He gave those to a porter asking him to wire ahead the flight number and time of arrival.

"At the terminal I was being paged," he said. "I thought it meant come back to camp, but it was Bob telling me to wait until he arrived. I said, 'Yes, Father'—and it sounded nice.

"Well, I missed the ordination, but I assisted at his First Mass the next morning. Since I had only a three-day leave Bob accompanied me back to New York. He wanted me to tell him where I was stationed but since that was a military secret I didn't dare. I didn't want to be comparing the cells in Leavenworth with those I knew in Korea."

Back at Camp Kilmer, he found that the engineers were passing around the rumor that it would be any day now. This rumor, unlike most in the army, turned out to be true. Chaplain Henry, still flinching at the memory of the two-and-a-half month voyage from Yokohama to New York, climbed the gangplank dreading the sea trip more than the war at the other end.

To his surprise nothing unusual happened on the crossing. By then the technique of avoiding submarines was well perfected. From time to time, destroyers took off from the convoy to drop depth charges. Air cover was perfect except for about a day and a half in the middle of the trip.

When the combat engineers reached Liverpool, they went by train to Henley-on-Thames, the town famous for its regattas. There Chaplain Henry, a captain, was assigned to share a room with a lieutenant colonel and a colonel. Before dawn each morning Colonel Rowland lighted the few rationed coals so that the room would be less chilly when the lower ranks touched feet to floor.

Time and again Archbishop Henry observed, "He certainly lived the Gospel's teaching that the higher you go, the greater servant you must be. It was the kind of thing Father Harris used to talk about in Ireland."

Again it was a case of adaptation. Harold Henry had adapted to the ways of Catholics, Irish, Koreans, Japanese, and GIs, and now he had to adapt to the British. Part of his work was to arrange for combat engineers to visit British families. He always made sure that the troops took cans of food with them as gifts when visiting homes that took butlers and beautifully set tables for granted, but that knew hunger all too well.

Something happened one morning on the train from Henley to London that made the Chaplain realize he and the other Americans had adapted better than they knew. While riding in a compartment with three Englishmen who had their heads buried in newspapers, he respected what he believed was a British custom, silence in the morning, and kept his mouth shut. For Harold Henry that was no mean achievement.

Finally, one man put his paper down and said, "I had one of your chaps in to see me the other day for some teeth work. I told him to go to one of his own dentists because if I did the work, some American dentist would ask who botched the job."

The chaplain complimented him on his humility.

The dentist continued, "The three of us have been traveling on this train for the last twenty years. We used to buy a newspaper, bury our heads in it, and begrudge each other a good morning. Since you chaps came along we find talking is rather pleasant in the morning. Yank, I don't care what any Englishman says, if you hadn't come over this time we would have been sunk."

What the Yanks had come for, of course, was the invasion of Europe. When would it happen and where? The combat engineers lived with that question every day as they marked time in Henley. Chaplain Henry noticed that his first thought each morning was, "Is this the day we go?"

One morning he saw a plane with yellow stripes on the wings, an identification mark used by allied planes in the invasion. He called his assistant, Bob Garneau, and they hurried over to a friend's house to listen to the radio. An American announcer was breathless in his description of the invasion. Later a BBC announcer spoke of it in measured tones and tied in the cricket scores with no change of pace.

The combat engineers wondered why they hadn't been invited to the invasion. They hardly had a chance to wonder when a telephone call came at two in the morning telling them to be at Portsmouth in four hours. Things got hectic, but they made the deadline. Just as Chaplain Henry's jeep was being hoisted aboard ship, the whistle blew for morning tea. The jeep stopped in its flight, twirled in mid-air, and sat there for the fifteen-minute tea break. Normandy could wait as far as the English dockhands were concerned.

The sky was dreary and the sea uneasy when the combat engineers crossed the English channel for Omaha Beach in Normandy. Their first taste of combat came when a V-2 rocket landed five hundred yards away. A few minutes later a German Messerschmitt 109 came out of the clouds and a green Coast Guard crew, manning the anti-aircraft guns on the next ship, shot it down. Two American P38s and a British Spitfire broke through the clouds a moment later, and the green crew shot them down also. It was rumored that the fleet commander signaled: "Marksmanship perfect; plane identification lousy." One of the grim jokes of war.

By night the shell cases and ammunition boxes stacked in clusters, formed a silhouette that resembled a miniature metropolis in the fields off Omaha Beach. After darkness Chaplain Henry lay down amid all those explosives and waited with apprehension for "Bed-check Charlie." That was the nickname the combat engineers gave a German plane that came over each night to drop a few bombs.

After the Saint Lo breakthrough, Colonel Rowland was informed that General George Patton was organizing the Third Army and that the 1103rd Combat Group would be attached to it. The engineers supported the Fifth and Ninety-fifth Divisions and the Seventh Armored Division. They belonged to the XX Corps under command of General Walton Walker, the spearhead corps for Patton's Third Army.

The combat engineers proceeded through Saint Lo and drove for thirty-six hours straight. They were delayed from time to time by some resistance, but the first real resistance the 1103rd experienced was at Arnaville on the Moselle River.

Colonel Rowland got his engineers into position so that by night they could put a pontoon bridge across the river. Infantry units and the Seventh Armored Division were crowding up for miles, waiting for the bridge to be finished so that they might cross and push ahead the twenty-five miles toward Metz.

In that area the Germans had every square yard of ground zeroed in. They could drop an 88-millimeter shell wherever they wanted it at any time. They would wait until the bridge was almost finished, and down would come a barrage of 88s and wipe out all that effort.

Finally, a chemical company was brought in to fog the area with smoke. Behind the smoke screen the bridge was completed and the troops crossed and were on the way to Metz, a town said never to be taken by frontal attack.

Metz was surrounded by forts with reinforced concrete walls two-yards thick and so sturdy that bombs and shells just chipped away at them but did no real damage. The Nazis, with German thoroughness, so plotted their positions that artillery, mortars, and crossing machine-gun fire surrounded the city with a shield of death.

General Patton said that if any soldier was killed in a frontal attack on Metz, that soldier's commanding officer would immediately be relieved of command. He gave the order to "run the gauntlet" around Metz and surround it, knowing that when the Germans inside the forts ran out of food they would surrender, as they did.

To run the gauntlet was tricky business, a game of Russian roulette. Vehicles didn't dare travel in usual convoy discipline, going at a fixed speed with equal distance between them. They shot across that deadly ground in spurts of varying speeds, anything to make it difficult for German gunners to get a lead on them.

On the eastern side of Metz, Colonel Rowland's engineers had another river to cross. They worked quietly all night building a Bailey Bridge, thinking that in the morning their infantry and tanks would cross it. To their surprise the first troops to use it were Germans, about 500 of them, who came out of the woods at dawn with their hands over their heads. Chaplain Henry long remembered the profanity of the engineers when they realized the Germans had been resting there all night, watching them work, and then when the job was finished walked across as though they had built it themselves.

It was at Saarlautern on the first line of defense of the Siegfried Line, that Chaplain Henry began wishing he had not listened to Bishop Cushing but had continued giving lectures in Boston. The combat engineers were at a crossroad on which six thousand rounds of artillery fell every twenty-four hours. No one dared be seen by daylight. The work had to be done at night.

Chaplain Henry and his assistant, Bob Garneau, parked the jeep by a wall. They noticed it could be seen by the enemy, so they moved it. A few minutes later an 88 shell hit the exact spot where the jeep had stood.

During the day Chaplain Henry ran the gauntlet offering Mass several places along the line. At night he would stay with the engineers wherever they were building. The river crossings were the most dangerous operations. The engineers first threw across a footbridge for the infantry, cleared mines for the spearhead, and blew up pillboxes. Next they built a more substantial bridge across the same river to get the tanks into action.

It was in one such operation that Chaplain Henry was decorated with the Bronze Star for Valor. The citation said that between December 5 and 17, 1944, his group built a bridge under a terrific barrage of direct small arms and artillery fire. "With no thought of his personal safety, Chaplain Henry made his way daily to the aid station, ministering to the wounded, and then moved forward to the site of construction to cheer and encourage the laboring soldiers. Casualties were heavy, yet Chaplain Henry did not let the enemy fire prevent him from visiting the area at least once every day and from remaining there for five consecutive nights to hearten and reassure his men. The fortitude, loyalty and professional attainment of Chaplain Henry reflect the highest credit upon himself and the Army of the United States."

"I didn't feel courageous," the archbishop admitted. "It was my conscience that pushed me. I think the soldiers really cared whether or not I was with them. Sometimes when the artillery was flying in a night river crossing somebody would say, 'It's O.K. The Padre's here!' I'm sure they could see my heart jumping through my uniform no matter how hard I tried to hide it.

"When anyone was killed I would write to his parents. I remember a clean-cut young man named Brennan who used to set up the altar on the front of the jeep and serve Mass. One day, a half hour after Mass, he was blown to bits while clearing a mined field. I told his parents what a fine young man he was. They replied in such a beautiful manner. They said he was their only son and that God had given them the destiny of creating a citizen for heaven and they had succeeded.

"I often thought about the parents of soldiers. What valor was asked of them! I feel the same way about the parents of missionaries. Nobody talks about the sacrifice they make. The missionary is engrossed in his work, he doesn't have time to fret about his lot. But the folks back home think about him living in mud huts, in danger, eating poor food. They worry."

At Christmas time in 1944, about the time Chaplain Henry was winning the Bronze Star, the Germans launched the Battle of the Bulge. The combat engineers were sent to Holland to the Ninth Army under British Marshal Montgomery to prepare for the Rhine crossing. Their job was to get the Thirtieth and Thirty-fifth Divisions across the river.

While Chaplain Henry was risking his life daily in Europe, some of his fellow Columbans were dying in the missions. On February 10, 1945, Japanese soldiers entered the Columban rectory in Manila and arrested Fathers John Henaghan, Patrick Kelly, Peter Fallon, and Joseph Monaghan. They were led away and never seen again. Stories of their executions were told among the Filipinos.

Looking back on the war thirty years later, Archbishop Henry remembered it as he remembered much of life, as a sharp vignette here and there. The main tidal wave was a blur, and slightly unreal, but there were those little details, a cry in the night or a face passing the window, that persisted in the memory with intensity.

Among his clearest memories were some excited French peasants, two suspicious hitchhikers, and a couple of encounters with General Patton, all minor incidents in his military career but for some reason his memory kept them in focus. The only reason to repeat them here is that the tidal wave of war is made up of many such small incidents.

The excited French peasants were gathered in front of a village church waiting for Chaplain Henry to come outside. They pointed to a farmhouse up the hill and repeated, "Boche, Boche!" This presented the chaplain with a problem he hadn't planned on: The Geneva Convention said that chaplains are to be considered noncombatants, but here were some French peasants trying to get him involved.

He reported the incident to the executive officer who mumbled something about the "the Geneva Convention." Chaplain Henry tried to justify himself by saying, "I'm not bearing arms."

"But you're bearing information."

"Yes, but our fellows think everything's clear around here. What if they go up there and get killed?"

The chaplain accompanied a combat patrol when it set out from the village for the farmhouse. They were joined by three French freedom fighters who knew every fold in the ground that gave the slightest protection. But there were few folds in the ground on that long walk across an open field. The chaplain kept wondering why he had got himself into this. He knew that a burst of machinegun fire could cut them down as the wheat stubble they were tramping on.

Suddenly, at a thicket twelve Germans stood up with their hands locked behind their heads. Chaplain Henry often recalled that he was never more frightened, even in situations more dangerous. He learned that one can only feel so much fright, and only so much pain, and when the limit is reached, that is it.

The three freedom fighters wanted to shoot the prisoners right there. The Chaplain intervened. He said to the Germans, "Don't be afraid. You go with the Americans. But do what they tell you, or they'll turn you over to the French."

Two suspicious hitchhikers entered the Chaplain's life at the time German soldiers were infiltrating the lines in United States Army uniforms to sabotage bridges and ammunition dumps. When two soldiers attempted to wave down his jeep, the thought crossed his mind that they might be Germans in GI uniforms.

He decided to give them the benefit of the doubt and told his driver to stop. One of them jumped in readily, but the other was clumsy in trying to climb over the spare tire at the rear. This aroused the Chaplain's suspicion, he had often observed that if there is one thing a GI can do with alacrity it is get in and out of a jeep. So he began to question his passengers. One answered all the questions, in acceptable midwestern English, but the clumsy soldier just grinned. As the jeep swept around a curve, a tank loomed on the road just ahead. It was a check point. The English-speaking passenger asked to be let off right there, right in the middle of nowhere, and so the driver stopped.

At the checkpoint Chaplain Henry said, "See those two fellows hurrying across the field, I think they are Germans."

A GI fired above their heads. They stopped, put up their hands and came slowly toward the checkpoint. They were Germans, all right.

On one of his meetings with Patton, Chaplain Henry was able to be helpful. It was in the area called Little Switzerland in Northern Luxembourg. The combat engineers had been enduring a terrific shelling for several days when a new chaplain came forward to allow Chaplain Henry to go to the rear for some rest.

Chaplain Henry was looking for one of the bath units that General Patton insisted the service engineers erect behind the front lines the moment there was a pause in forward movement. Any soldier passing by could go in, get a fresh towel and a bar of soap, a hot shower, and clean clothes. Patton insisted on hot showers and hot meals. Even when the fighting was most fierce at the front, he insisted that everyone get a hot meal every day, even if the cooks had to deliver it. He said the cooks could be shot at too. Before anyone was given a hot meal he had to take off his wet socks to avoid trench foot and put on the fresh ones which came with the meal.

Chaplain Henry lurched across a rutted road in Luxembourg anticipating the creature comforts that Father Harris used to speak of in the novitiate—a hot shower and a hot meal. He recalled the admonition that when you have them enjoy them, but when you don't have them don't complain. He remembered the soft-boiled eggs that were almost raw and tasted of garlic. There were times he could have eaten those with relish.

Suddenly Generals Patton, Walker, and Irwin loomed in front of him. General Patton, whom he had met several times before, waved him to a halt. He wanted to know where the bridge was being built for the tanks. The chaplain said, "I just came from there. About a mile down this road you come to a fork. Be sure to stay to the right. To the left there's nothing but Germans."

"Thank you, Padre," said Patton, "I appreciate this. It wouldn't pay to be caught by the Germans, would it?"

At another meeting between Chaplain Henry and Patton, the General was paying off a debt. He had promised that if a bridge were completed by a certain deadline he would give the combat engineers a case of whiskey. Each time the bridge was near completion, the Germans would bring down salvos of 88s atop it, and the work had to begin anew.

It was during this frustrating and frightening operation, that a black soldier said to Chaplain Henry, "When I get home—*if* I get home—I'm gonna change my counting. I'll say 85, 86, 87, 89. No more 88!"

The engineers made the deadline, and Patton kept his promise. In the course of the conversation on that occasion, Patton said to Harold Henry, "Padre, you're a goddam fine chaplain!"

CHAPTER

12

The Period of Letdown

AFTER THE RHINE CROSSING, the war was practically over. Chaplain Henry and his assistant traveled around Germany without troop protection and, much to their surprise, were welcomed as liberators. When the American chaplain asked German pastors what time the church was available for him to offer Mass for American troops, the answer was always, "You are the conqueror, you name the time and we will arrange the schedules." When he objected to this attitude, saying they needed no permission from him in arranging affairs of the parish, they expressed amazement, admitting that this was much better than conditions under the Nazis.

When the war in Europe was ended, Chaplain Henry did not foresee that the war in the Far East would end as soon as it did. Still embedded in his consciousness were the hours at the radio in Naju listening to accounts of how easily the Japanese military machine rolled across China, and the days in Mokpo and Naju jails listening to the Japanese brag of their invincibility. But, of course, he had not heard of the atom bomb.

He wanted to get to the Orient. After pulling strings for transfer he was assigned to the 10th Replacement Depot near Rheims. It was the first time he ever benefitted by volunteering for something; when Japan suddenly surrendered, the troops in the replacement depot were not needed in Southeast Asia, and so were returned to the States immediately.

Father Henry wanted to return to Korea but his superior general asked him to wait a while. He was to be a delegate from Korea at the Columban Fathers' General Chapter in Ireland in July of 1947. Since it was practically impossible for a civilian to get accommodations to and from the Orient on a troop ship, he was told to mark time at St. Columban's Minor Seminary, which had opened that year, 1945, in Milton, Massachusetts.

This was perhaps the only "ordinary" time in Harold Henry's life and for him the least satisfying. He was going through that uneasy period of adjustment that every soldier suffers upon returning to civilian life. The period of high excitement is past and the nervous reaction follows, usually a deep melancholy.

The archbishop spoke of those months without pleasure. "I ended up with all the subjects that the other priests didn't want—Greek, French, Latin, and History. A few other odd jobs, such as director of the infirmary, were tossed in. It took all of my time just to keep two pages ahead of the students."

To settle his nerves he returned to his first love, sports. He began coaching teams and started a campaign with the rector and the council to let him introduce real football instead of settling for touch football. They gave in to him, rather ungraciously he thought, for one game. In that game a student split his eyelid, not bad enough to cause permanent damage but bad enough to require plastic surgery. The rector said to the coach, "That ends your Knute Rockne career."

In August 1947, when Father Henry returned to Milton from the Columban Chapter meeting in Ireland, he started pulling strings with more intensity than he had ever pulled before. Everywhere he turned he was told that civilians were not permitted to return to Korea, the situation there was too "unstable," a vague word much used in bureaucracy. The military did not want to bother with civilians because it would have to provide them with food and postal service and there were already enough problems without adding these.

Finally someone told Harold Henry to go to the top, something he had been doing all of his life. Apply to the Joint Chiefs of Staff. They might give him permission if the commanding general of the military government in Korea authorized it.

Along with the application he sent a personal letter that was a study in salesmanship. In it he described specific incidents in which Columban missionaries had helped the military during the war. He was saying, in effect: here is your chance to say thanks for past favors and to take out some insurance for similar favors in the future.

He told how Bishop Patrick Cleary, his old rector in Ireland, had been helpful to General Doolittle's flyers after they had bombed Tokyo in 1942. One of the B-25s crashed in the hills above Nancheng, Kiangsi Province, Bishop Cleary's headquarters. With the help of some Chinese, five of the crew who had bailed out made their way to the Columban compound. One airman, painfully injured, was treated at the Columban Sisters' Hospital by a doctor, a refugee from Nazi Germany. Other Doolittle crews came through Nancheng on their way to safety. The general himself came to thank Bishop Cleary and the sisters for their help, saying he hoped there would be no retaliation. A month later the Japanese captured Nancheng and threatened to kill the bishop, priests, and sisters. Bishop Cleary stood up to them, explaining that the hospital would treat anybody in need, Japanese included. The Japanese burned the hospital, destroyed whatever supplies they could not take with them, and left the town in ruins.

Father Henry's letter also described how helpful the Columbans had been in Burma where the Allies fought to build the Ledo Road and to reopen the Burma road. The missionaries had helped both foot soldiers and pilots. When Americans flying "the Hump" between India and China found it impossible to lift their crippled planes over the Himalayas and bailed out, the Columbans went into action. They would lead the pilots to the nearest American unit whether in India, Burma, or China. In such rescue operations Father James Stuart, an Irish Columban, and his Kachin parishioners became legends among the American troops along the Ledo Road in Burma. On one occasion a flyer mistook a Kachin for a Japanese. He ran to the Irrawaddy River, swam it, and hid in a bamboo thicket. A few moments later the bamboo parted and there stood the Kachin. He handed the exhausted pilot a note that Father Stuart had written: "I am a friend, follow me."

Within a few days a wire came from the Joint Chiefs of Staff saying that Harold Henry had permission to return to Korea on a troop transport. He could bring three tons of luggage! And also Father Patrick Monaghan.

CHAPTER
13

Back to Korea

WHEN THE TROOP SHIP docked at Inchon, Father Patrick Monaghan was standing at the rail beside Father Henry. The priests noticed that the *yungkams* on the dock, smoking long-stemmed pipes and surrounded by their own serenity, seemed to enjoy the hectic spectacle as the dependents of military men disembarked. There was a twinkle in their eyes as they watched a platoon of GIs who had been assigned to carry infants from ship to shore, the kind of assignment no Korean man of their own generation would have accepted.

They watched the freighters unloading chemical fertilizer from the States, the fertilizer communist propagandists had called poison, saying it would destroy the crops. So the Korean farmers, at the suggestion of the *yungkams*, scattered a little in one corner of the field, and, lo, the corner of barley grew higher than the rest.

Someone asked one of the *yungkams* what he thought of all of this commotion down on the dock. The old man puffed his long-stemmed pipe meditatively and said, "Korea must be a wonderful country. The Chinese wanted it. The Japanese wanted it. The Russians wanted it. And now the Americans want it. A wonderful country, indeed!"

Archbishop Henry said that when he saw the American flag flying at the port of Inchon that morning in late November of 1947, it gave him a new realization of freedom. Never had he expected to live in Korea without being hounded by the Thought Control Police. And now he could.

Oh, he had heard rumors about trouble brewing now that the country was divided in half, but there are always prophets of doom. Certainly, he was not prepared to believe that in less than three years Columbans would suffer in Korea more severely than they had during World War II. That word "martyr," that Father MacPolin had used the first morning in Korea, was one he himself would use often. Certainly he was unprepared to believe that he would nearly be killed because of the priest standing next to him at the ship's railing, or that a Columban's martyrdom would give to his life a new direction by placing a burden on him he had never expected to bear.

During the twenty-five-mile trip from Inchon to Seoul the Columbans began to realize that the Japanese had run an efficient railroad. They realized it still more when they found that what used to be a seven-hour trip from Seoul to Mokpo now took eighteen hours. When the efficient Japanese, known as the Germans of the East, left the railroad system in the hands of the Koreans, known as the Irish of the East, the latter were unprepared for the job. Every station master and every engineer had been Japanese; the firemen had been Korean, and now the firemen were running the show.

The equipment was in need of repair. Wartime shortages had made up-keep difficult. And at the end of the war some Koreans had damaged trains, had even destroyed some, to show their resentment against the Japanese for developing an efficient system at Korean expense.

In Mokpo, Monsignor MacPolin greeted the two priests with enthusiasm, saying how glad he was for the sight of them. Now, after fourteen years in Korea with no break whatever since that Sunday in October of 1933 when he had escorted the pioneering priests to their first assignments, he could go back to Ireland for a holiday.

Father Henry was startled to see the change five years had brought. The monsignor was nearing sixty, but looked older. There was a sagging in the features and in the spirit that had not been there before, not even during those days in the crowded cell in Mokpo.

Monsignor MacPolin said Father Henry was to be vicar general until his return. In the event that anything unforeseen happened he was to be pro-prefect apostolic.

Although Father Henry had pulled strings to be allowed to return to Korea, now that he was back he was painfully homesick. He hadn't realized how much he had come to accept the soft life of the States. Now as he took on the burdens of the new job, not knowing where to begin, he had to keep reminding himself of the things Father Harris had taught in the novitiate: You have to be open-minded to God's will, and willing to be led; those are conditions of divine guidance. Once caught up in the purposes of God, horizons of Korea had shrunk since he had gone away. He believed that if he per-

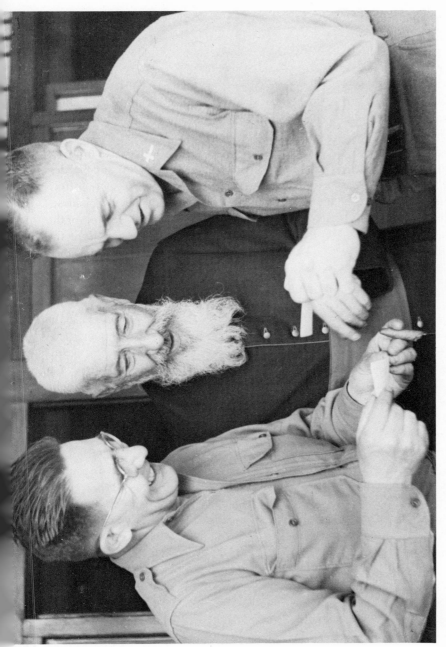

An old friend, Bishop Germain Mousser, shows photographs to Fathers Patrick Dawson and Harold Henry in Seoul at the end of the Korean conflict.

severed there would come a sense of freedom. Following a destiny, no matter how demanding, is more liberating than purposeless freedom. He never doubted his destiny—but, oh, he was homesick!

The terrible homesickness that the two priests felt upon their return to Korea is reflected in a letter Father Monaghan wrote at the time: "The very day we got into Kwangju we got our assignments. Harold went to Mokpo to take over Monsignor MacPolin's job, and I took over Kwangju from Tom Cusack. Just as well we weren't given time to sit and think. My heart went to my boots on landing and stayed right there all the time on the long trip from port to Kwangju. Thirteen years in the country didn't seem to help a bit.

"They were glad to see us back and started right away to make their own plans for the trip to Ireland. Monsignor had fourteen years in Korea without a break and came here direct from China where he had been for eight years. Fr. Cusack had completed his thirteenth year in Korea so that they both needed and deserved a rest and a change. We had ours. Within a week they were both on their way and we were so busy getting into our new jobs that we didn't have time to be homesick."

Father Henry took the train from Mokpo to Seoul—this time the trip took twenty-nine hours, from three o'clock one morning to eight o'clock the next—to see Monsignor MacPolin off on his home leave which would begin by military ship. In Seoul they came upon a Maryknoll missionary, stalled because of a jeep's frozen gas line. Father Henry, recalling a trick his father had taught him in Northfield, crawled under the vehicle to thaw the ice with a candle.

He felt a kick on his foot. It was Monsignor MacPolin.

"I just got a call to hurry to the staging area. Don't bother to come out from under there."

"How long will you be gone?"

"About a year."

Within six months, Monsignor MacPolin asked to be relieved of all responsibilities in Korea. He later became an American citizen and until his death in 1963 spent most of the time teaching French and History in the Columban Seminary at Milton, Massachusetts.

When Father Henry learned that the monsignor would never return, he wrote him a letter that was not the most charitable he had composed. He complained of the sorry state of affairs he inherited: Upon opening the safe he had found less than $100 in Korean money. While it was true that Korea had been cut from the Columban budget during the war, still the war had been over for more than two years and no budget applied for. The Koreans were too poor to support their pastors, who often lacked money for food.

Then there were those IOUs that Monsignor MacPolin had signed for food in Kwangju, promising to pay back the debt in rice after the war. Father Henry was determined to redeem the IOUs as soon as possible.

He applied to the Columbans for a budget. He also asked help from Rome and received $12,000 from that request.

"We were certainly grateful to the United States troops in those lean days," said Archbishop Henry. "They knew we didn't have anything, and so they said we were welcome to eat in their mess halls and buy in the PX. The Columbans had acted as interpreters and advisers to the military government and had let the military use their parish facilities, and now they were showing their appreciation."

With that letter off his chest, Father Henry braced himself to carry the burden of pro-prefect apostolic of the Prefecture of Kwangju for an indefinite period. Years later Archbishop Henry admitted that it was the most effective title he ever had because it was an unfamiliar one in the States. Whenever he approached a monsignor of a large American parish, seeking permission to talk to his congregation about the missions in Korea, the monsignor, unwilling to reveal his ignorance about the title, and taking for granted it meant something grand, gave permission for the pro-prefect apostolic to speak at all the Masses.

(A pro-prefect apostolic is someone doing the work until a prefect apostolic can be appointed, who is usually a monsignor with the jurisdiction of a bishop but without a bishop's consecration. As for the title, Prefecture, that, like the title Vicariate, is the name given an area that does not have enough Catholics to be raised to the status of diocese.)

Six months after having the temporary appointment thrust upon him, Father Henry wrote to Chester and Marie Rowland: "Conditions for conversions are not as good as before the war but can be regarded as fair. The minds of the people are in turmoil: a government is in process of being formed and all the conflicting elements are busy with their propaganda; then with the huge inflation, the people use most of their energies to make ends meet and to find jobs by outwitting their neighbors. The minds of the people being so volatile, they have no perseverance in a fixed idea. For this reason, even though we have many catechumens, baptisms have been proportionately few.

"If only the police would treat the people decently; i.e., act as protectors instead of oppressors—several innocent people right in this area have been beaten to death by the police—we would have little fear from Communism within. But many are so antagonized by the police that they join the Communists out of spite, not because they believe in its philosophy."

A year after Monsignor MacPolin left Korea, Rome appointed Father Patrick Brennan as prefect apostolic with the title of Right Reverend Monsignor. At Christmas of 1948 Monsignor Brennan arrived in Korea and the very sight of him made Father Henry feel this was the best Christmas gift he had ever had. Here was the same Patrick Brennan who had returned on the *Gripsholm* with him and had also volunteered as an army chaplain instead of lecturing in the Boston area as Father Waldron had planned. After the war, as Columban superior of China and Korea he had lived in Shanghai.

"Pere" Brennan, as the Columbans called him, had been a secular priest in the Archdiocese of Chicago before becoming a Columban. For ten years he preached on the mission band, going from place to place in the Chicago area conducting spiritual retreats for religious and lay people.

One Sunday a Columban missionary, Father Michael Mee, was preaching at Father Brennan's Mass. Each time the visiting priest made a gesture, he exposed a big rip under the sleeve of his cassock. The rip haunted Father Brennan; it became a symbol of a life more rugged than the one he was leading. Preaching on the mission band was difficult psychologically, but physically he was growing soft—the food was good and the housing more than adequate. He needed the kind of life that demanded more of him in every way. When he joined the Columbans he got it.

When Pere Brennan loomed on the scene, Father Henry thought he could say goodbye to desk work and once more mount his bicycle to go from village to village as in the days before the war. Before he could cherish this thought for long, Monsignor Brennan appointed him vicar general, chancellor, secretary, and treasurer. When put more simply this means he was the right-hand man for the new prefect apostolic.

Shortly after Monsignor Brennan's arrival, the superior general of the Columbans, Father Jeremiah Dennehy, came on a visitation to Korea. Back in Ireland the feeling was that not too many young priests should be sent to Korea because more than likely it would become another China, with the Communists expelling all religious groups. Father Dennehy held that opinion as firmly as anyone.

Monsignor Brennan hadn't spent those ten years on the Chicago mission band in vain. In dealing with Father Dennehy he pulled out all the stops on his great store of eloquence. In no time he had the superior general agreeing to send fifteen new priests within the next eighteen months.

The optimism that came so naturally to Father Henry was beginning to wane. He wrote to a friend in the States: "Korea has changed considerably—for the worse. It is really in a terrible condition from every point of view. The Communists are busy night and day with their propaganda. They have freedom of activity in the country places where they cannot be watched so closely. The people join the party through fear, dreading the reprisals if they do not. Many Koreans who call themselves Communists are not the atheistic kind. They think that Communism means they will get the former Japanese land free. The propaganda is sufficiently vague to fool the people and get votes for Communist leaders."

Perhaps Monsignor Brennan had some doubts, too, because on July 8, 1949, he wrote to Father Dennehy apologizing for his request for fifteen more priests. He spoke of the problem as a financial one rather than one that was politically explosive. He said he realized that "it is not so easy from your end of the business—and it sure is a business when it comes to putting cold cash on the line for boat and train fare and the complete outfitting of the fifteen. That is only one of your many worries, Doc, and by no means a little matter. But as we know, God is good and so are God's children. Some of God's children have given themselves for this grand work of saving souls out here in the Orient, and others will not forget them. It is the old story of the two books—the prayer book and the check book. It is a big business, the business of salvation and a good investment for all concerned—God's children who labor in the field afar and those who help them by their prayers and financial aid. If we keep the prayer books in circulation, the rest of God's children will keep the checks in circulation. I feel we won't be disappointed, Doc, and we will have priests out here year after year, and we will have friends at home who will not forget."

The new priests came and brought Father Henry a chore he had not planned on: Monsignor Brennan after having listened to his assistant complain once too often about the sorry training he had had in Taegu, told him to develop a language course that would be more effective. And so he did. While taking a Berlitz course in French, Father Henry had decided that the same system could be used in teaching Korean. With his French book in hand he set about adapting the lessons to his needs.

For forty-five minutes each morning he would drill the young priests in one new construction and ten new words. He never permitted them to write anything down, feeling that learning a language is in great part memory, and so what they needed most was to train the memory to record sounds and retain them. With the Berlitz book as a guide, he composed sentences in Korean and had the students learn expression after expression by rote. Next he held up objects—books, teacup, hat—and had the students call out the names.

After this brisk warm-up, Gregory Kim would put the young priests through more subtle paces for the next six hours. He did little with the

Korean alphabet; the stress was on the spoken word; reading would have to wait. It worked. Within two and a half months, the young priests could hear confessions in Korean, something the pioneering Columbans could scarcely do after a year.

Monsignor Brennan was impatient for the new priests to learn the language; he was getting ready for what he called "the big push." His ambition was to set up parishes in most of the twenty-two counties in the province of Cholla Nam Do, where the Church was unknown. There was one parish in Kwangju City when he arrived. When he dedicated the second, with a Korean priest in charge, his excitement and enthusiasm was downright boyish.

Monsignor Brennan flinched each time Father Henry mounted his bike with the Whizzer motor attached. He believed in living larger than life; his recurring motto was, "no nickel-and-dime show here." He insisted on buying a jeep. It was the first owned by a Columban, even though the society had been in Korea for seventeen years. This was a far cry from that plane Father Henry had dreamed of. The old jeep from Okinawa, that the army sold for $300, was in such a sad condition that Father Henry, with all the mechanical magic his father had taught him, could scarcely keep it in service. He was giving it too much attention for a man with the title of vicar general, chancellor, secretary, and treasurer. He said later, "I was too much of a screwdriver priest in those days. Now I discourage my young priests from doing things like that."

After getting stalled once too often, Pere Brennan decided that if this was not going to be a nickel-and-dime show, he had better get a new jeep from the States. Father Henry went to Seoul to pick it up and drive it to Kwangju. As he bounced across the rutted roads—he had four flats on the way—he little thought that this maroon Willys would soon save his life.

"The 38th parallel" was an expression Father Henry had heard often since returning to Korea. At first the expression sounded strange to his ears because in the old days nobody seemed to know or care what latitudes and longitudes Korea fit into. Now the 38th parallel was destined to become a part of history, and all because Russia entered the war against Japan a few days before the end of World War II.

Korea was never intended to be a divided country. The Russians were to accept the surrender of the Japanese Army north of the 38th parallel and the Americans were to accept the surrender south of it. Afterward the two military governments were to arrange a general election for a united Korea. Instead, Russia established a Communist regime in the North, while the

United States conducted elections to establish a civilian government in the South.

Father Henry didn't take the situation too seriously until he read in the newspaper that Secretary of State Dean Acheson had said that Korea would not be the outer perimeter of the United States military defense. He knew that this would be handing over an unprepared South Korea to the Communists of North Korea.

The darkness of the situation shows in a letter he wrote October 26, 1948, to the editor of *The Far East:* "On Tuesday, elements of the Korean army left their posts and, according to plan, attacked the police stations and guard posts in the Sunchon-Yosu area. Police were tied up and killed as well as people who were active anti-Communists. High school students were given guns, and they set up their own courts and liquidated any students or teachers they did not like or who were expressly anti-Communist.

"Sunchon was held for two full days and Yosu for almost a week. The rebels did not enter our church grounds, but the house has a few bullet marks. A few bullets hit Father Brandon's bed but he had ducked down. After the loyalists recaptured these places, they in turn rounded up any who showed favoritism to the rebels and did away with them. Corpses are strewn all over the place. Father Brandon has gone to Yosu to help collect and bury bodies while Father Moran and Father Kim are working in the Sunchon area.

"The rebels are in the mountains around Sunchon now and the police and the Korean Army are trying to route them. Many army personnel deserted to the rebels as was expected. We feel that this is only the beginning. Things have been quiet. Incidentally, the last American troops pulled out of here less than a week before the uprising began!

"I am very proud to report that all our Catholics remained loyal and have organized relief work in helping the afflicted families and collecting the bodies. I believe a few Catholics were killed by the rebels, but I do not have the facts yet."

All through 1949 and the early months of 1950 the letters and reports from Korea were filled with distress. And then one morning the young priests came to language class all excited, bearing the most distressing news of all: at dawn the armies of the North Korean Communists had come down across the 38th parallel.

Father Henry told them not to worry, there are always skirmishes up there. They assured him that this was not a skirmish, but the real thing. He kept saying, "No, no." He didn't want to believe it. There he stood on June 25, 1950, only a few feet from the spot where he had heard the news of Pearl

Harbor on December 8, 1941. He was not ready to face another war. He had seen enough of the rubble of battle in his time to think often of the Chinese proverb: "What cannot be made in a hundred years can be spoiled in less than a morning."

CHAPTER
14

Another War

MISSIONARIES along the 38th parallel began drifting southward to get out of the crossfire. Two of them, Father Frank McGann, a Columban, and Father Patrick Cleary, a Maryknoll priest, came as far south as Mokpo, where Monsignor Brennan invited them to unpack their suitcases in the Columban residence.

The visitors brought no great fears. They believed that within a few weeks the conflict would end, especially since United States troops were getting into it. As Father McGann said, years later, "Nobody knew North Korea had such a fantastic army! We thought our stay in Mokpo would be a brief holiday and in no time we would be back in our parishes."

On July 5, ten days after the invasion, Monsignor Brennan wrote to the superior general in Ireland, "There is no need to worry. In fact, some of the padres are out digging up the ground for a good crop of tomatoes."

Father Brian Geraghty, though, wasn't so optimistic. He had been one of the pioneering Columbans who entered Korea that dreary Sunday in 1933, and was now the Columban superior in Korea with residence in Seoul. At the time of the Communist invasion he went from Seoul to Mokpo feeling uneasy enough to decide that the student priests studying Korean under Father Henry's new system ought to be moved to Pusan. From there, if things got ugly, they could be readily transferred to Japan. He himself left for Pusan to look for housing, requesting Monsignor Brennan to make arrangements for the young priests to follow.

After dinner one evening, the two visitors, Fathers McGann and Cleary, challenged "the old Mokpo hands," Pere Brennan and Father Henry, to a game of bridge. As the cards were being shuffled someone observed that Korea had always been something of a lightning rod surrounded by thunderheads: Its three neighbors—China, Russia, and Japan—had long fought back and forth across its soil, and now that the United Nations was involved, troops from several other countries were becoming a part of the dreary history.

The bridge game had just begun when the Korean houseboy, John Ri, told Monsignor Brennan that a visitor was at the door. Soon Pere returned and said, "Well, boys, this is it." He introduced the visitor, a disheveled young man named McDonald, an official of the United States Embassy who had come to Mokpo to warn all foreigners to leave the area because it could not be defended. He assured them that the area would be retaken within two or three months and that everybody could then return for business as usual.

Monsignor Brennan invited the young man to have something to eat and drink and suggested he go to bed for the night. It was evident he needed the rest, having repaired seven flat tires on his trip down by jeep. Then the monsignor took Father Henry aside and told him to make arrangements to get the student priests to Pusan.

Fortunately, the Korean naval commander, Admiral Chung Kuk Mo, was a friend of Father Henry's and so the priest drove his maroon jeep through the dark streets of Mokpo down to the port to determine what chances there were to get the young priests to Pusan. The admiral said that a ship then under repair would be ready to take them in the morning, but that they should board about midnight.

Father Henry hurried back up the steep hill to urge Pere Brennan to leave for Pusan, too; but Pere said, no, it was his duty to stay. Fathers Thomas Cusack and John O'Brien said they would also stay. Father Cusack was pastor and Father John O'Brien was assistant pastor of the church on the hill, the church the Japanese had rushed to the night of Pearl Harbor to arrest two other Columbans.

When the young priests reached the Mokpo dock a little after midnight, they were told that the Korean ship was still under repair and that the time of its departure was uncertain. Just as they heard the bad news, a United States Air Force crash boat came roaring into the harbor. The young Columbans hitched a ride on it, and that slam-bang ride out of the Yellow Sea, across the southern end of Korea, and on up the Sea of Japan to Pusan was one they always remembered.

At two o'clock in the morning Monsignor Brennan called Father Henry to his room and said, "When the Communists come they'll take the jeep. So I

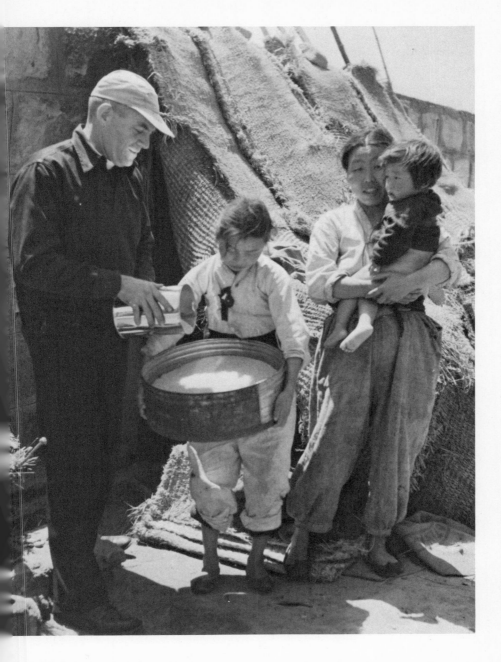

Beside fleeing Communist guerillas during the Korean war, Father Henry directed a rice distribution program.

want you to get it out of here. Take it to Pusan. Along the way stop at the country parishes and pick up the priests. With your army experience you ought to get through." He was referring to the Mount Chiri area that was said to have 20,000 guerrillas operating in it.

Father Henry protested, saying he would stay unless the monsignor went with him. Pere was firm. "Don't worry," he said, "if things get bad I'll go to one of the islands. We'll be seeing you back here soon."

Father Henry awakened Mr. McDonald and the two visitors from up near the 38th parallel, Fathers McGann and Cleary, to suggest that they help form a convoy. Fortunately, Father Cleary had driven down to Mokpo in a jeep.

While things were being packed, Dr. Herbert Codington, a Presbyterian missionary living in Mokpo, drove up the hill in his jeep to hear what the Columbans planned to do. They suggested he "join the push to Pusan," and he decided he would. So shortly after dawn four jeeps driven by Fathers Henry and Cleary, and by Dr. Codington and Mr. McDonald, formed a convoy on the road from Mokpo to Kwangju.

They had planned to stop at Kwangju to pick up some priests, but the stop was unnecessary because en route they met a jeep filled with Columbans on the way to Mokpo. The driver, Father Sean Savage, said he could not accompany the convoy because he wanted to return to Kwangju to stay with his pastor, Father Patrick Monaghan, who had refused to leave. His passengers, Fathers Frank Woods, Kevin Mangan, and Michael Conneely joined the Pusan-bound convoy which later picked up Fathers Vincent Carroll and Oliver C. Kennedy in Sunchon.

As the Columban convoy approached the area where the guerrillas were most active it came upon convoys of the Korean army and the Korean police retreating from the Communists. The four jeeps joined the retreat as far as Chinju. Having lurched for twenty-four hours without rest over the worst roads imaginable, through mountains dark, sharp and barren, everyone in the Columban convoy was exhausted. Father Henry decided that it was safe now to rest because they were beginning to meet advance elements of United States troops who had landed at Pusan. So he made arrangements for his refugees to sleep with the medics of the Twenty-fourth Division in Chinju.

At the end of the 220-mile trip that took nearly three days, Father Henry led his four-jeep convoy into Pusan. There he learned that Father Brian Geraghty had "commandeered" the house owned by the Maryknoll Sisters, the nuns having left for Japan shortly after the start of the war. The small house was filling fast; in time it would shelter twenty Columbans and twelve French missionaries.

Father McGann recalled that the house became so crowded that he and another Columban had to sleep in a jeep. They awakened one morning to find the jeep had been jacked up during the night and three tires stolen. This was typical of the stories American soldiers would soon be telling about the "slicky-slicky boys," those Koreans who could cut quietly through the wire of a perimeter fence, avoid an armed guard, roam at will through the GI area, take their pick of anything that wasn't nailed down, and depart as quietly as they had come.

One legend of the "slicky-slicky" boys revolved around two American guards who were court-martialed. During the trial they swore that all through the night they had carefully patrolled around the warehouse. Never had they relaxed for a moment. Then how come two metal doors had been lifted from their hinges and a truck backed into the warehouse? "I dunno, sir! I shoore dunno!"

Although the slicky-slicky boys were operating freely in hectic Pusan, they were the least of Father Henry's worries. He thought that he had been busy in Mokpo as vicar-general, chancellor, secretary, and treasurer, but now he suddenly found himself the liaison officer with the United States forces, quartermaster general and transportation officer of a band of missionary refugees.

A few days after the Columban convoy had arrived in Pusan, Father Sean Savage came to town with a jeep overflowing with Koreans. He said that after leaving the Columban convoy on the road between Mokpo and Kwangju, he had returned to Kwangju to find Father Monaghan as determined as ever to stand his ground.

Soon a French missionary arrived at the Kwangju rectory, having ridden down from the north on a bicycle. Father Savage was awakened in the night by the sound of an argument between the Frenchman and Father Monaghan. The Frenchman was insisting that the pastor and his assistant leave at once for Pusan, but the pastor wasn't giving an inch.

At dawn Father Monaghan went to the church and prayed for half an hour. He returned to the rectory, pointed a severe finger at Father Savage and said, "You take the jeep and go to Pusan. If the Reds get near I'll come by motorbike. I want you to take some Koreans with you. I was going to give the jeep to them." The Koreans he referred to were known anti-Communists whose lives would end abruptly if they should fall into the enemy's hands.

Several days later in Pusan a truck driver searched out Father Savage and handed him a letter. It was from Father Monaghan, saying the motorbike had broken down in Sunchon and that he would walk as far as Chinju. Come, pick him up there. Father Henry volunteered to go along.

In the maroon jeep the two priests lurched across an impossible road and reached Chinju at midnight. No one there had seen Father Monaghan and so they decided to hurry on to Sunchon where the letter had been written. However, the Korean police refused to let them proceed before dawn.

Things went well enough until they reached Hadong, about twenty-five miles from Sunchon. A Korean major stopped them to ask where they were going. When they told him, he said they had better hurry because North Korean troops were only ten miles north of Sunchon.

The Columbans nearly wrecked the jeep forcing it at the greatest possible speed across miserable roads to cover twenty-five miles before the enemy could cover ten. Sunchon was deserted. The doors of the houses had been left open, which increased the sense of emptiness, of abandonment.

Suddenly, three soldiers stepped from a building. The priests were terrified, thinking they had come upon North Koreans. The soldiers only said, "Get out fast!" The priests rushed to the deserted church. They yelled, "Pat, Pat where are you?" There was the broken motorbike, but Father Monaghan was nowhere in sight.

They returned to their Pusan residence fatigued and with nerves on edge, feeling they had failed Father Monaghan. When they walked in the door, there he sat. He said he feared that Father Savage wouldn't arrive in time, so he had hitched a ride on a truck to Yosu and had taken a boat from there to Pusan.

Fathers Henry and Savage did not realize how very close they had come to getting killed until a few hours after returning from Sunchon. Father Henry was called to United States military headquarters to report everything he had seen on that jinxed trip. During the conversation an American officer happened to mention that Hadong had been captured yesterday.

"That's impossible," said Father Henry, "I was there yesterday. I picked up a French missionary there."

"What time?"

"About noon. Maybe a little after."

"The Communists took it at one o'clock."

The Columbans were kept busy in Pusan. Every day three or four troop ships arrived, many without chaplains, and so the refugee priests went to the piers to hear confessions and say Mass for troops about to go into battle. Often in the middle of a meal the cry would come, "Ship's in!" and the missionaries would hurry from the table leaving the food to grow cold as they rushed to the docks.

Some of the priests joined combat units as volunteer chaplains, adding to their duties that of interpreter. Probably the most famous volunteer was Father Frank Woods, the ex-bartender Harold Henry admired so much when they were seminarians in Ireland. He joined the Second Battalion, Thirty-first Regiment, of the Second Infantry Division because he knew the commanding officer from the military government days after World War II. His unit was twice surrounded by Communists. For his conduct in action he received the highest decoration which can be given a non-American citizen, the Medal of Freedom with Silver Palm.

The citation reads that he climbed a hill and shouted at the Communists in Korean to give themselves up. It was thought only two wounded were there. About seventy-five stood up, their hands over their heads. The citation concludes that with no thought of his personal safety Father Woods arranged for the surrender, reflecting the highest credit on himself and the United States Army.

While the Columbans were showing courage beyond the call of duty, many of their parishioners were doing the same. The story of Paul Kim, the seventy-year-old head catechist in Mokpo, might be used as an example.

Paul had a friend who was a disenchanted Communist. Because the friend had once been active he was still welcome without suspicion at the party's high echelon meetings in Mokpo. He would inform Paul of people scheduled to be arrested, possibly executed. Paul would inform those people; and when the Communist military police arrived in the early morning, their victims would be gone. Sensing that there was collusion, the police put spies at various Catholic homes. It soon became evident that whenever Paul Kim made a visit, people began to slip away quietly one by one.

Paul was arrested and tortured but refused to reveal the name of his informant. He was sentenced to be executed. A Communist soldier, who looked no more than seventeen, tied him up and brought him to the quarry behind the jail for execution. On the way the soldier said, "Honorable Old Man, I know you are a good man. Authorities make many mistakes. I'll fire my gun in the air and report that I executed and buried you. You hide in the country."

Paul hid in a village in which he had friends, about seven miles from Mokpo. After a few days his conscience began bothering him. He was an old man and had led a full life; he ought to take his chances back in Mokpo serving as a catechist.

Through a third party he reestablished contact with his Communist friend. He resumed visiting Catholic homes under cover of darkness and again was apprehended.

The local commander flew into a rage, saying that if he couldn't trust subordinates, he would execute this renegade himself. He ordered Paul tied up, thrown into a truck and he and the driver went to the quarry. While they were walking the 200 yards from the road to the quarry, an American P-51 fighter plane came in low, strafed the truck, killing the driver and the commander. Paul walked away to die peacefully in his home ten years later.

In Pusan Father Henry attached himself to the 1054th Evacuation Hospital that had no Catholic chaplain. Each night from eight until three in the morning a minimum of a thousand casualties were brought in. Those not needing immediate surgery were sent by ship to Japan. Later, the navy hospital ship Consolation and a MASH unit arrived without Catholic chaplains, so Father Henry was kept busy making the rounds of three hospitals.

Quite often he talked with wounded captured Communist soldiers who were astonished at the expert medical treatment they received. They often asked the priest to thank the American doctors.

"I asked several why they fought so doggedly," said Archbishop Henry. "The answer was always the same: They were told the Americans would cut off their ears or their tongues. Also that if they surrendered they would be shot from behind by their own officers, and that their relatives would be made to suffer. I asked them if they really believed that about the Americans. They said not any more. Now they knew better.

"After the war only twenty-five percent of the North Korean and Chinese 'volunteers' chose to return to their countries. I think that was a great condemnation of Communism."

One day while making the rounds at the hospital, Father Henry was asked if he would consider working for the air force in Japan as a consultant on Korean translations. He agreed, providing he would be permitted to return to Mokpo as soon as the troops had cleared that area.

On September 16, 1950, United States troops landed at Inchon and other UN forces broke out of the Pusan perimeter. On October 1, Korean marines landed at Mokpo and the Communists withdrew rapidly northward.

The air force kept its word, even making available to Father Henry a special plane so he could take back to Mokpo five Columbans. They had been assigned to Japan because the superiors in Ireland thought Korea was finished as a mission country.

Getting back to Mokpo was not without frustrations. The special plane left the six priests in Pusan, where, they were told, a plane loaded with mortar shells would pick them up and take them to Kwangju. They waited a week but no such plane appeared.

Father Henry went to the Korean Naval Headquarters to learn if a ship might take the Columbans and their jeep home. After a short wait they were put on one of the first ships to carry passengers to Mokpo. The trip was made on a sea so rough that even the sailors got seasick, and to add to the discomfort the captain had everyone standing watch for floating mines the Communists might have left around.

From the Mokpo harbor the six priests hurried to the Columban residence wondering what they might find. In Pusan they had heard from a Korean priest, Father Oh, that Monsignor Brennan and Fathers Cusack and O'Brien had been captured, but as they rode up the hill the hope grew that, with all the combat of recent weeks, perhaps the three Columbans had escaped and were back in the big red building doing business as usual.

Instead, they found the house occupied by three Korean marines. One of them, a Catholic, said that upon landing he had asked a Korean civilian where the Catholic church was located and was directed to this house. When he and a friend arrived, they caught four Communist soldiers setting fire to the place. A fight ensued during which one Communist was shot, and the others fled. The marine said he had then gone around town to the various offices the Communists had established to collect furniture stolen from the house.

He said that one of the houseboys, John Ri, helped to identify the furniture. John said that when he had objected to the theft while it was in progress, the Communists took him to the front yard and told him to dig his own grave. After he had dug it, they walked off and left him standing there.

Almost the first sight to confront the returning priest was a large black anchor that the marines had painted on the dining room wall. He didn't know it at the time but it would take many repaintings over many years before the anchor would cease to bleed through. He hurried to his office and found it bare except for a shelf of books; behind the books he found the typewriter he had hidden the day he departed, and so he knew the Communists had not spent much time reading. The doors to some of the bedrooms bore the scars of bullet holes because the Communists sometimes fired through a door before opening it. The building would eventually become the convent of the Columban sisters and to this day may be the only convent in the world with bullet holes in the doors of the nuns' bedrooms.

Outside, the building bore some scars from shrapnel. The garage, in which forty-nine Koreans had been confined awaiting execution, was a shambles.

Dominic, the cook, came forward to greet the priest with whom he had weathered so many rough days. He told a touching story of his brother, Gregory, a seminarian at the outbreak of the war. Gregory and another seminarian were arrested and locked in a cell with a Korean nun. When they were told that they would be executed in the morning Gregory said at the evening meal, "Let's enjoy this meal as though it were a banquet. We are

going to heaven. This should be the most cheerful meal we have ever had."
The nun was released. The two seminarians were beaten to death with clubs
the following morning.

Dominic said that quite suddenly and unexpectedly the Communists had
arrived in Mokpo, from Kwangju, early in the morning of July 24. A truck
load of shouting soldiers pulled up to the front door, and when Dominic told
Monsignor Brennan that the Reds had arrived, he knelt down and began to
say the rosary. When the Communists were told that this was a church, they
said they were not against religious freedom and went away. The next day
they returned and took Fathers O'Brien and Cusack prisoners long enough to
march them around town. They then returned them to the rectory, saying
they were not going to interfere with anyone's religion. This turned out to be
a ruse; they wanted the Catholics of Mokpo to feel at ease so that they might
more easily find out who the Catholics were.

A few days later the three Columbans were taken the fifty-six miles to
Kwangju by motorcycle. The monsignor and Father O'Brien rode as best
they could in the sidecar and Father Cusack rode the handlebars.

A few weeks later a prisoner of war, Lieutenant Alexander G. Ma-
karounis, and two other United States infantrymen, met the three Columbans in the Kwangju jail. The lieutenant later wrote an account of their experience for the May 1951 issue of *The Far East*. Following are some excerpts
from that article.

There were heavy iron doors on the row of cells which we saw dimly in the gloom.
One of these doors was opened and we were motioned to go in. We could tell by the
movement inside that someone was there already, but this cell didn't seem as crowded
as the others. Then the iron door creaked shut behind us. The lock snapped tight.

We stumbled around in the darkness. Then a friendly, you might even say fa-
therly, voice said, 'Everything is okay, Mac; we'll talk about it in the morning.'
Within the next few minutes, our eyes got accustomed to the darkness a little, and we
saw that there were four others in the cell. The man who spoke was Monsignor Patrick Brennan, a Columban missionary. With him were two other Columbans, Fathers
Thomas Cusack and John O'Brien. The fourth was a South Korean police official.

It was a cold night, for August, and there were no blankets for us in the cell. There
were only three blankets in all, but these were immediately shared with us by the missionaries. It was the first of many acts of kindness and consideration the priests were
to show us during the dreadful days we were to go through. . . .

When we first met the priests, they had been prisoners for about five weeks. As the
meals consisted of only a small bowl of barley with a small slice of pickled turnip, the
priests had all lost a great deal of weight.

Monsignor Brennan and Father Cusack were wearing black trousers and black
shoes. The Monsignor had on a black shirt; Father Cusack a blue one. They also had
their collars and cassocks. Father O'Brien was all in white; he had white trousers, a

white T-shirt and a white cassock. They kept their cassocks rolled up and out of the way most of the time—I guess they didn't want to lose them.

It would be hard to tell you just what these men did for our morale—they boosted it by at least 500 per cent! Monsignor, for instance, would stand at the cell window and listen to the birds chirping merrily outside, then he'd turn and cheer us up by telling us a singing bird was a messenger of hope.

At other times, he'd encourage Father O'Brien to sing us a song and do one of his Irish jigs. Father O'Brien had a good voice and the way he sang 'Far Away Places,' sort of made you forget you were cooped up in a prison cell and sent your thoughts flying back home.

Each day, U.N. planes flew over Kwangju, strafing and bombing this north-Korean stronghold. At the times of these raids, I could see the lips of the missionaries moving in prayer and, although we could hear the crashing of bombs all around, we came through without a scratch.

On the second day we were there, the south Korean police official was taken out of our cell. We don't know what happened to him. This gave us a little more room in the cell which was about 14 feet long and 10 feet wide. In one corner of the cell was a water faucet that we could use twice a day.

One day, we three soldiers were taken out and brought to a little church which the Reds were using as a headquarters. After questioning us, they told us they were sending us to a prisoner-of-war camp in Seoul. They put us on a broken-down truck, and we were happy to find that the priests were going with us—along with other prisoners who made thirty-two altogether. Among these were two more G.I.'s, Privates Steger and Miller.

In preparation for the journey, the priests' hands were tied with ropes. The hands of the military people were fastened with hand-irons and ropes. We traveled only at night to escape allied bombers, and spent the days in jails along the way. On the second and following nights, the Fathers' hands were untied.

We were on this truck three nights straight and then, when we were approaching the city of Taejon, the truck broke down for good. We were told to get off and walk. Father Cusack, who knew this part of the country well, told us we were about seven miles outside the city.

What a seven miles! Privates Steger and Miller did not have shoes, and their feet were soon badly cut by the sharp stones on the road. The guards set a fast pace, too fast for men who were exhausted from wounds and malnutrition. However, the guns pointing at us told us we must keep up with the pack.

Monsignor Brennan and myself found it most difficult of all. He was the oldest, and his strength was gone. My wounds made walking a torture. We asked the guards to slacken off the pace a little, but they refused. The Monsignor, thinking more of me than himself, he was puffing with over-exertion, told me to take it easy—to fall down and rest. Father Cusack overheard him; he told me to do no such thing because he had heard the guards saying in Korean that they would shoot anyone who did.

Then Father O'Brien helped me along, and Father Cusack lent a hand to Monsignor Brennan. It was a sad procession!

We approached a river and could see the city of Taejon about a mile away. We had to cross a bridge. It was now daylight—about 8 A.M. Suddenly a flight of U.N. light bombers appeared overhead, and we all scattered for cover under the bridge where piled rocks led down to the water. I was so exhausted that I guess I blacked-out for a moment when I hit the ground. Monsignor Brennan must have done the same because he began to slide down the rocks into the water. Father O'Brien reached out just in time and pulled him back. We lay there panting for breath for about ten minutes; it was a welcome relief.

Then the planes were gone, and we were reassembled on the road. The guards saw that Monsignor Brennan and myself were in bad shape and would never be able to make it into Taejon at the pace set. They told us to fall out; I thought this was the end. I could see the Monsignor's lips moving as he prayed. But they didn't shoot us; instead, the guard motioned with his gun that we could walk slower—the others continued on ahead.

We were reunited in the city of Taejon where we were put in a small building, but not before we were made to sit out in the open for about 30 minutes while a Korean with a small camera took pictures of us. We were then put on display for about two hours while hundreds of North Koreans, army people and others, came in to look at us.

When we could keep our eyes open no longer, we all fell fast asleep from sheer exhaustion. About noon, a Korean came in, woke up us five soldiers and took us out to another building where we met close to a hundred other U.N. prisoners. . . .

For us, the story of the missionaries ends in the prison of Taejon. We do not know what happened after we were taken from the cell. But wherever they are, I shall always remember them for the comfort, cheerfulness, kindness and courage they somehow communicated to us when they were no better off themselves.

Monsignor Brennan used to say to us, 'Trust in God and everything will come out all right in the end.' I'm sure everything did.

The next news of the three Columbans came from the wife of a Korean judge. She said she had been confined in the same room with the three priests from Mokpo at the Franciscan Monastery in Taejon. She was released on the afternoon of September 24, and that night there was a massacre at the monastery as Red troops prepared to hurry north so as not to be cut off by advancing United Nations troops.

Later neither Father George Carroll, M.M., nor Father Beaudevin, M.E.P., could recognize any of the Columbans among more than a thousand corpses piled up in the monastery garden. The bodies were so decomposed and swollen that the two priests had difficulty recognizing Father Pollet, a man they had known by sight. A well in the monastery garden was filled with bodies that neither priest had had a chance to inspect.

Eight years later Father John Vaughan of Dunedin, New Zealand, was walking along a crowded, narrow street of Seoul when he chanced upon a small bookstall. He absent-mindedly fingered through an odd assortment on the remote chance that he might find something of interest. He picked up a small black volume; it was the summer quarter of the Divine Office. Opening the cover to see to whom the book might have belonged, on the flyleaf he found written, "P. Brennan 18 Dec. 1926."

Hope sprang up again among the Columbans, but nothing more was heard. So in the archives of the Society of St. Columban, Monsignor Brennan and Fathers O'Brien and Cusack are recorded as having died in the massacre of Taejon on September 24, 1950.

CHAPTER

15

The Death March

WHEN THE KOREAN WAR broke out, forty-one Columbans were working in Korea. They were divided between two mission territories—the Prefecture of Kwangju, under direction of Monsignor Brennan, and the Prefecture of Chunchon, under direction of Monsignor Thomas Quinlan (of "propter pontem" memory).

All through the war Father Henry wondered what was happening in the Prefecture of Chunchon, a territory especially vulnerable because it overlapped the thirty-eighth parallel. He heard fragments of rumors from time to time but the details were not known until Monsignor Quinlan was released from prison in 1953. Briefly, this is what had happened.

Since Monsignor Quinlan's headquarters at Chunchon, Kangwondo, was only twelve miles from the thirty-eighth parallel, he heard gunfire within two hours after the North Koreans crossed the border at four o'clock Sunday morning, June 25, 1950. Throughout the day no mention of an invasion came over the radio, and so he considered it just another skirmish, a little more prolonged and intense than usual. At six o'clock that evening an official announcement of the invasion was made by radio and instantly the townspeople of Chunchon began to flee by train and truck to Seoul.

Father Anthony Collier, whose parish was across town, visited Monsignor Quinlan late that evening to say that a few Koreans near his church had been wounded by stray bullets and that he had given them first aid treatment. His church overlooked a bridge which the Red army would have to cross to enter the city. The monsignor, feeling there would be severe fighting around the bridge, invited the young priest to stay with him for the time being.

Father Collier said, "I prefer to stay with my parishioners. Short of a direct hit I ought to be safe. If the Reds capture the city, I might be of some help to my people."

Two days later Father Collier and his house boy, Gabriel Kim, were siezed by Communist soldiers as they walked toward the post office. The two were bound together with ropes and marched toward the river. On the way, without warning, one of the soldiers opened fire on them with a submachine gun. In falling, Father Collier pulled Gabriel to the ground with him.

The soldiers left the two for dead. Gabriel had wounds in the shoulder and throat and lay beside the body of Father Collier a day and two nights, working feebly to free his tied hands from those of the dead priest. When at last he succeeded, he made his way painfully to Pusan. To this day he is badly scarred.

A few days later two other Columbans in the vicinity were executed. Father James Maginn, pastor at Sam Chock, and Patrick Reilly, pastor at Mukho, could have escaped but preferred to remain with their parishioners, mostly new Catholics who were afraid of the Communists.

On the fourth of July, the soldiers took Father Maginn as he was praying in his little one-room church. They beat him, and then, three days later they shot him to death on a hill just outside the town. They then put pressure on his parishioners to declare themselves Communists, but none went over to them.

Father Reilly played hide and seek in the hills for a month and could have continued evading the soldiers had not a Korean, to curry favor with the Communists, betrayed him. They came at night and got him and, after keeping him in prison for a few days, shot him on the roadside, leaving his body there. The local people buried it.

A year after their deaths, Father Henry attended the funeral of Fathers Collier and O'Reilly in Chunchon. They were buried amid the stone ruins of what was to be the cathedral; it was destroyed a few weeks before the day set for the dedication. Later the body of Father Maginn would also be buried among the ruins. Eventually three new churches—in North Chunchon, in Mukho, and in Sam Chock—would mark the places where the three had died.

On the dreary day of the funeral, Father Henry met Gabriel Kim, the house boy who had been left for dead, and heard him tell of the dreadful thirty-six hours he lay tied to his dead pastor. He met an acolyte, Stephen Park, whose father had been killed by the Communists, and whose brother had died in prison. In the congregation stood Lieutenant Colonel C. S. Hoge, of Olathe, Kansas, who had come down from Seoul to the funeral. He told Father Henry how he had urged Father Collier to escape with him but the missionary had only repeated, "No, thank you, my place is here."

Shortly after the start of the invasion, Colonel Hoge, the United States Military adviser of the South Korean forces in Kangwondo, also asked Monsignor Quinlan and his assistant, Father Francis Canavan, if they didn't want to go south with him to Wonju. The monsignor thanked the American for his thoughtfulness, saying he felt it was his duty to stay, but said to Father Canavan, "You're free to go. You're not responsible for this district. I'll give you my blessing and think as much of you as if you stayed."

Father Canavan preferred to stay. Colonel Hoge said goodbye and left.

A week after the invasion, while Monsignor Quinlan was saying his Sunday Mass, the Communist soldiers came for him. After shooting up the church, they marched the monsignor and Father Canavan to the first of several prisons. Later they were joined by another Columban, Father Philip Crosbie.

From Chunchon the priests were moved to Seoul, later to Pyongyang, and in October were transferred to an internment camp at Manpo in the far north of Korea. On the evening of October 31 all the prisoners in the camp were told to pack their blankets and get ready to march. The priests didn't know it at the time but this march was part of the Communist army's retreat before advancing units of the United States Infantry.

No transportation was provided for what became known as "the Death March." Several hundred prisoners—soldiers, journalists, missionaries, civil servants—were lined up on a Korean morning that was especially cold, in a snow that was especially deep. Some were old, many were sick, and all were feeble from near starvation.

Commissioner Lord of the Salvation Army went to see the Communist commander, inown to the prisoners as "the Tiger." "These people will die if they have to march!" protested Commissioner Lord.

"Then let them march until they die. This is a military order," said the Tiger.

Ninety-eight of them did die. Some from weakness and exhaustion and others from bullets when they could drag themselves no farther. Monsignor Quinlan saw the Tiger himself fire a bullet into an American lieutenant's head. The lieutenant's offense was that he had allowed his men to rest because a guard had given him permission to do so.

The march lasted ten days and ended more than a hundred miles farther north, at a village called Chung-Kang. Father Canavan had contracted pneumonia on the march and, although he was ill for some three or four weeks, he seemed to have recovered when suddenly he had a relapse and died on December 6.

Monsignor Quinlan was released April 9, 1953, three and a half months before the truce was signed. When Father Crosbie was released some months later he wrote a book about his nearly three years of imprisonment. It was called *Pencilling Prisoner* when published in England; *Three Winters Cold*, in Australia; and *March Till They Die* in the United States.

During the war the Columbans lost seven priests, several seminarians, at least 2,000 parishioners, and half of their buildings. All in all, the Communists had put to death 5 bishops, 82 priests, and 150 religious and seminarians.

CHAPTER
16

The New Job

WHEN FATHER HENRY returned to Mokpo, the war was just getting started, although he and everyone he talked with thought surely it would be over by Christmas. Once more it fell to his lot to administer the Apostolic Prefecture of Kwangju, assuming again the high-sounding title of pro-prefect apostolic.

According to Church law, anyone in such a temporary office is not to make any major changes. Locked into such a position, Harold Henry felt thwarted. To make no major changes was unfulfilling to the man who had the word *change* ground into the core of his being.

Although he eventually got permission from the apostolic delegate to make necessary changes, it turned out he could not make as many as he would have liked. Changes for him meant starting new projects, the kind of activity he would pursue with such zest after 1953. For the time being, though, travel was unsafe even in the southern province. When the Chinese volunteers entered the war it began to look as though his prefecture might once again be overrun. Even if the main force did not penetrate to the south, there were still the guerrillas to contend with. Many north Korean Communists and civilians who had cooperated with the invaders had been trapped in the south after the Inchon invasion and could not get up to the thirty-eighth parallel. So they fled to the mountains to establish bases from which they conducted guerrilla raiding expeditions.

Even more frightening were some of the blatant murders within the towns. Father Henry wrote of this in a report to his superior shortly after returning

Had it not been for the missionaries the Koreans would have suffered even more than they did from 1950 to 1953.

to Mokpo: "When the Red Army left the town, the local Reds with masks and knives went about killing and looting. The unfortunate part is that these are getting away scot free by bribing police officials and even the ROK soldiers."

In August of 1951 Father Henry reported other dangers in the southernmost part of Korea: "We cannot send a priest permanently to Noan in the country as the guerrillas enter the village every night for taxes and rice. A Korean priest sneaks in there occasionally to give the sacraments. A ROK regiment used to be here but has moved to the front: results, the guerrillas have become quite bold. Ask Father Savage, who was in Naju one night when they attacked. The city office was burned down—less than fifty yards from the house where Father Savage slept. He did not sleep in the church as it is too exposed. One Red with a machine gun stood outside the door of the house in which he was staying, firing like mad, unaware of the prize within."

Although many Columbans had returned to their parishes they continued to visit isolated army units. Usually they traveled by military aircraft. To facilitate this, Father Henry had twenty-five copies of travel orders made out in his name each month. He would give these to different priests so that on some days Harold Henry, according to the names on the manifests, was appearing in three places at once.

Even in those darkest days of the war, the happy events of the great decade from 1953 to 1963 were already beginning to cast their shadows before them. The apathetic spirit that Harold Henry had found in Korea when he returned from World War II would soon give way to a spiritual vivacity the like of which no missionary had dreamed of.

The signs were beginning to show even as early as the Christmas of 1950, when Father Henry reported to his superior: "For the first time since the Christmas after Pearl Harbor (when we were all in a Japanese jail) we were unable to offer Midnight Mass. But the curfew was lifted at 6:30 Christmas morning and every Mass was packed. As there was not sufficient room in the church, the people had to gather at the windows for Benediction after the last Mass. Our churches are crowded for daily Mass and the Rosary, and we have many under instruction."

During these uneasy days Father Henry depended more than ever on his catechists. Being Korean, they could move about more freely and blend more readily into the landscape than a western missionary. He thanked God that the priests in South Korea had selected and trained as catechists some remarkable men and women. Father Francis Herlihy, a Columban, described the ideal catechist:

"He is the missioner's mouthpiece; his representative, his messenger; his alter ego. He has access to places and persons that the missioner cannot reach. He has command of intricacies of language that a foreigner may never hope to equal."

When the superior general of the Columbans, Father Timothy Connolly, visited Korea early in 1953, he was impressed with the high spirit and optimism he found there in spite of the destructive war. His report reflects his satisfaction with the work Harold Henry was doing:

"Finally I came to Mokpo, where the pro-prefect of this South Korean mission field, Father Harold Henry from Minneapolis, has his headquarters and is ably assisted by Father Tom Moran and Father Oliver C. Kennedy.

"Father Henry has seen the prefecture under Japanese rule—when he was expelled from it; he has seen it under the stress of army occupation when priests had to deal with problems of relations between the occupying forces and the civilian population and had to keep on good terms with both; and he has seen it overrun and ruined by Red invasion. Twice he has had to shoulder the government of the prefecture: once when it was deprived of Monsignor MacPolin, and again when his successor Monsignor Brennan was taken and died in the hands of the Reds. It is not strange that Father Henry, like all of these priests, is more mature than his years.

"But his wisdom is not acquired by the process of sitting and thinking, for he is continually on the go from morning to night. He is bedevilled by money worries, vacant parishes for which he has no priests, children for whom he has no schools, a vast multitude of potential Catholics whom he cannot win for lack of these missionary munitions. Withal, he is the happy warrior for whom no detail of the struggle for souls is too small to neglect, no problem too big to tackle, no worry too all-absorbing to wipe away the smile from his friendly face, no day long enough for all he has to do, and all he has to do still not enough to keep him from doing more."

When the Korean war ended, Father Henry made arrangements to return to the States to collect money and supplies for the needs of the Prefecture of Kwangju. On December 3, 1954, he had lunch with Monsignor Paul Taggart in Wilmington, Delaware, and after lunch he set out for Philadelphia. At the Wilmington Memorial Bridge he had just paid his toll when a policeman ran out shouting, "Stop that car! I'm looking for that man." Father Henry's only thought was that perhaps he had hit someone without knowing it.

After what seemed like an eternity of fumbling through his pockets, the policeman pulled out a scrap of paper and said that Monsignor Taggert had phoned to say that Father Henry should call operator 50 in Omaha. He offered the use of the phone provided the call was collect. So there in the toll booth, a place that specializes in collecting money, he learned that Rome had appointed him Prefect Apostolic of Kwangju. When he hung up the phone he had a new title, Monsignor, and had just been set free, officially, to make changes galore.

CHAPTER
17

Amazing Growth

AN OLD Irish missionary said, "When we went to the Orient to harvest souls, all of us took scythes and rakes—except Harold Henry. He took a Caterpillar tractor and a McCormick reaper."

Although the remark was humorous, it was based on serious statistics. Harold Henry had been responsible for forty-six new churches, well over a hundred mission stations, a hospital, three clinics, a major seminary, a retreat center, nine high schools, and twelve kindergartens. He had encouraged dozens of self-help programs to make life more livable for the old, the orphaned, the maimed, and the poor. To help the Columbans with all of this, he brought to the Prefecture of Kwangju thirteen religious communities from all over the world.

When Father Henry took over the administrative burden of the prefecture, at the time of Monsignor Brennan's death, there were only eight parishes and little else of church-sponsored activity. Even that which existed was badly in need of reconstruction as the result of two wars.

Then quite suddenly it happened. After the truce was signed in 1953, the Catholic Church in Korea enjoyed a decade of growth beyond all imagining. During those years Harold Henry grew, too, as suggested by his rapidly changing titles: Father Henry became a monsignor on December 3, 1954, a bishop on May 11, 1957 and an archbishop on March 25, 1962.

Looking back later on that decade of feverish activity, Archbishop Henry tried to explain what happened: "I believe that this unparalleled outpouring of grace came as a result of the Church's agony on Korean soil. A sort of

reimbursement for suffering. I'm not just thinking of the seven Columbans
who died. I remember Patrick J. Byrne, a Maryknoll bishop, who died in
captivity after the Death March. And that 76-year-old French nun, Sister
Beatrice, who was shot on the Death March. Bishop Boniface Sauer, a Bene-
dictine, and one of his German priests died in prison. Twelve priests of the
Paris Foreign Missions were killed or died of ill-treatment. Bishop Francis
Hong disappeared in captivity. Five Korean priests are known to have been
killed, one died in prison, and between twenty-five and forty are missing in
Communist hands. Several Korean sisters were killed. Two Carmelite nuns
died in captivity. Innumerable Catholics and Protestants were killed, died in
prison, or just disappeared as captives. We had more than 400 Catholics who
could have saved their lives by denying their faith, but they chose the firing
squad instead. It is interesting to note that the majority had been baptized
within the previous three years. So the remark, 'They are rice Christians' is
not apt here. Rice Christians do not die for their faith. Yes, those of us who
survived were reimbursed for our sacrifices, most of which we'll never even
know about."

Another reason that religion flourished, Archbishop Henry believed, is
that in South Korea the Communists were their own worst enemies. Many
Koreans who toyed with the idea that maybe communism offered solutions
to the troubles of life found that the Reds brought only chaos and destruc-
tion. As Father Austin Sweeney wrote from Cheju Island, "One thing certainly is clear in all this mix-up: Communist propaganda will not deceive the
people of Cheju again. They have seen that the freedom and peace which
Communism promised them is the freedom of slavery and the peace of the
grave." Five years after the truce, Father Bernard Smyth wrote, "It is an interesting fact that only in Pusan in southeast Korea, which was never under
Communist rule, have you any large number of Communist sympathizers."
The Koreans saw that the Reds were determined to stamp out all religion,
especially Catholicism, and some may have turned to the Church as a flight
from something they had come to dread.

Archbishop Henry believed that another reason for the amazing growth
was the friendship that grew between priests and people during the long
agony, the kind of deep friendship that only shared ordeals can generate. The
Koreans were impressed that foreign priests shared their anguish when they
really did not have to. They were also impressed that the poor received help
just because they were poor and not for any advantage the giver might receive. Koreans became curious about a Church that gave something for
nothing.

Another thing in the Church's favor was the good example set by the

Harold Henry checks with the foreman at one of the 46 churches he built in Korea.

United States army GI. "Young Korean men were attracted to the Church because they saw a high percentage of the American soldiers attending services," said Archbishop Henry. "It was quite impressive when you considered that nearly thirty percent of the American troops were Catholic. Koreans watched battle-tired, muddy soldiers kneeling in the icy wind to attend Mass. And so many starving refugees were nourished back to life by the generosity of Catholic servicemen. The soldiers helped build churches, too. When they left, they left behind the memory of a virile faith and of an unbounded charity. It never dawned on them that they also were missionaries. They would have been surprised and embarrassed to have been told that. I remember that under the Japanese regime the Church was just tolerated and very few men were attracted to it. With the coming of the American troops the Korean youth began to see Christianity in a new light. This gave 'face' to the Church, and nothing can succeed in the Orient without 'face'."

The more the Church enjoyed "face" the more it attracted sophisticated Koreans. For generations it had been the "potters' church." The potters were on the lowest rung of the social ladder, one step below the butchers. Their ancestors, many of them wealthy men, had fled to unpromising southwestern Korea hoping to escape religious persecution in the nineteenth century. There they began to work in clay. This image of the "potters' church" changed after the Korean War. Prince and Princess Lee, members of the Korean dynasty that had been dethroned by the Japanese, became attracted to Catholicism. Before long missionaries were being approached by judges, teachers, physicians, merchants, and military men seeking admission into the Church. This continued until, in time, the Columbans found that their parishioners represented all levels of society.

The more the Church flourished the heavier grew the burden that Harold Henry carried. No one was more aware of this than his secretary, Rita Kriess, who with her husband, a retired naval officer, had come to Korea to do two years of volunteer work. In a magazine article in 1959, Mrs. Kriess wrote: "The bishop's residence is more than just a chancery office for the vicariate and living quarters for the bishop and his staff. After spending a few days observing the routine of a normal day's work, you realize the real purpose of its being. Supplies must be secured for the feeding and clothing of the hungry and the poor; sums of money must be continuously doled out to pay for upkeep and maintenance of the various parishes, which in the missions are not self-supporting; monthly payrolls for the catechists must be met; reports for Rome and Columban headquarters compiled; correspondence from almost every part of the world must be answered."

In his administrative burden it was the meetings that were hardest on

Harold Henry's morale, especially after Vatican II, when meetings proliferated throughout the Church. Typical of his response to them was a remark in a letter to the Rowlands in March of 1965: "I went to the bishops' meeting in Seoul for three consecutive days of hot air from 10 A.M. to 12:30 P.M. and from 2 P.M. to 6:30 P.M. It took me three days to get back to normal."

As bureaucracy in the Church became more involved, Harold Henry seemed to mellow a little, judging from something he wrote to friends in the States in December of 1967: "I have twelve subcommissions on my pastoral council which is supposed to study ways and means of making our apostolate more effective. All sent their reports. I'll either have to get a computer to sift and evaluate the information or form another commission to do so. When I get it all evaluated, I submit it to the Senate of Priests and their evaluation will be submitted to my diocesan consultants. After that, as one priest said, 'And then you'll do what you intended to do anyway.' [Then came the mellow admission.] "Truly I received some very helpful suggestions—all made with the greatest of good will."

Meetings and desk work made him restless because the athlete inside was always eager to be set free. He sometimes paused and stared into space remembering the days he rode a bike from village to village and climbed steep mountain trails to some remote mission station. Whenever the chafing became too severe he found an excuse to slip away from the chancery office and then, as always, adventure found him. Typhoons, blizzards, wrecks, and near-misses seemed to search him out. As an example, he wrote to the Rowlands: "On the way back we had engine trouble and the fuel pressure warning light was flickering on and off. So the pilot flew along the Nak Dong River so we could land on a sand bank if necessary. We made Taegu and changed planes for the flight over the Chiri Mountains. The pilot, a Captain Lee, ROK army, told us there was no sweat, that he had been shot down twice in Vietnam and succeeded both times in making a forced landing."

Within five years after the end of the Korean War, Henry had so many pressures on him that he didn't know which way to turn. Rita Kreiss wrote in 1959: "Bishop Henry has vacant sites in many towns but can see no possibility of setting up a parish in these places in spite of the potential Catholics there. He is at his wit's end to keep pace with the converts and to find enough money to build churches. This is all the more pitiful when you stop to ponder a moment exactly what a priest and his church can accomplish in a few years in any given town in Korea."

Take the case of Huk San as an example of the kind of pressure put on the bishop. Huk San meant two things: the name of a windswept, rocky island sixty-five miles out of Mokpo and also the name of a cluster of sixteen islands dotting several thousand square miles of the Yellow Sea, islands that wanted to be united into a parish.

There wasn't a Catholic on the islands until about 1950. Then three Catholics, fleeing the Communists, arrived from Mokpo. Converts themselves, they had friends on Huk San to whom they spoke of the faith. The friends proved interested, catechisms were purchased, and classes began. About the time of the start of the Korean war, Father Thomas Moran visited Huk San, found thirty well-instructed catechumens, and baptized three of them before he left. Later a permanent, paid catechist was assigned to the islands, and successive visiting priests baptized larger and yet larger groups.

Deputations from the islands put such pressure on Bishop Henry that in November of 1957 he sent Father Sean Brazil to Huk San as its first permanent pastor. Father Brazil was no stranger to the archipelago; while visiting the islands he had baptized many of the 472 Catholics and had instructed many of the 1,900 catechumens. In fact, when the pressure was being put on the bishop, Father Brazil asked to be assigned to Huk San because he liked the honest, hard-working fisher folk and felt he could do successful work with them.

Father Brazil was not long on his new assignment when he presented the Bishop with another problem, one he had not had before: He needed a motorboat. "There is little inter-island traffic," he wrote, "and the locals have only sailing and row boats which take eighteen hours on a trip that a motor-powered boat could do in six. As things stand I can visit each of my stations only three or four times a year. I want to visit every one of them each fortnight. And to do that I must have a substantial boat with a reliable engine."

"Where can I get $1,800 for a motor boat?" the bishop said to his secretary on one of those days he was at wit's end. To make matters worse, his old friend, Father Frank Woods, was also putting pressure on him. In Father Woods's parish in Changseng, the postwar years brought an increased flow of converts. The trickle of the old days grew to a stream and suddenly the stream became a torrent. A village of 1,200, where there were no Catholics, begged Father Woods to come to it, or at least send a catechist. A second, larger village sent a deputation making the same request. A third and a fourth followed closely on these two.

Father Woods turned to Bishop Henry for another priest. He was told, as indeed he already knew, that a priest could not be spared. He next asked for help to employ additional catechists and was told that for lack of money he would have to make do with the catechists he had.

He passed on the bad news to the four villages. Maybe later, he said, holding out a hope he really didn't feel. The villagers refused to wait. If Father

Woods couldn't instruct them, they would do it themselves. And so, after buying a few catechisms, the group leader in each village set about teaching his fellow villagers, learning himself as he went along.

In face of such determination, Father Woods took action. He arranged for the instruction of the group leaders; in two villages he contrived also to have catechism classes held. A simple church, built by voluntary labor on a donated site, went up in one village; a second church was under way in another. At this point five additional villages came along with similar requests. Thousands of people were clamoring for instruction. Right now! Immediately!

Sometimes the laymen would put pressure on the bishop face-to-face and sometimes through his priests. For instance, Granny Im, an old Korean woman, never approached the bishop, but she got what she wanted indirectly. She used to walk four miles, leading her family and neighbors, from Hwasun to Father Michael Pak's church in Kwangju city to attend Mass. She kept haunting Father Pak to send a catechist to live in Hwasun where the church was little-known, saying that she had made eleven converts and knew of many other people who would welcome the faith if only someone told them about it.

Father Pak listened, was impressed, and sent a catechist in March of 1956. The catechist, an old lady named Agatha Yu, found the eleven converts and ten other Catholics that had migrated to the area from other parts of Korea. Conversions grew so rapidly and so much pressure was put on Bishop Henry through Father Pak that two years later he sent Father William Gallagher to Hwasun. Five years later the town had 500 Catholics, with 300 more under instruction, and a brick church that would hold 700. The church, donated by Colonel and Mrs. Rowland, is named St. Martin's in memory of Marie Rowland's father.

Every Columban in Korea felt desperation from time to time during that period of rapid growth. How to care for so many with so little! One priest, to provide shelter for his ever-growing flock, sold his shotgun, radio, and watch. He thought twice before selling the shotgun because it helped supplement a meager diet. In his pursuit of food, he and other missionaries had learned to disguise themselves as Korean farmers so that they might get close to birds without attracting attention. They wore white coveralls and moved with the slow rhythmic pace of farmers, until the ducks, geese, or pheasants were properly aligned, and then felled several with a single shot. After selling his shotgun the missionary became a vegetarian.

When he was suffering most acutely from a shortage of priests, Harold Henry received a letter from Bishop Alonso Escalante, the founder and superior general of the Missioners of Guadalupe, the Mexican National Mission

Society. The Mexican bishop said he was coming to Korea to see if it was possible for some of his priests to work in Kwangju. Archbishop Henry reread the letter several times just to make sure it said what it seemed to say. He immediately thought of Sunchon and the great area surrounding it.

He wrote: "When the bishop arrived I was marooned on an island. Bad weather. The priests at the chancery took him over the entire territory. About four hundred miles over dusty roads in two days. That's the equivalent of a thousand miles at home. When he returned at about five in the evening I was back in my house. He disappeared to have a much-needed shower. When he returned to my office he came bearing a bottle of Johnny Walker Black Label. He had picked it up in the duty-free airport at Hong Kong. He said he needed something to wash the dust out of his throat. I said I had salt spray in mine.

"By 9:30 that night we had a contract drawn up to submit to the Holy See. He promised to send seventeen priests to Korea within three years! We toasted the agreement. Next morning I told him he was the easiest catch I ever made!"

When need for more and more churches haunted Bishop Henry, he showed his usual imagination and flair. He found a partial answer to his problem in geodesic domes invented by Buckminster Fuller. A newly patented plywood model seemed to best suit his needs.

In July of 1957 the manufacture of the first geodesic dome designed specifically for a church began. When finished it was shipped to the Columban headquarters, near Omaha, for exhibition.

When Bishop Henry arrived for the inspection he decided that this new style of church would ease the financial strain in Kwangju. Here was a church to hold 400 parishioners at a cost of $2,300, while a conventional church in Korea with the same floor space would cost about $12,000.

The bishop was so pleased with what he saw he immediately ordered another, with a larger dome, at $5,500, one that could seat about 1,200. This was the last of the domes, however, for the shipping costs were too high and the acoustics in the church were poor. They had been worth buying, though, if for no other reason than that they increased Harold Henry's image as a man of ideas, an image worth having when he was raising funds.

Looking back over his years in Korea, Archbishop Henry said that one of the things he was most proud of was the way he organized the lay apostolate. He gives unstinting credit for an abundance of conversions to the lay people who worked as catechists and as members of the Legion of Mary.

"I divided my catechists into two categories, ambulatory and residential," said Archbishop Henry. "An ambulatory catechist is on salary and has a full-time job with the church. He is called 'ambulatory' because he is a contact man who lives with the poeple and tries to interest them in the Church. He spends most of his time conducting classes for catechumens and giving private instruction in the homes of those unable to come to the church.

"The residential catechist receives no salary and works only part-time. He represents the priest in the mission station or does such work around the rectory as keeping parish records up to date, organizing workers for church projects, and distributing relief food and clothing."

The catechists were so effective that the November 1955 issue of *The Far East* quoted Monsignor Henry as saying, "Our problem in Kwangju boils down to two essentials—more catechists and more money to hire more catechists. We are swamped with people demanding instruction in the faith; we need full-time catechists to give them that instruction. Even where new churches and schools are an urgent necessity, I prefer to spend money hiring catechists. We can do without the building if we have to."

In August of 1953 Father Henry, with Father Tom Moran, pastor of Mokpo, organized the Legion of Mary in two parishes in Mokpo. From a dozen or so members, the organization grew until within five years it numbered well over 10,000 and is now in every diocese in Korea, except one. Marie Rowland deserves credit for this. A talk that she gave in Japan about the Legion of Mary convinced Father Henry he needed such an organization in Korea.

To understand the work of the Legion of Mary it is necessary to understand how a catechumen is prepared for baptism. The first section of every Korean catechism includes twelve prayers that a prospective convert must know before his name is placed on the list of catechumens. After that, his course of instruction lasts a minimum of six months. During this time he takes three examinations in the catechism given by a priest. The first section of the Korean catechism deals with doctrine, what a Catholic believes; the second part deals with morals, what a Catholic does; and the final section speaks of grace and the sacraments. All in all, the requirements are exacting.

Since many older Koreans cannot read or write they have difficulty in learning the prayers and studying the catechism. Here the Legion of Mary proves to be especially effective. A member gathers together several of the older people each evening and spends thirty minutes or more reciting aloud the prayers and the answers to the catechism, until by sheer dint of listening the oldsters memorize the necessary minimum.

Successful missionary work involves not merely bringing catechumens to the point where they are ready for baptism, but keeping in close personal touch with them afterwards until they have really found their feet as Catholics. This important function of keeping in touch is also performed by the Legion of Mary. Every new convert is visited once a month for the first six months after being baptized.

The Legion of Mary does other work, too, but these two functions, teaching and visiting, have been emphasized because of their importance. Archbishop Henry asked the members of the organization to specialize in those functions because it is then possible to take care of large numbers of catechumens without a proportionately large number of priests. As the archbishop said, "The Legion of Mary brings nothing but work to a priest, but that's the kind of work a priest is here to do."

CHAPTER
18

Healing the Sick

WITH ALL THE PROBLEMS—rebuilding, instructing catechumens, feeding and clothing thousands—it would seem that Harold Henry would not go out of his way to create new ones, but he did. He decided he needed hospitals and clinics. When his friends looked at him as though he couldn't be serious, he flaunted his "no sweat" attitude, and wrote an appealing letter asking for helping hands. He sent the letter to the motherhouse of the Sisters of St. Columban at Cahiracon, Ennis, County Clare. He explained in the letter that a missionary must help the body as well as the soul.

The letter was appealing enough to receive a favorable reply. Monsignor Henry was so elated that he was in Boston to meet the sisters when they reached the United States on their way to Korea in September of 1954. With them he planned an itinerary to collect drug supplies and hospital equipment which the Catholic Relief Services promised to ship to Korea free of charge.

The four sisters reached Korea on January 17, 1955: Sister Enda, a medical doctor from County Mayo; Sister Mary Martha, a nurse from County Longford; Sister Dorothy, a nurse from St. Paul, Minnesota; and Sister Rosarii, a dietitian from County Mayo.

When the four arrived in Mokpo they were welcomed by Father Tom Kane; Monsignor Henry was still in the States collecting money to build a boys' high school. Father Kane, who had been Harold Henry's cell mate in the Naju jail and was now his vicar general, introduced the sisters to their new home, a tiny Korean hut with mud walls, mud floor, and four rooms each about seven by eight feet. Olive drab army blankets covered four army cots and another blanket hung across the window to impede somewhat the penetrating wind coming in off the sea on a January night. For light they had a candle stuck onto a nail that had been driven through a jagged block of wood.

The next morning the four Columban sisters faced up to the Korean language. Father Sean Savage, at that time a pastor in Mokpo, offered to conduct classes. Between classes the nuns walked down the steep hill to visit the harbor, trying to make some sort of contact with the people. Wherever they went they attracted attention. The Koreans seemed pleased to see "the ladies in white who have long noses and are always smiling."

Soon they realized that they would not be able to give as much time to the language as they had hoped for, for the Koreans were putting on pressure for a new clinic right away. Several things happened to make Sister Enda feel she should not delay. For one, the first shipment of drugs and equipment arrived in March, sooner than expected. A gift ambulance came from the States as a surprise in June. Also in June, Sister David, a medical doctor from County Galway, and Sister Philomena, a nurse from County Cork, reached Mokpo.

Sister Enda decided she would open the doors of a clinic on July 5, the feast of Blessed Andrew Kim, first Korean martyr. In the little mud hut the sisters designated one room for registration, one for examination, one for a pharmacy, and one for treatment. Outside the back door a pressure cooker atop a kerosene stove was used for sterilization. On the first day thirty-seven patients arrived. Each morning thereafter the numbers grew. The Koreans began to line up at the door at four o'clock in the morning. Even though the rain might be beating down and a cold wind coming in off the Yellow Sea, the sick stood there patiently. Some had come as far as seventy miles and some from the hundreds of islands that dot the sea on the southwest coast.

Sister Enda said, "Often they went home to their villages in the hills by bus or train or on foot and told their friends and neighbors about the strange foreign ladies in white who wore crucifixes and talked bad Korean with a strange accent." The more they talked the larger the crowds grew. The sister attended to patients all morning and afternoon, and in the evening she made house calls. Each day it became more evident that with 1,200,000 people in the area, floor space, equipment, and helping hands were needed.

Whenever the situation was especially frustrating something happened to give the sisters new strength. Sister Enda tells anecdotes to illustrate the times the seemingly impossible suddenly became possible. Describing one such occasion, she said, "We started to pray because we needed lumbar puncture needles for a spinal tap in meningitis; Luer-Lock syringes, morphia, plaster of paris for fractures, ethyl chloride for short general anesthesia, catgut to suture wounds, and a host of other things. A few days later we heard that a United States Army camp had sent us some supplies and they were waiting at the railway station. It was a huge crate, and we couldn't believe our eyes when it was opened—the lumbar puncture needles, and the plaster of paris, the catgut, the ethyl chloride, and the other things. Our Guardian Angels—even though they had to don a United States Army uniform—had checked our list and sent us our hearts' desire."

Back in the States, friends and relatives were busy collecting medical samples and bandages to ship through Catholic Relief Services and so avoid customs duty. Friends and relatives in Ireland followed the lead and soon doctors and druggists were sending their samples to 35 Fitzwilliam Square, Dublin, for shipping to Korea.

"We started to build a clinic," said Sister Enda, "but we simply didn't have the money for it. We used to pay the workmen every Friday. About $300. That was an awful lot then. One Friday I had no money. I got to thinking of the families of those men with no money for the weekend. There came a knock at the door. It was a man I had given some junk to—broken beds, bits of machinery, and such, junk from the army in Pusan. He said he had sold it and handed me $300.

"Three weeks later the same problem arose. No money for the Friday payroll. I was ashamed to think that maybe, just maybe, something might come again out of the blue. A knock at the door and the same man. I said he had already paid me for the junk. He explained that only today he had sold all of it. Again he handed me the money for the exact amount I needed."

Unusual things continued to happen. One morning Sister Enda saw an unexpected bus pull up close to the door of the clinic. All the passengers were lame or limping or maimed in some way.

"Some of them were polio victims and were limping with a stick or crutches," as she recalls the sight. "Some of them were cases of TB spine or TB hip, bent in two, with wasted but hopeful faces. Some of them had never walked and never would . . . cases of cerebral palsy . . . hopeless. Still their faces had the look of hope. Somehow they might be cured or helped. They had heard that an American surgeon from Ohio was coming to the clinic to work for the month of October."

Dr. McNamara came and worked a few minor miracles. His field was general surgery, not orthopedics, which is what that busload of patients needed. They needed both physiotherapy and psychotherapy.

"And this is where Susan came in," said Sister Enda. "Susan is a Peace Corps worker from Chicago who had been working as a physiotherapist in an orthopedic hospital run by American Presbyterians in Sunchon, about 130 miles from Mokpo. She gets five days off every month and these she spends with us, taking care of polio and spastic cases."

When Susan saw that the Columban sisters could give only limited help to those patients who had come fifty miles by bus, she asked her boss, Dr. Topple, an American Presbyterian doctor, to lend a hand and this he did magnificently.

He put together a surgical team: himself; Dr. Yoo, a Korean orthopedic surgeon; Dr. Wolbrink from the Presbyterian hospital in Kwangju, a graduate of the Mayo Clinic; two paramedical workers, one to make splints and braces, the other to do the plasters.

In a landrover they drove over the bumpy roads from Sunchon to Kwangju and then to Mokpo. They stayed for three days, examined fifty patients, did extensive reconstructive surgery for twelve, got braces and splints for twelve more, and physiotherapy for all.

"What this team and Susan did for our patients cannot be put in words," said Sister Enda. "They brought health and hope. I will always remember the eleven-year-old boy with polio in both upper and lower limbs. After the operation he stood for the first time in his life. The look on his face!

"The team has come back every month. We owe them more than we can express. We owe thanks to Captain Donald Bishop of the United States Air Force who provided the bus free of charge. He came and stayed till every patient was checked and treated. At Christmas he sent us a check for fifty dollars to buy crutches for those who couldn't afford them. Especially, we thank Susan."

Harold Henry was behind the sisters helping every inch of the way. As Sister Enda recalls, "He would give you everything. He kept nothing for himself. And when he gave you something there were no strings attached. When he gives something he gives it. So I was always careful not to ask for too much.

"I remember the electricity from the city was bad. So we got an Onan generator. Only ten kilowatts. Nobody here could tell the archbishop how to connect the automatic start-stop mechanism, necessary if there was a power failure during surgery. So he kept writing to the firm in Minnesota until he got it installed. If anything went wrong with anything, he was the one to fix it. He was so active. Nothing was work for him. One Christmas we gave him a pair of overalls."

The day the two-story clinic was finished and paid for, it was already too small. The patients kept coming, most on foot but some on the backs of their friends. A common sight was a wife with her husband on her back, arriving after an exhausting journey over the hills in the burning heat. The fatigues and the delays in this form of transportation were among the reasons many of the patients, once they arrived, were too ill to help medically.

As one of the sisters wrote back to Ireland, "It's so easy to be sensible about seeing your doctor in time when a bus or a car is at your service and your doctor is within easy reach. It's not easy when the only doctor you know of is miles away, and the only means you have of getting there is by walking, or getting a 'lift' on somebody's back."

When Harold Henry saw that the new clinic was too cramped, he offered his own big, three-story house to the Columban sisters to turn into operating rooms and wards. Sister Enda felt embarrassed at putting him out of his own home, but he said, "No sweat." He would build a place in Kwangju and move there, and so he did. He assured her the move made sense because Kwangju was more centrally located and his priests could reach him more readily.

What had at one time seemed impossible to the sisters now seemed at least probable. Once they caught the archbishop's no-sweat attitude, things happened fast. Sister Clare, at that time the superior of Mokpo, started writing letters to friends in the United States and Europe explaining the need for a new hospital. The principal contributors were: the League of Austrian Women, $25,000; the diocese of Innsbruck, $85,000; the bishops of Holland, $25,000; the bishops of Germany, through Misereor, $390,000. The hospital was free of debt the day it was blessed, the Feast of Our Lady, March 25, 1968.

To help overcome the shortage of nurses in South Korea—one nurse for every 20,000 people—the sisters turned the clinic into a Junior Nursing College. The nursing school, with an average enrollment of about 120 students, was put under the direction of Sister Frances Therese, a Columban from the Philippines who had earned her master's degree in nursing education in the United States.

Before long the students at St. Columban's Nursing School caught the Columban spirit which Archbishop Henry condensed into the harsh expression, "No sweat!" For example, many of the students gave up a part of their summer vacation to bring medical services to remote villages in the hills of southwest Korea.

With some medical students from Chunnam University the young women organized the expedition to the last detail. Some fifty future doctors and nurses set out for the village of Miari with the Columbans' ambulance and three volunteers, Sisters Mary McHugh and Laurentia, and Father Anthony Mortell, the chaplain.

Sister Mary said, "We hope this project makes some of our future doctors and nurses sensitive to the needs of people almost destitute of medical care. Only twenty percent of Korea's doctors practice in country places where sixty percent of the people live."

The students set up their first field clinic in a shabby primary school. They covered desks with clean white paper; wooden tables served as examination couches; a small kerosene stove, on which a basin of water boiled, was the sterilizer for syringes and minor surgical equipment. In no time a miniature laboratory and a pharmacy were in operation.

Before the field clinic was ready to function the word had spread. All day long they came. Through the rice paddies mothers carried children on their backs and sick adults lurched along in carts. Many had been blind from birth. Many were deformed from TB of the chest, bones, and joints. The children badly crippled by polio were later taken to the Columbans' hospital in Mokpo to be helped by an American specialist in reconstructive surgery.

The volume of work grew heavier. Although the temperature inside the schoolhouse rose to 106 degrees, the students worked efficiently and calmly. Often they had to repeat the same instructions ten times to one person, but they did it with deference and respect.

"Medical students are not as deft at finding the disease as seasoned practitioners," said Sister Mary. "So it often took them a long time to examine a patient. But the patients didn't mind. They liked having their abdomens and livers palpated at length, and the longer the future doctor took to listen to their chests the happier they were."

At about seven o'clock in the evening the crowds began to dwindle. The students had a chance to organize their supplies for the next day. They were also ready to eat.

The next morning the crowds were bigger. By the third day vaccines, medicines, and dressings were running out. The only thing to do was to hurry back to St. Columban's and beg for more supplies, enough for two more days. After that the clinic closed. The admissions records showed that the students had cared for 1,200 patients.

"Sister Laurentia and I were a great curiosity," said Sister Mary. "The village people were shy at first, but once they heard us speak their language, all barriers vanished. The questions came pouring in: What made us leave our homes to work in such a poor place? Did we miss our families and our parents? What medicine did we use to keep our skin so white?

"We tried to explain what our life meant. Why we were concerned about them. We tried to help them in their attitude toward death, those beyond medical aid. Both the patient and his family would listen gratefully. They seemed to grasp the fact of God so easily. One feels the Spirit of God working in their lives."

Harold Henry regretted leaving all that enthusiasm in Mopko, but he was not long in Kwangju before he also had a thriving clinic there. The idea for it did not come from him but from a brother in Ireland. In a way it grew out of his consecration as a bishop in the spring of 1957. After the ceremony, Bishop Henry went to Rome, as is the custom, to pay his respects to Pope Pius XII. From there he flew to Ireland to visit the Columban headquarters and it was there the idea for the clinic was put before him.

"About an hour before I was scheduled to leave for the airport," Archbishop Henry reported later, "the provincial of the Brothers of St. John of God visited me. The brothers have their Irish headquarters in Stillorgan, just outside of Dublin. He practically got down on his knees begging me to permit the brothers to start a clinic in Kwangju. This was a new experience for me; I was the one doing the begging all my life. Anyway, it was a nice experience and I didn't play hard to get. I agreed with his plan, agreed heartily. But secretly I was worried. What in the world would we use for a clinic?

"I was hardly back in Kwangju when I knew the answer. It came to me during my installation as bishop. The installation was most unusual. The ceremony is usually held in a cathedral, but ours would hold only 400 people. At least 3,000 wanted to attend.

"While I had been away, Father Eugene Ryan, who handled finance and building for me in Kwangju, bought a piece of property with an abandoned textile factory on it. So we held the installation ceremony in the abandoned factory. Straw bags were strewn on the floor for the people to sit on. Right in the middle of the ceremony my heart gave a leap. The factory could be turned into a clinic!"

The five Brothers of St. John of God fell in love with the building when they came to Korea in December of 1958. With the help of a Korean contractor, Patrick Kim, and several German engineers who were building a fertilizer plant for the Korean government, they converted the old textile factory into a modern twenty-two-room clinic. Of course, the clinic was not long in operation when it became evident that the floor space would need to be doubled.

Besides working in the clinic, the brothers visited the sick in the area. They served the 500 inmates at the Kwangju Beggars' Camp. It took a special kind of courage to face the degradation inside that camp. The inmates were literally dumped into the compound; some were brought on the garbage trucks in the morning—the insane, the tubercular, street urchins, the mentally retarded, indigents, and the maimed.

The brothers also visited a leper colony at Naju, twenty miles away. The ordinary cases were treated at the colony but the more serious ones were brought to the clinic. The Korean government supplied medicine for leprosy treatment, but the brothers supplied medicine for all other sicknesses.

They also visited what was popularly known as "The Shoe Shine Home." Officially it was called the Kwangju Boys' Center for Vocational Guidance. The home was started in 1953 by the Kwangju police to get orphans off the streets and to teach them to be useful members of society. The 350 boys helped support the home by shining shoes throughout the city. Their main work, though, was to study academic and vocational subjects under the guidance of volunteer teachers.

To help the brothers get off to a good start, three volunteer doctors came from abroad: Dr. James Carr of Dublin; Dr. James Walsh of Waterbury, Connecticut; and Dr. James Kavanaugh of Montreal. They soon found that their practices in Korea were unlike those back home in that now they were treating more tubercular patients than anything else.

Diseases of the pulmonary tract were common; the Korean way of life encouraged such. First of all, it was usual for a Korean to grow up in a family with nine or ten in one room—a nest for infectious disease. This early conditioning seemed to give the Korean a preference for crowded places. A missionary said, "Watch a Korean board a bus. He will pause and look all around and if he doesn't see someone he knows, his face will fall. He likes to be near somebody."

The dust of summer also damaged the breathing apparatus. Many people living in houses along the road threw water on the dust, but that helped little for the water immediately evaporated in the burning sun. A high incidence of sinus infection was the result.

A poor diet brought many patients to the clinic. One of the western doctors was appalled his first day there to meet a woman and her five children who had been living on boiled grass. Stomach disorders, of course, were common. Food, greasy or raw, encouraged intestinal parasites. Ulcers were usual and stomach cancer was widespread.

The volunteer doctors from Ireland, Canada, and the United States soon learned that Koreans love needles, a carry-over from Chinese acupuncture. So they began giving a shot of vitamins along with a packet of pills just to make sure the patient felt he was properly cared for. Sometimes this needlework was not sufficient to please the patient. For instance, when Kim Munog lay seriously ill in the hospital, he was getting the best that modern Western medicine could offer, but it wasn't helping much. In advanced stages of emphysema, his breathing was so labored that everybody knew his days were numbered. Suddenly the nurses heard screams coming from his room. They rushed in to find an acupuncturist twirling needles in the chest of the critically ill man. Kim Munog's family, deciding that Western medicine was getting nowhere, had smuggled in the practitioner. It would be nice to give a happy ending to the story and say that the acupuncturist cured Kim Munog, but he didn't.

The St. Isidore Clinic in Hallim, on Cheju Island, was started when Father P. J. McGlinchey's tractor driver was injured. As Father McGlinchey said at the time, "First you get yourself a tractor and then you need yourself a clinic." Now two Columban sisters with a staff of twenty care for nearly a hundred patients a day. Their biggest problem is what to do about surgical needs. A small fund established by a priest's bequest makes it possible for them to send needy cases to the mainland for operations.

Out of the blue the archbishop got an excellent small clinic he hadn't planned on. He said: "The Providence of God continued. I received a letter from the St. Charles Borromeo sisters in Germany asking whether there was a possibility of starting a clinic. I said I have over nine thousand square miles to cover and would be very happy if they would start one at Sunchon where we had no medical or education projects. The sisters built a beautiful clinic and carried a burden out of all proportion to their small staff. In 1974 they donated the clinic to the Caritas sisters of Kwangju."

When Harold Henry arrived in Korea in 1933 he was not aware of the country's 30,000 lepers. Certainly he did not think of them as parishioners, even though as a boy he read with interest everything written about leper colonies in the Columbans' magazine, *The Far East*. In time, though, he began to see the lepers as the most needy of the needy. They haunted him to such an extent that his secretary wrote, "If the bishop shows any partiality whatever to his flock, I believe it is to them."

Eventually he established a colony that the lepers named Hyun Ae Won in his honor, Hyun being Henry in Korean. There he provided housing and livestock for some four hundred families, mainly burnt-out cases that were forced out of the leprosarium. A burnt-out case is a leper who is cured only after the disease has eaten away everything that can be eaten away. Since few people have the magnanimity to treat the loathsome as brothers, such cases are not accepted in society because they are too disfigured.

The archbishop also provided financial aid for three other leper colonies, Changsong; Ho Ae Wond, also known as Sin-Do-Ri; and Youn Am. While such aid was hard to come by, even harder to find were helping hands. When the Korean government asked that he assign nuns to the work, he found that he could spare a few Caritas sisters and that was all. Yet the need kept haunting him.

One day while visiting in Pusan, he met Bishop Wechner, of Innsbruck, Austria. Bishop Henry spoke with such feeling of his need for helping hands that the Austrian bishop asked to visit Sorokdo, a leper colony 400 miles away. Appalled by what he saw there, he returned to Austria to send three nurses, Marianne Stöger, Margaret Pissarek, and Maria Dittrich, to Korea to establish a nursery for nonleper children of leprous parents.

The nurses began work at the largest leper colony in the world, located on Sorokdo, a beautifully wooded island in the Yellow Sea, a half mile off the coast of southern Korea. Many of the 5,500 lepers live in their own small homes grouped in seven villages where they garden and raise pigs and chickens. Only the acutely ill and the helpless are cared for in the hospital.

Catholicism was established on the island through the efforts of one leper who undertook the task of catechist in his own village. Six others, each in his village, did the same under the supervision of the first man. Soon Father Henry, as pro-prefect apostolic, sent a missionary to open a mission station. When the number of Catholics on the island grew beyond a thousand he built a rectory and a church on Sorokdo and sent a pastor there.

In describing the first Mass that she attended in that church, Sister Jeremy wrote: "A man, swinging both arms for balance, briskly slid forward on some padding tied to his knees. Another middle-aged man felt his way along the wall to the front, apparently counting each window until he knew where to crouch in his place. From behind came a sound that was odd for an August morning—the distinct, rhythmic crunch of footsteps on snow. It was produced by the wad of bandages added to the stub of an old lady's foot."

Although in recent years a cure has been found for the physical disease— weekly use of D.D.S. tablets—leprosy still remains a psychological problem. R. V. Wardekar describes the problem in a pamphlet about leprosy: "Within limits of normality, every individual loves himself. In cases where he has a deformity or abnormality or develops it later, his own aesthetic sense revolts and he develops a sort of disgust towards himself. Though with time he becomes reconciled to his deformities, it is only at the conscious level. His subconscious mind, which continues to bear the mark of the injury, brings about certain changes in his whole personality, making him suspicious of society."

The psychological problem is evident in a few words that a Columban wrote from a leper colony in Korea: "The lepers are sensitive, and quick to notice that a priest does not shrink from them. When they are being baptized or confirmed, all watch the minister of the sacrament closely to see if he will touch them, and their hearts are won when he does." A missionary has no place in a leprosarium unless he is able to overcome his repugnance to the point where he can advance without shuddering. Knowing this, Archbishop Henry never assigned a missionary to a leper colony without more than usual deliberation.

The archbishop, a born raconteur, could go on for hours telling anecdotes about the leper colonies, hospitals, and clinics. Such stories abound in the newsletter he used to publish in Kwangju and in the letters he writes to friends.

In the newsletter of March 1964 he told of Sophia Kim, a girl on Cheju Island: "I went to Hallim for Confirmation and after the ceremony I was having a cup of coffee in the rectory when the catechist came in saying Sophia Kim was in church crying her eyes out. She had arrived too late for Confirmation. I told him to have her at the altar rail and I would come right over and confirm her. I found her near the railing sitting on the floor. I didn't know until then that she was badly crippled. She apologized for being late; her parents had to carry her down the mountain and it was a slow process. It so happened that some Columban sisters from the hospital in Mokpo were visiting in Hallim. I asked if they could help Sophia. They said they would take her back to the mainland with them to see what could be done. In time, I received a letter from Sophia. She says she is back on Cheju and is now walking to church. Sometimes it pays to be late!"

In spite of everything described so far, and of all that will be described in the following pages, Archbishop Henry did not consider himself a builder. He seemed to think of a builder as someone who raises great cathedrals—something he was against in mission territory. His feeling about his building program was reflected in a wry remark: "When I come before the seat of judgment, if God doesn't ask me what I have built, I won't bring up the subject."

The devil, according to the archbishop, has three ways of tempting a priest. "First by drink. If that fails, he tries women. Failing that, he tempts the priest to build something, a monument to himself. This completed, the priest says, *'Hic dormiam et requiescam'* (here I will sleep and take my rest) and so he does nothing else for the rest of his life."

CHAPTER

19

Concern for the Mind

HAROLD HENRY wasn't satisfied with caring for the body with hospitals and for the soul with churches, he wanted to do something for the mind, too, and that meant schools. He had a warm spot in his heart for schools ever since those discouraging days in Naju when the success of his parish school kept him from quitting Korea to seek an appointment as a curate back home in Minnesota. His affection for his Naju pupils shows in a letter he wrote at the time:

"The bell has rung, and all the youngsters line up in front of my school for morning drill and exercise, which takes about ten minutes. The few lazy ones who come late have to stand in front of the others and do their exercises, and then be reprimanded by the teacher.

"To the lively air of my gramophone they march to the classrooms like veterans, not forgetting to leave off their shoes before entering the room. My classrooms are only twenty-four feet square, but we squeeze between seventy-five and ninety pupils into each. The desks are simple affairs—just two planks, one to serve as a seat and the other as a support for reading and writing.

"In studying their lessons our Korean children shout them at the top of their voices. Ki Sou, who is sitting in the front seat, in not very clever, and he shouts to Soon Ki, who sits in the back of the classroom, asking how the problem should be done. Soon Ki shouts back the required information, and the teacher looks on, quite proud of both boys who manifest such an interest in their studies."

An interest in studies is traditional among Koreans as among all orientals. To go to school a poor Korean will often expend an admirable amount of initiative and energy. This always pleased the archbishop because nothing impressed him more than someone working hard to improve his own lot.

Peter Yung, a thirteen-year-old farm boy, was the kind of student Harold Henry always went out of his way to help. When Peter finished primary school his world collapsed, for his father, like many Korean farmers, could not afford to pay the tuition for middle school. So Peter dropped out.

He dropped out of society, too. Since he could not wear the national school uniform, he was forever labeled as too poor or too stupid to continue his education. He ached for the uniform that identifies all middle- and high-school students, a uniform worn in public even during holidays. For girls it is dark blue or black, with a white collar; for boys it is black with a peaked cap. On the breast pocket is sewn a name tag; on one side of the collar is pinned the name of the school and on the other the class year.

Somehow or other Peter heard of Father Patrick Brandon's night school for poor children, one of several the Columbans operated in Korea, and so he walked from the farm to Kwangju with only enough money to buy a shoeshine kit. With the kit he worked the streets from dawn to dark every day so that he might go to school for half the night.

Although twice as many seek admission as can be accepted at the Sacred Heart Vocational School, Father Brandon somehow found room for Peter. The shoeshine boy joined 300 others who spent four hours a night studying the usual middle-school courses and some vocational subjects, all taught by teachers who volunteer help. It was these volunteers who proposed to Archbishop Henry that he start the school in an old wooden house he owned. When the student body outgrew the house, he built six classrooms in Father Brandon's parish and named Father Brandon principal.

The Korean's desire for an education was the first thing to impress Sister Pauline Nagle, a Columban medical doctor from Ireland. While practicing in Mokpo she observed, "It is difficult to get a child with a fever of 102° to stay in bed. He doesn't want to miss school. The young Korean has his heart set on the professions; he doesn't want to do manual labor. Unfortunately, the Koreans are so intent about education that the suicide rate is high among young people during exam periods."

The pressure that Koreans put on missionaries for more and more schools was described by Father Thomas Neligan some years ago when he wrote: "The teachers met me with expressions of despair on their faces. 'Father,' they said, 'we cannot possibly accommodate them all. We think an entrance examination would eliminate the weaker intellects.' I readily consented, and gave the full powers to examine, with the proviso that we should confine our-selves to a hundred children.

"The teachers returned to me after some hours with the information that they had already passed the hundred mark, but that the parents of the unsuc-cessful candidates refused to be turned down and were waiting to plead the cause of their children before me in person. Even as they were speaking a procession of mothers arrived accompanied by weeping children, and I was stormed with requests to take just one more. But I was compelled to be firm, as we already outnumbered our quota. Some of the parents remained till eve-ning and even offered to buy desks for their children, while others returned next morning to repeat their requests. This persistence had one effect: it con-vinced us of the necessity of a larger building for the following year."

Archbishop Henry noticed that whenever the pressure became severe enough something happened so that all of a sudden his wish would be granted. For example, he received $150,000 from American GIs to start the Kapaun Boys' Middle and High School. It came like manna from heaven when the soldiers collected the money to build something in Korea as a me-morial to Father Kapaun, a chaplain who had been a hero in World War II and had died in the Korean War. The Salesian fathers administered the school.

On another occasion the archbishop stopped at Greensburg, Pennsylvania, to ask the Sisters of Charity of Mother Seton to start a girls' high school in Korea. It was a wild gamble and he knew it. "I played a little poker in my life, but when I talked to Mother General and her council I didn't get the slightest reaction. I left the meeting feeling that I had failed in convincing them. But at breakfast the next morning the sister who served me was all smiles. She said that Mother General Claudia had announced to the commu-nity that morning at meditation that they were starting a mission in Kwangju. Ninety sisters volunteered, four were chosen as the first group to come to Korea."

The Seton sisters thought they would start their girls' school in Mokpo and went there to study language, but something unforeseen happened to change their plans. The change of direction began one day when Father David Richers, the pastor of Kang Jin, came to Kwangju full of excitement. He said that a group of Koreans in his town had started a girls' school but could nei-ther finance the expansion nor afford the operating expense. They were willing to sell it to the Catholic Church "for the price of a bit of tobacco," the Korean equivalent of "for a song."

"When asked the price of the 'tobacco,' " said the Archbishop, "we were told it was $20,000. I said we couldn't afford that and would have to pass up the offer even though it was a bargain. I was approached again and this time the price of the 'tobacco' was so reduced that I put on a small celebration in honor of the donors, because it really was a donation.

"Who would take charge of the school? Sister Mary Agnes Carey, the superior of the Setons, offered the services of the sisters. They could run the school until I found someone; she said it would be a good experience for them when they started their school in Mokpo.

"They rented a mud hut with a thatched roof in Kang Jin. One room—kitchen, dining room, and recreation room—was nine by twelve. The two bedrooms were nine by nine. I enlarged the school so that they could live in a few classrooms. More and more students came and the sisters were evicted. So I built them a convent.

"The sisters fell in love with Kang Jin and the students and people of Kang Jin fell in love with them. Their 'temporary' tenure became permanent. They are running one of the finest girls' schools in the province. We eventually built a new school and demolished the old buildings; they were in danger of falling down."

Out of the blue the archbishop got another helping hand just when he needed it most—this time it was teachers he hadn't planned on. It started when a Salesian priest came to him saying that in Japan there was a community of Caritas sisters in which there were seven Korean nuns. Largely because of them the Caritas sisters wanted to start a foundation in Korea.

"At that time I had a one-track mind," said Archbishop Henry. "When I had to find a place for them to live I thought of the abandoned factory that had worked so well when the brothers came from Ireland. Just down the road from my headquarters was another abandoned factory and so I bought it. You would be surprised at what a beautiful chapel the boiler building made. The nuns fixed up the place as only nuns can, with a little paint and tons of floor wax made from old candles. As they began to receive postulants I built them a new convent and novitiate."

Within fifteen years the original seven grew to a community of one hundred professed nuns in Korea. Their primary work was teaching in high schools and in parishes. They also operated a small hospital and clinic. At first they helped only in Kwangju, but soon they were working in four dioceses.

Of all the schools that Archbishop Henry helped start none put more demands on his time and energy and nervous system than the seminary. The pressure to start it came neither from the Koreans nor from his own priests, but from Rome.

Within three days after Monsignor Egano Righi-Lambertini had arrived in

Korea as the new apostolic delegate, he came to Kwangju to visit Harold Henry. He came determined to sell the idea that a major seminary should be built in Kwangju. The reasons he gave were those that Harold Henry knew all too well: The only major seminary in Korea, in Seoul, was equipped to handle at most 200 students; however, it accepted 300 and turned away fifty or sixty each year.

"Where was the money to come from? That was all I wanted to know," said the archbishop. "He said that since I was an American I could go to the United States and pick the golden apples off the trees. For a year I kept telling him this was an impossible undertaking for one man.

"Then one night when I was in Seoul he invited me to the apostolic delegation for dinner. Well, with Chianti and a good spaghetti dinner I began to think how wonderful it was that the Holy Father had papal representatives around the world to give the likes of me such a pleasant evening.

"Then he must have slipped me a Micky Finn! He said, 'Now, about this seminary; you will do it for the Holy Father, won't you?' And before I knew what I was saying I said I would try.

"He asked me to write a letter to Cardinal Agagianian, the prefect of the Congregation for the Evangelization of Nations, saying that I would *try*. He wanted the letter the next morning!

"Well, within two weeks we had a letter from the Cardinal saying I was a wonderful bishop. He said that a major seminary was 'the most urgent need of the Church in Korea today.' "

Armed with that letter, Harold Henry set out for the United States to pick the golden apples from the trees. The project turned into a nightmare, as will be related later.

When the money was raised and the day for beginning construction arrived, something unusual happened. Just as workmen were about to start digging, an agitated Korean rushed up and yelled, "Stop!" He said that as a veteran of the Korean War he knew that a hundred mortar shells were buried at the spot they were about to dig. He offered to dig for the shells himself, if he could keep the scrap iron to sell.

Army and police officials were called in. After long disputation, they agreed that a civilian should not be allowed to own mortar shells. They directed the workmen to dig "under official guidance."

They removed some seven hundred shells.

When the seminary was dedicated, in March of 1962, it was given the name of Daegun-Brennan Memorial Theological College: Daegun, in memory of Father Daegun Kim, the first martyred Korean priest, and Brennan, in memory of Monsignor Patrick Brennan, one of the most recent of Columban martyrs. With 291 students and 16 faculty members, the seminary is crowded. It would be even more so except that at any given time about seventy seminarians are away doing their three years of required military service.

Father Hugh O'Rourke, the superior at the Columban headquarters in Omaha, said that what he most admired about Harold Henry was his ability to change. This sensitivity to change helped the archbishop see the possibilities of education continuing on and on beyond the classroom. He saw the possibilities in such things as exhibits, radio and television broadcasts, and retreat centers.

As for exhibits, it was Archbishop Henry who urged Father Thomas Moran to design a booth for the Provincial Industrial Exhibition in Kwangju. This took a little doing because nothing like it had been done before, and so the organizers of the exhibition weren't sure if they should give space to such a display.

When permission was finally granted, the opening date was only two weeks away. Father Moran and his staff of young Koreans worked around the clock to develop as their visual theme the seven sacraments reflected in everyday life.

A tape recorder played Gregorian chant sung by the monks of the famed Solesmes Abbey. Leaflets explained to visitors why the Catholic Church found it fitting to have a booth at an industrial exhibition. Two Caritas sisters and a half dozen laymen worked as guides at the booth from 9 A.M. to 9 P.M. each day for a month.

"The guides operated on certain well-defined lines," said Father Moran. "Each visitor to the booth was to be treated with respect and humility. There was to be no taking advantage of his presence in order to impose explanations or doctrine. Visitors were left free to look and pass on. If any individual had a query or comment to make, he was listened to with friendliness. Our guides were warned against speaking too much; better to leave questions with a margin of curiosity than to try to explain or instruct completely. Aggressiveness or argument of any kind was to be avoided."

For a long time the need for a retreat center haunted Harold Henry. He felt that if converts were to mature in their spiritual lives they needed to grow beyond the memorized catechism. A place for spiritual retreat was especially needed now that the Church attracted more sophisticated Koreans. And yet he couldn't ask any of his own priests to establish and operate such a center; they were already working to the edge of exhaustion.

In 1962 he suddenly saw a way of getting his dream to come true. In that year Father William Westhoven, C.P., came out from the States to conduct a spiritual retreat for Columban priests at the Columban House in Seoul. It so happened that when Father Westhoven saw Korea it was a case of love at first sight. As soon as Harold Henry observed this romance he knew he had an ally.

The archbishop wrote to Father Westhoven's provincial explaining the need for a retreat center in Kwangju, one established and staffed by the provincial's own order. He said that when the Korean War ended in 1953 there were 180,000 Catholics below the 38th parallel and that by 1960 this number had grown to 800,000. He explained that it is easier to make a convert than to help a new Catholic to grow in religious sensitivity while maturing in the life of the spirit.

The archbishop and Father Westhoven were so persuasive that the provincial agreed to their requests, and so the retreat center was dedicated on August 14, 1966.

Architecturally it is a striking building that blends the modern West with the ancient East. Amid oriental landscaping it perches atop a cliff, like an eagle's nest, and is approached by a steep, tortuous road, symbolic of the journey a soul takes if it is to get where it ought to go.

Since the average Asian in 1976 is 17, the retreat center has a special concern for youth. The aim is to help the young see the danger of letting religion become a dreary habit instead of an exciting creative experience. All in all, it stresses quality rather than quantity, a shift of emphasis from the pioneering days in Korea when the statistics of "how many" were much quoted.

The archbishop's next educational project was to be a new girls' high school in Cheju City. Not long before his death he built a girls' middle school at the edge of the city.

All who knew him well felt that somehow he would get the school built. As Marie Rowland said, "The Archbishop is the kind of man who if you give him a penny will make plans that cost a dollar. And if he gets a dollar he makes plans that cost a hundred dollars. He believes that whatever he gets and plants, with prayer and good intentions, large things will grow from it. It has certainly worked that way."

CHAPTER
20

Something for the Body

A T THE END of the Korean war Monsignor Henry realized more fully than ever the wisdom of an admonition attributed to St. Teresa of Avila: "If a hungry man asks you to teach him how to pray, you had better feed him first." That was something he had probably heard during one of those spiritual conferences in the old mansion on the River Shannon in County Clare, for it was the kind of admonition that Father Harris would be apt to repeat.

By now Harold Henry was also beginning to realize that Father Harris had an advantage over most spiritual directors because his sermons were directed toward young men destined to be missionaries in the Far East. A missionary is apt to learn more readily than a young curate in the United States, or even one in Ireland, about the interaction between body and soul.

Like other Americans, Monsignor Henry had grown up aware of inlets of poverty, but not of vast oceans of it. He knew it was possible to go year after year in the States without coming upon somebody truly destitute; he soon learned that, excepting Japan, no one can visit the Orient for so much as a morning without seeing and smelling and hearing the multitudes who are poorer than the poorest in the States.

Poverty is so dramatic in the Orient that a perceptive young missionary might begin to sense, even before unpacking his suitcase, that the material and the spiritual are not readily separated. As one spiritual writer said, "Bread for myself is a material question; bread for my neighbor is a spiritual question."

In trying to help the seminarians see how the soul is reached through the body, Father Harris had read to them a letter written by Bishop Galvin during those days of great floods and bandit harrassment in China:

"The idea of the Church as something kindly and helpful and charitable has been firmly established in the minds of the people. In any pagan country where the masses have no clear conception of God and only vague, uninspiring ideas of the next life, they must first be attracted by something that they can see and feel. It is through some medium helpful to their bodies that one must reach their souls. If you speak to a pagan about serving God and attaining eternal salvation, you leave him quite cold. He does not understand you. But he does understand charity and sympathy and friendship."

Monsignor Henry learned that while he ought not to care about the spirit alone, it is just as true that he dare not care about the body alone. He observed that anyone who comes bringing bread alone won't be loved for it, for this matter of helping people is touchy business. The starving body and the starving soul need to be worried about simultaneously. Anyone who acts as though only one hunger is worthy of concern will, in time, be resented, even hated.

It had been Monsignor Henry's observation that a missionary senses sooner than a bureaucrat this need for a delicate balance—the right amount for the body and the right amount for the soul. Perhaps it is because a missionary works person-to-person instead of organization-to-organization that he soon sees he must help people organize their outward lives if he wants to help them organize their inward lives, and vice versa. Circumstances forced him to admit that the outward and the inward are inseparable, of a piece, each influencing the other.

The theory that the best way to help the poor is to teach them to help themselves is threadbare from too much quoting. Monsignor Henry found through the years that the theory was more quoted than acted upon because to put it into practice takes effort, patience, and, above all, imagination. Although Harold Henry was sometimes short on patience he had an abundance of willingness to make the effort and an imagination that soared. Fortunately, he was blessed with some lively young priests who had the zest and inspiration to help keep the outer and inner man all of a piece. That is exactly what he needed at the end of the Korean war when he carried the administrative burden inherited from Monsignor Brennan. And what a burden it was! So much to be administered and so little to do it with.

Each year the poor of Korea endure a period called "spring suffering." The kimchi pots outside the mud huts are empty, the rice has been eaten, and now they search the hills for herbs and grasses, for anything edible, until the crops come again. At the end of the Korean war "the spring suffering" ex-

The parishioners closest to Harold Henry's heart were the lepers.

tended to all seasons. People on the run don't plant and harvest. If something was planted it was often harvested by Communist guerrillas who lived off the land. On top of all of this, a drought caused one bad growing season. Famine became a way of life.

Harold Henry got through those dreary days thanks to the Catholic Relief Services of the National Catholic Welfare Conference (now the United States Catholic Conference). The relief agency, with headquarters in New York, sent him tons of grain, flour, cotton seed oil, and cheese supplied by the United States Government; and wearing apparel collected by the United States Bishops' Annual Clothing Drive. All items were distributed on the basis of need, not creed.

Some Korean Catholics revealed they were less than charitable by showing resentment when their pagan neighbors came to the parish church to receive food and clothing. The missionaries found themselves in hot water by insisting that the distribution be by need not creed, and sometimes the water got so hot the pastors wished they had never had the burden of distribution thrust upon them.

Next the Korean government began to complain about the manner of distribution. It expressed its gratitude to the Americans who were feeding and clothing the needy, but said that this should not be done as hand-outs. The official attitude was: you are making beggars of our people; have them do some work for the food and clothing.

This attitude coincided with Monsignor Henry's. He realized it was easier to hand out supplies and forget it than to use the imagination and effort to start projects, but that in the long run the self-help system was worth the effort.

He used relief flour and cornmeal to pay laborers to build a road and two reservoirs in Noan and to shore up the banks of a river in Kwangju where erosion threatened to topple eight houses into the stream.

"In any project I always try to make the Koreans self-supporting. Even the lepers." In the leper colony Hyun Ae Won, the 425 negative cases who would not be accepted in society live on self-sufficient farms. They sell pigs, chickens, eggs, vegetables, and cereals. At another leper colony Monsignor Henry used money sent by the Friends of the Lepers in Sacramento, California, to buy chestnut trees. The harvest of chestnuts helps supplement the lepers' income.

He bought land and built a chapel at Sin-Do-Ri, a leper village near Kwangju. Most of the 500 lepers there were arrested cases, and no possible danger to anyone, but if one of them was caught sneaking into town, he'd be stoned and driven out. Later Father Anthony O'Leary came along seeking ways to help the lepers help themselves. He began by encouraging them to start a cooperative and he financed their first enterprise, a tiny co-op store.

Next he started a pig-raising project to supplement family incomes. The pigs could be purchased through interest-free loans from the co-op. Since the loans were repayable, they helped strengthen the spirit of self-help. Soon 108 out of 140 families in the village were participating.

The lepers also have other plans. Two ponds will supply them with fish; a chicken hatchery will give each family a flock, and an animal bank will supply cattle and rabbits to any farmer looking for breeding stock.

At the end of the Korean war, in 1953, Huk San Island, sixty miles off the southwest coast of Korea, was in an especially desperate state. To escape starvation the islanders were scraping bark off the trees and boiling it for soup.

Monsignor Henry sent food and clothing and some young priests to help the people become self-sufficient. This was an especially difficult assignment because there was nothing to work with. There wasn't a wheeled vehicle on the island, not even a cart or a bicycle. Not even a road. The only transportation the islanders had were a few boats. (When the islanders saw automobiles in Mokpo they spoke of them as "boats on wheels.")

Using help from the relief program, a road was built. Then with United States Army surplus supplies and $20,000 collected by the Columban Fathers, a generator was set up and the island wired for electricity.

Monsignor Henry made sure a junior high school was started on Huk San and within a decade it had 400 students. To help make the school self-supporting, he gave it the profits from a credit union which he helped get started by putting in $3,000 and asking the island people to add as much as they could afford.

With all of this Huk San was still so far behind that in 1967 a government survey declared it the most economically depressed region in Korea. About that time a young Columban, Father John Russell, from County Meath, took a good hard look at the situation and let his imagination take wing.

This is how he saw it: Huk San is an archipelago of eleven islands sitting in the Yellow Sea, comparatively rich in fish—mackerel, shark, abalone, oysters. The land is anything but rich. Volcanic in origin, it can yield, at best, about one-third of the food that the population needs. So forget dreaming up new projects for the land; start projects for the sea.

The Yellow Sea, though, is so fierce it has defied the islanders through the centuries. It has one of the highest and fastest tides in the world, and contrary winds against a high fast tide cause heavy seas. This, in addition to typhoons and dense fogs, makes fishing a hazard. A former missionary on

Huk San, Father John Quinn, said, "A fisherman told me that every time he went out he vomited. It wasn't seasickness. He was sick with fear. Imagine living that way year after year."

Father Russell, in turning his thoughts to the sea, was all too aware of its viciousness. He said, "Many a fisherman's dream has been dashed on the rocks, and many children were left without fathers in this Yellow Sea. Two years ago fifty-three men died in one storm; last year two boats were lost with just a sole survivor. Every year takes its toll. A sea that should be a harvest field is a merciless killer."

The trouble, he decided, lies not so much with the sea as with the structure of Huk San's boats. "They are small, poorly powered and flat bottomed," he said. "In other words, the few boats there are, are built for a fine day. To build for a storm, more design, more keel, and more power are needed."

As a beginning, a shipyard was built. Archbishop Henry approved the project; the Society of St. Columban raised the money.

In making a survey of the situation, Father Russell had learned that in the nineteen villages there were a total of twenty-five boats. Five of these were over ten tons and the rest around five tons. Most were old and spent much of the year in dry dock being repaired.

During its first year of operation the shipyard built twenty-four fishing boats. Only two stayed at Huk San, the rest were sold in mainland ports because the islanders could not afford them.

"To build boats as we know them," said Father Russell, "tons of expensive cedar wood are required. This is an import item in Korea, bought with dollars. During 1971 alone the price of cedar increased by twenty-five percent. The poor man's chances are getting grimmer. He must catch fish to make money; to catch fish he needs a boat; to build a boat he needs money. The Huk San fisherman is in 'the-dog-following-his-tail' economic circle.

"With this problem in mind, I went to Seoul in April of 1971 to see a good friend in Catholic Relief Services, Bob Fleischman. He happened to know a boat 'fanatic' in the United States Eighth Army by the name of Colonel Robert J. Kriwanek. I went to hear what he had to say and a new hope appeared on the horizon.

"At the time he was talking in unbelievable terms. 'Build boats of concrete,' he said. 'It is an old idea that is just being perfected these days.' After giving me all the literature he had on the subject he sent me back to my island to study. To make a long story short, I was converted. I saw the possibility of Huk San fishermen owning well-designed, strong, and economically maintainable fishing boats at a third of the cost of comparable timber hulls."

Most people, especially Huk San fishermen, gave a sceptical laugh at the mention of ferro-cement boats. In the middle of all the skeptical laughter, Father Russell's home parish in Nobber, County Meath, gave him $1,500; the Australian Catholic Relief gave him a sizeable grant, as did Columban benefactors in the United States; and the Huk San shipyard started building a seventy-foot motor vessel out of concrete. The design and specifications, down to the last detail, were supplied by Cyril Chisholm, naval architect to the Irish Sea Fisheries Board.

Nothing in the history of the Huk San archipelago caused so much excitement as the boat's maiden voyage. There it was—floating! A ferro-concrete boat that will not rust, scale, or deteriorate in salt water. A boat that is fireproof and one that rot or worms will not touch. Here was a cheaper, safer, and lighter boat than the fisherman of Huk San ever dreamed of owning.

The Huk San Credit Union used the experimental boat to introduce the Danish seine-fishing method which had proved successful in the West. Backward Huk San started to revolutionize fishing all around the Korean Peninsula.

CHAPTER

2 1

Do-It-Yourself Catholics

THE MOST DRAMATIC STORY that Archbishop Henry told of helping people help themselves had as its setting Cheju Island, 90 miles off the southern coast of Korea. The principal character was Patrick J. McGlinchey, a tall, red-headed priest from County Donegal. When he and three other newly ordained priests landed at Pusan on April 14, 1953, they were the first Columbans to arrive in Korea since the start of the war, nearly three years earlier. They felt more nervous than most new missionaries because as their plane sped down the airstrip it moved between rows of black, snub-nosed B-17 bombers and airmen were loading bombs into the bomb racks.

In Mokpo, Father McGlinchey struggled with the language for several months and served as an assistant in Sunchon for a short time. Although the young priest had been in Korea for scarcely a year, Monsignor Henry decided to send him to Cheju Island to start a new parish at Hallim.

If ever a people needed to be given the courage to stand on their own feet again it was the Cheju islanders. Even before the start of the Korean war, Communist guerrillas terrorized the islanders. Some 60,000 islanders and guerrillas were killed in the fighting.

When he reached Hallim, in time for Palm Sunday of 1954—exactly one year after arriving in Korea—Father McGlinchey was appalled by the burned-out villages, the barren land, and the dehumanizing poverty. He said, "I know a starving man isn't inclined to get down on his knees except to hunt for something to eat. My own roots are in the soil, so I said, 'Why not put kneeling to work in two ways—planting and praying?' "

From Cheju City to Hallim, Father McGlinchey rode by jeep over a nearly nonexistent road. He found his "parish church," a small Korean shack, ten-by-twenty-five feet. Behind it were two small rooms each measuring six-by-eight feet. They were occupied by the catechist, Maria Kim, and her husband, Marcello. The two Koreans and the priest went out to inspect a nearby piece of land that Monsignor Henry had bought on his last confirmation tour. A crop of barley was growing on it; the Catholics—only twenty-five of them in the parish—had decided to put the land to good use while waiting for the church to be built.

Father McGlinchey stood there wondering how many barley crops would come and go before he could afford to build a church. He had a check in his pocket for $1,000, the most Monsignor Henry could afford to give him.

What happened next is best told in Father McGlinchey's own words:

"At that time the war in Indo-China was in full swing and the Communists were crashing their way toward Hanoi. The Americans were supplying the French with bombs and ammunition and had a 9,000 ton freighter, the *San Mateo*, fitted out specially for the purpose, plying between Japan and Indo-China. In the month of April 1954 this ship was returning to Japan to pick up another load of ammunition. Something went wrong with its radar mechanism and one dark rainy night it ran full steam onto the rocks some distance from the site we had picked for our church. The mishap to the *San Mateo* proved a godsend to us in our plight. The ship was imbedded in rock for a whole month and great holes were torn in her hull. As she was a very important vessel, and the need for her services were so urgent, teams of divers worked day and night blasting away the rock to allow her to be pulled clear. In the meantime I went on board very frequently and acquainted the officers with the situation in my parish. They reacted with typical American generosity. On board ship were large amounts of dunnage timber which was used to hold the ammunition cases in place. When the time came for pulling the *San Mateo* back into the sea, the lower holds would fill with water and all this timber would become waterlogged and have to be discarded. I was told to take as much of it as I could unload.

"It was at this point that I got my first inkling of the caliber of the island people. If I had had to depend on my Catholic congregation alone we couldn't have got much timber off that ship. But word spread of our need, and hundreds of pagan men and women turned out and worked very hard carrying the heavy beams across the dangerous rocks."

Things began to go well. A company of American marines that had been based on the island pulled out and turned over their buildings to Father McGlinchey. A United States Air Force chaplain, George B. Gerner, saw the dire needs of Cheju Island and, along with his Catholic GIs, raised ten thousand dollars. Father McGlinchey was able to build a church in Hallim that seated 1,000—on the floor; another in Kosan for 600, and one in Kwi Tek for 400. In no time the Catholic population had grown to 3,000.

All of this time Father McGlinchey was distributing food and clothing supplied by the American Catholic Relief Services, but he was not satisfied with that arrangement. He was forever talking with farmers, fishermen, officials, schoolteachers, and shopkeepers, always haunting them with the same question: how to raise the standard of living on the island?

Their answers were discouraging: People are too poor and have no access to capital, and besides they are too busy scraping a living from day to day to take time off to think up schemes for improving themselves.

Father McGlinchey shook his head at these pessimistic answers. He felt that what the islanders needed more than capital was some imagination, some know-how. Having grown up on a farm in Ireland, he was appalled at how poorly the islanders did things.

For example, they didn't lime the land even though the island soil was highly acid because of its volcanic origin. And yet lime galore was available if only the seashells on the shore were ground into powder. Manuring was neglected, too. The result was that tens of thousands of acres of grasslands lay barren when they could support herds of cattle, sheep, goats and pigs. Potatoes, something every Irishman knows about, were sown in holes dug in the soil, instead of in drills, and so heavy rains caused the crops to grow sodden and rot.

"This list could run on indefinitely," said Father McGlinchey. "Briefly, I may say that practically every phase of farming on the island was primitive and unenlightened. The result was that though the people worked very hard—and very cheerfully—they could reach no more than a bare subsistence. The same remark applies to their fishing industry."

One morning Father McGlinchey saw an American on the streets of Hallim, an unusual sight in those days. He introduced himself, learned the visitor's name was Charles A. Anderson, and invited him to the presbytery for a talk. By noon he knew the answer to the question of how to help the islanders help themselves.

Anderson, a retired army colonel, was in Cheju inspecting some 4-H clubs. Shortly after World War II he had introduced Korean youths to 4-H, a society for young farming folk of school age who are anxious to learn better farming methods. While Anderson was military governor of Kyenggi the idea caught on and cooperative farmers in the States shipped cattle, hogs, chickens, and rabbits by the boatload to Korea.

The Communist attack of 1950 undid all the work of those early years, but after the armistice, 4-H was reorganized and Colonel Anderson, now retired from military service, came back to Korea at the request of the American-Korean Foundation to act as national 4-H consultant.

The colonel made trips to Japan and the States to bring back high-grade cattle, hogs, goats, and sheep. All over the country, 4-H clubs sprang up. But a club will not thrive for long without the services of a dedicated local leader. For lack of such leadership, the colonel said that many of the island's clubs were steadily deteriorating, and others had already disappeared.

Father McGlinchey saw instantly that 4-H was the kind of movement needed in Hallim and he believed he could supply the energy and enthusiasm. He read all the literature the colonel gave him and visited a few of the best clubs near Seoul.

When he started the movement in Hallim parish, in February of 1958, he knew he would have to provide his 4-H club members with quality animals and seed. What was to develop in time into a thriving animal and seed bank started with one good Yorkshire sow bought in a distant village and consigned to the tender care of the boys and girls of Hallim.

"The youngsters were delighted with their sow," said Father McGlinchey. "They spent long hours in cleaning the pen, washing the pig, or simply watching it. The big moment came when the sow had its first litter, and there was great excitement. We distributed the young pigs among the members with strict instructions to put into practice what they had learned about the proper care and feeding of pigs at our club meetings.

"The idea was that each youngster should rear his newly acquired pig at his own home; that, when the first litter arrived, he should pay back two of the litter into the club's animal bank; and, at that point, would become absolute owner of his sow, and of the remainder of her litter. The piglets returned to our bank would be distributed among other members and the project would proceed to multiply itself."

Harold Henry, by then a bishop, was so pleased with the way Father McGlinchey was helping his people help themselves that he sent some money to buy a small plot of ground—at a respectable distance from the church—so that the pig-raising operation could develop still further. Besides, by now Father McGlinchey was beginning to have visions of chickens, sheep, and cattle.

Some years later, with money received from the Columban Fathers and their friends, the young missionary went out east of Hallim and bought 1,200 acres of dark, brooding land reminiscent of the American West at its most desolate. The young priest said that he was attracted to the land because it reminded him of the west of Ireland. He could buy the land for less than two dollars an acre because the Koreans considered it useless. If he was to prove to the farmers that they could make better use of what they had it would be best to prove it with the very land they most despaired of.

Two things happened that helped keep up the enthusiasm. For one, Monsignor George Carroll, Director of the Catholic Relief Services, National Catholic Welfare Council, approved large shipments of yellow corn under a Public Law 480 project. The corn had been spoiled in warehouses, and although unfit for human use the pigs thrived on it. Next, two American air force sergeants visited the pig yard and returned with a truck load of war surplus supplies—circular steel frames used to build Quonset huts, and steel slats used in constructing runways. With this they built a series of pig pens.

Father McGlinchey wanted more purebred stock. He didn't want to keep putting time and energy into the rundown island breed. Just about then he received some money from the German Bishops. He used it to buy purebreds—Durocs and Chester Whites.

He convinced officials of the United States Catholic Relief Services that the project should be expanded into a major program to help more farmers help themselves. The relief services arranged for 41,000 tons of grain to be delivered over a five-year period through the United States Food for Peace program. The arrangement was, under Public Law 480, Title II, that corn meal, fortified with the vitamins and other ingredients required for a balanced diet, should be sold to participating farmers. The proceeds were used to establish farms of twenty-five acres each. The recipients had ten years to pay for the farm and the money repaid became part of a revolving fund that, in time, would establish 500 farms. By 1976 some 300 farms had been started. The recipients of the funds were those who showed initiative and responsibility while in training.

As an example of what this meant to the farmers: Peter Kim lived with his wife and four children in a cave with a burlap sack over the opening. His income was about fifty dollars a year. During the first year on his own farm he cleared about one quarter of the twenty-five acres and planted sweet potatoes and raised pigs. His income that year was $1,125. He told Archbishop Henry that the following year, with half the land cleared, he will double that income. "And then," he said, grinning the widest possible grin, "I'll be able to send my daughter to the university."

At one time Father McGlinchey found it necessary to make a personal visit to Washington to convince AID officials that it was possible for a missionary to know quite a lot about pigs. Help also came from such relief agencies as

Misereor in Germany, Oxfam in England, Gorta in Ireland, and Corso in New Zealand.

That one pig given such tender loving care by the 4-H club children in 1958 has developed to quite an enterprise by 1976. Now the farm raises more than 15,000 pigs annually.

After teaching the islanders to raise pigs Father McGlinchey had to teach them how to raise chickens. They were not aware of the need for insulation against draughts and so suffered great losses. He tried to tell farmers of a better way but they just shrugged their shoulders and continued to lose chickens. So he decided to show them.

"We started off by building a stone house twelve feet wide and forty-two feet long, divided into three sections. We faced the house southward to catch the sun for most of the day and put large glass windows at the front. We started with twenty hens and a wooden incubator. Things didn't go so well the first year; there was an epidemic of Newcastle's disease in the area and we lost 200 chicks. The following year we produced 800 chicks, and the year after that, 2,000.

"We acquired more incubators and set up chicken runs with the purpose of keeping 200 purebred Leghorns and New Hampshires as a source of young chicks for distribution. The plan is that the farmer pays back two eggs for every chick he gets from the bank."

The value of liming the land was something else Father McGlinchey could prove only by demonstration. When he came to Hallim he used to say, "Why don't you put lime on your land?" and was told that in the first place farmers don't recognize the need for lime, and in the second place there is no lime to be had.

"I pointed out that the coast abounded in seashells, and these shells, if crushed into powder, make good lime. People grinned, said it was interesting, but added they didn't believe a word of it.

"I got our 4-H boys to draw shells from the shore, crush them into powder, and dress their plots with it. I offered a prize of a thoroughbred hog to the boy who produced the biggest crop of barley on his newly limed plot, and a second prize of a crossbred hog to the boy with the next best crop. The boy who carried off first prize reaped exactly twice the amount of barley yielded by unlimed plots of the same size."

As a result there is now a large plant on Cheju Island that processes the white sand that is a product of seashells.

About that time, 1960, Father McGlinchey wrote to friends in the United States and Ireland who were helping his program financially: "We also installed a series of hotbeds which produce about 10,000 young plants, such as tomatoes and cabbages, for distribution among club members. Here again we avoid anything in the nature of a mere give-away program. Our youngsters are required to cultivate their seeds or young plants, as the case may be, according to instructions. And when the crops have matured, they are further required to pay back twice the original amount they received, for redistribution among other members. In marketing, we try to help individuals to secure better prices for their produce by getting them to sell in groups, rather than singly."

Since Father McGlinchey is from County Donegal, it was reasonable that he think of sheep and weaving when casting about for other ways to help his parishioners help themselves. The parishioners again were skeptical, pointing to the unpromising pasture land around Hallim and repeating over and over that the Japanese had failed in an attempt to raise sheep there.

Still the missionary went ahead and imported a few Corriedale sheep from Japan in 1958 and distributed them to farmers willing to take a chance at fattening them with hand-feeding and grazing on the rough local grasses. At the same time he sent a girl from his parish, Agatha Ri, to a spinning factory in Cheju City to learn how to card and spin yarn. She returned to teach fifteen women and girls. They began with a few sets of hand carders and three spinning wheels made, in part, from bicycles. The first wool used came from outside sources and the first yarn spun was turned into sweaters that were imitations of the sweaters knitted in the Aran Islands off the west coast of Ireland.

Now Father McGlinchey had something definite to show; it was no longer just a dream. He tried his best to raise funds for expansion but for some reason one lead after another failed to materialize. Bishop Henry decided to see what he could do for the young priest and asked help from Misereor, the German bishops' organization for giving aid abroad. The director of the fund sent a German priest from Hong Kong to make an on-the-spot survey. He liked what he saw and soon a check arrived from Germany that helped with the expansion.

Norman De Haan, on loan to the Korean government from the American firm of Smith, Scherr & McDermot to advise on the development of small handcrafts, took a generous interest in the Hallim experiment. He made arrangements to send Susanna An and Cecilia Kim to a Protestant school of cotton weaving in Seoul. There Miss Anne Davidson, of Church World Services, was more than helpful.

Anthony Ford, of the United States Overseas Mission, helped procure Hallim's first weaving loom. Ford was so excited by the imaginative project that he came to Cheju and helped install the loom, and with it as a model, several Korean carpenters built three more. When Cecilia and Susanna returned from Seoul they trained Columba Kang and Philomena Kim. The four girls wove the first bales of Hallim tweed cloth.

The first four looms, suitable only for narrow-width cloth, were gradually replaced by fifteen large looms built by local carpenters. Five new Quonset huts were needed to house the larger looms and processing equipment.

Water and power were needed. A well was dug, a water tower erected, and boilers installed. The generator that operated the Grain Mill—another McGlinchey project—provided electricity.

The most important step in the development of the handweaving industry was the arrival of the Columban sisters from Ireland in 1962. They came to run the factory and to look after the ever-growing number of girls who worked there. The first three sisters to reach Hallim were Sisters Mary Ligouri Taffe and Mary Ethna Kenny, both from Clare, and Sister Rosarii McTigue from Foxford. They were joined within a year by Sisters Declan O'Dea from Clare, and Imelda Crowley of Cork.

In factories and handcraft schools in Ireland the sisters had learned the art of weaving the delicate patterns and bright color combinations found in Irish tweed. Kim Samuel, an artist, mastered the secrets of the dyer's art which the sisters had learned from experts in Dublin, Artane, Avoca, and Foxford. Another artist, Athanasius Im, a former catechist, was hired as a designer.

The success and expansion of the textile plant gave impetus to sheep-breeding on the island. In 1975 there were 1,300 sheep on the main farm thanks largely to a gift in 1966 of 400 Romney Marsh ewes and 14 rams from Corso.

A year later Corso sent a young sheep expert, Geoff Lee, to give advice and to help establish permanent pastures of imported clover and rye grass. Geoff set up a system for frequent dipping because of the prevalence of ticks on the island.

When the time came to shear the sheep the farmers did not know how to do the job properly. Instead of shearing away the wool in one piece they snipped it off in lumps making the processing unnecessarily difficult. Father McGlinchey imported a dozen pairs of hand shears from Japan, and he imported from the Korean mainland Father Peter Tierney, an old hand at shearing on his father's farm in Galway. He taught the farmers of Cheju how to shear properly.

Hallim products sell well largely because they are of such quality that they attract favorable publicity. Norah Noh, Seoul's leading designer, was principally responsible for calling attention to Hallim. Her mannequins displayed the clothes to good advantage at fashion shows in Seoul. When she moved to Hawaii, her successor, Miss Park, and her dress stylists continued to promote Hallim tweed. When the United States ambassador and his wife, Mr. and Mrs. Winthrope Browne, selected the tweed for their spring suits, the story was carried in the press and soon Americans working in Korea began buying Hallim products as gifts to friends back home. Miss Korea helped popularize Hallim tweed by including it in her wardrobe when she set out for the United States.

Sales are so good that eighty girls are employed at the factory making blankets, wall hangings, fringed rugs, and tartan skirts; and approximately 300 women and girls work at home knitting sweaters, vests, coats, dresses, scarves, caps, mittens, afghans, and ponchos, all of 100 percent wool.

Almost all the girls are selected on the basis of need. They are usually supporting large, impoverished families. Some are partial cripples who would not be able to get other employment because there is little work around Hallim except farm work and gathering seaweed and shellfish.

The girls themselves feel that one of the greatest helps is having the sisters take a personal interest in them, counseling them in their problems, and inspiring them with the example of dedicated lives. The girls say their families benefit financially, socially, and spiritually. It is evident that when their lot is improved it restores a sense of their own dignity.

By 1963 things were happening so fast around Hallim that the various projects were brought together under the head of the Isidore Development Association. The association was put under the patronage of a Spaniard, St. Isidore, the patron of farmers. Archbishop Henry was named president; Father McGlinchey, director; and three Koreans were appointed to the board of directors.

Isidore Development Association grew rapidly to 2,000 reclaimed acres with its 428 participating farm families owning an additional 4,500 acres. To help members of the association to get on their feet economically, a credit union was established that now has 2,500 members with outstanding loans of a quarter of a million dollars. The average farm income has grown from $300 to $2,000 a year. An agricultural school on the Isidore farm has replaced the 4-H clubs. Here each year 137 young men learn the latest methods in farming. To help them, and to bring more professionalism to the entire Isidore program, experts volunteer to come to Cheju to serve two-year terms: Kevin and Josephine Bell, both veterinarians from Melbourne; Terence Fogarty, a veterinary surgeon, and his wife, Mary, a nurse, from County Tipperary; Francis Eivers and Patrick White, farm machine mechanics from County Meath; Michael Pierse and Seamus O'Donoghue, agriculture graduates from

University College, Dublin; Robert Stuart Thow, from Aberdeen, a specialist in raising pigs; Chris Burgen, a cattle breeder from New Zealand. With the help of such volunteers the island saw more advancement in farming and livestock management methods in the past decade than in the preceding thousand years.

Father McGlinchey remembers how he used to lean on a black stone wall, the kind that surrounds each tiny field on Cheju, and watch farmers do things the hard way. For example, he was amused and saddened at the way they used wild ponies during planting season. When the seeds were scattered over the field, the farmer and his wife and children would chase a herd of ponies around and around, chanting a haunting song, until the seeds were covered and the ground smooth and packed.

"When you see a man scratching the surface of the land with an ox-drawn wooden plough your first inclination is to laugh," said Father McGlinchey. "But when you see the beads of sweat stand out on his forehead as with grim determination he pushes and wrestles the plough unevenly behind the slow unwilling animal, and when you realize that this man is literally fighting to feed himself and his family, your feelings change first to sympathy and then to anger that things should be so in our day.

"I decided that come hell or high water a way would have to be found to show the people of Cheju that there are easier and better ways to battle the land. A way was found and it was Oxfam who found it. They gave me the funds to buy the first tractor, plough and disc harrow ever seen on Cheju."

The tractor had hardly arrived when the first driver—who, unknown to Father McGlinchey, was an epileptic—turned it over, nearly killing himself. As Father McGlinchey rushed the boy to a makeshift clinic in Hallim, he vowed he would see to it that Hallim soon had a first-rate clinic.

Isidore farm soon owned twenty-five tractors in its farm equipment pool, and Hallim had a first-rate clinic. To start it, Father McGlinchey used the $1,850 which he received with one of his citations from the President of Korea. The three Columban sisters who operated the clinic were assisted by a staff of nineteen, which included two doctors and two registered nurses. About 1,000 patients register each month.

Father McGlinchey brought his cattle to Cheju with the same dramatic flair he brings to everything. To get the project rolling on Isidore farm he needed 450 head, for which Misereor promised to finance seventy-five percent of the cost. Since it is economically unsound to ship less than 1,000 head over the 5,000-mile route from Australia to Korea, the question arose as to what to do about the 550 cattle that the farm could not afford.

Father McGlinchey interested Korean Air Lines in taking 300 head for its farm on Cheju, but he was still 250 head short of 1,000. Off he flew to Australia where, after long negotiation, the company agreed to sell him the 250 more on credit, and Archbishop Henry asked the Columban fathers to guarantee the loan.

Then came the problem of how to get the cattle ashore. The huge freighter would have to drop anchor far out in deep water. The plan had been to have the cattle arrive in summer and swim ashore, but all the dickering had delayed the project so that the cattle arrived in December, a month of dangerous, choppy water.

The missionary turned to the United States Army for barges and tugboats. It turned out to be an armada silhouetted on the horizon—the huge freighter carrying 1,000 purebred Australian cattle, flanked by barges and tugboats. To the people of Cheju it was an exciting sight. "The cattle are coming! The cattle are coming!" was a cry that echoed across the hills.

Father Jeremiah Kelly, who witnessed the spectacle, said, "Father Pat McGlinchey was the calmest man in the crowd. He kept looking around, wondering if he had forgotten anything. The logistics of moving 1,000 head of cattle safely ashore and then trailing them twelve miles across the hills to the Isidore 2,000-acre ranch were frightening. It had meant transforming the wharf of a Korean fishing village into a huge temporary stockyard. Corrals had to be built, hay and grain provided, temporary water and power lines set up."

Father McGlinchey saw the barges move into position to load the reluctant cattle. "God has blessed us again," he said. "Look at that tranquil water—hardly a ripple. You seldom see that in December."

Father McGlinchey and Archbishop Henry had much in common—unbounded energy, freewheeling ideas, and an impatience with the slowness of the way things move. The archbishop said, "Father McGlinchey has twenty-two ideas in one day. My task is to hold him down to two a month. When he has $10,000 promised for cattle next month, he wants to spend it this month. Once an idea is decided on though, I allow him to follow it without interference. He likes that. I learned in the army that you give a man an assignment but don't tell him how to carry it out."

When the archbishop spoke of Father McGlinchey's tendency to let his ideas run away with him, he knew this was one of his own problems, too. When he heard this complaint being made against himself he wrote with amusement in 1966 to his old commanding officer, Colonel Rowland: "A bookkeeper at the chancery said to the procurator, 'You had better talk to the bishop. He's spending money like he's got it, and he hasn't. Don't let him make any more commitments. I have butterflies in my stomach already.' "

Both Archbishop Henry and Father McGlinchey agreed that no one should confine his aspirations only to worldly matters, because there could not really be a kingdom of heaven on earth. Material advantages seem like the trappings of paradise until boredom sets in. Something spiritual is needed or life gets out of balance. Both were aware of the warning in the Acts of the Apostles: "If what they are planning and doing is of no more than human origin, it will come to nothing."

To help keep a balance in Cheju's beehive of socioeconomic betterment, Archbishop Henry did something dramatic: He brought from the United States a contemplative order of nuns to establish a monastery on the farmland he bought adjacent to the Isidore Development Association. It was in Minneapolis that he approached a foundation of the Sisters of St. Clare, usually called the Poor Clares, to ask if they would be willing to come to Korea.

On February 8, 1974, Archbishop Henry went jolting across a rocky, rutted road to the monastery that stands alone in the middle of vast, windswept acreage. During his Mass that day, in thanksgiving for the completion of the monastery, he repeated what he had stressed in Minneapolis—that the sisters should not engage in an "active" apostolate. He said, "I did not ask the Sisters of St. Clare to come to Korea for catechetical purposes. Rather they must sacrifice themselves every day in their lives of sacrifice and prayer. Rather than tell people about God they are to tell God about the people. In this way truly they will be the leaven in the community, invisibly transforming it, moulding it along the lines He wants."

The sisters are "active" in that they operate a small farm as a way of keeping body and soul together and as a way of keeping that part of the Rule of St. Clare which says: "Let the Sisters labor . . . in such a way that, while idleness, the enemy of the soul is banished, they may not extinguish the spirit of holy prayer to which other temporal things should be subservient." Although active in some temporal things, they keep the balance tilted on the side of prayer, sacrifice, and contemplation.

That prayerful oasis out there in the middle of nowhere is bearing fruit. According to Father Jeremiah Kelly, of the Isidore Development Association, "The wisdom of the archbishop's decision is already becoming evident. Attendance at Mass is greatly increased, and the children, though not instructed directly by the sisters, have a greater awareness of, and appetite for, their religious doctrine classes. The leaven is working."

Everything and everybody seem to be working well on that wild western end of Cheju Island. It is one of the reasons Archbishop Henry referred to Korea as "the land of do-it-yourself Catholics."

CHAPTER

2 2

Prayer Book and
Check Book

WHILE a newly arrived missionary was complaining that the seminary had not given him a course in accounting, Father Tom Neligan, an old Korea hand, opened a notebook in which he kept expenditures and income. He ran the stem of his pipe down one page and said, "Now here, for instance, Tchoi Marcu, who has the wee field below all year, landed in here on October 20 with a half sack of potatoes. That's his rent. We've eaten them. Would you tell me now, what column ought that go in?"

Another old hand, Father George Carroll, a Maryknoll Father, recalled that his first Christmas collection included five fresh eggs, a dozen tangerines, ten dried persimmons, a live chicken, a dead pheasant, and a dozen apples packed in a bag made of newspaper.

In describing the poverty of his parishioners, Father Maurice Foley, a Columban, told the story of Josephine. Her day, he said, starts at three in the morning when she makes breakfast for the family. At four o'clock, with a baby on her back, she catches a train to a town twenty-five miles away. She arrives at six when the vegetables are coming in. Buying continues until nine, and she has time for a little rest and some lunch before the return train leaves at one. Josephine boards it loaded down with vegetables. When she reaches her home village at three she goes from shop to shop selling the vegetables. Home at five. Dinner at six. Washing-up, cleaning the house, taking care of

With Cardinal Agagianian and Archbishop Fulton Sheen at the Second Vatican Council.

the baby brings her to eight or nine at night. The profit for the day's transactions—about one United States dollar.

From the beginning Harold Henry was resigned to this "financial frost," a Korean expression for hard times. He realized that if he was to build churches, schools, convents, rectories, hospitals, leper colonies, and self-help projects, he would have to look elsewhere. He focused his efforts on collecting money in his native United States, where he gave to fund-raising all of the determination, enthusiasm, and courage that he had expended on sports a quarter century earlier.

Since his advancement to bishop had some influences on Harold Henry's success in fund-raising, perhaps it is best to tell here of events surrounding his episcopal consecration. Everything about it was off-beat, as might be expected.

Before a priest becomes a bishop, he is notified of the date on which Rome will release the news of his nomination. He is expected to keep this information secret until the official announcement. Keeping secrets for Harold Henry was filed under the "no sweat" category reserved for all other difficulties.

He got quite a jolt at dinner one evening when Peter, the waiter, rushed into the dining room to offer congratulations. "What for?" asked the monsignor. "Bishop! Bishop!" gasped the excited Peter.

The monsignor's first thought was uncharitable. He suspected that Peter had found the key to the strong box that held the secret document. Before he could say anything, though, Peter explained, "On radio in kitchen."

That night congratulatory cablegrams began coming in from all over the world, especially from the United States. A few days later a delayed airmail letter reached Korea from Rome telling the date of the official announcement, a date now past.

Since Archbishop Cushing had been so kind through the years, Monsignor Henry decided to ask if he would perform the episcopal consecration in Boston. Cushing agreed and set the date for May 11, 1957.

Three weeks before that date, Monsignor Henry arrived in San Francisco planning to stop here and there visiting relatives and friends while moving by easy stages toward Boston. A message from Archbishop Cushing changed that: He was told to come to Boston immediately to address the Serra International, a club of business and professional men who foster religious vocations.

"After the talk, Archbishop Cushing was kind enough to say it was a good one and told me to come to his residence the following morning," recalled

Archbishop Henry. "What a costly morning for him! He called a tailor and told him I would be down for a fitting for all my paraphernalia—the bill to be sent to Archbishop Cushing. Then he called the Franciscan Sisters of Mary and told them to make the three required mitres and send the bill to him. He called a hotel and told the manager he was making a man a bishop on May 11 and required 600 places for a luncheon to follow the ceremony—the bill to be sent to him. He took me to his sacristy and gave me about a dozen zucchettos, those red beanies, and a beautiful ceremonial bishop's ring that had been given to him. Then he lined up Bishop John Wright, now a cardinal, and Bishop Jeremiah Minihan to be co-consecrators at the ceremony. What a morning!"

At the luncheon Archbishop Cushing said he would speak only for ten minutes. Anyone who heard him give the invocation at President Kennedy's inauguration can guess that he spoke longer, so much longer that when it came time for Harold Henry to speak, Archbishop Cushing said, "Just thank the Pope for nominating you, the bishops for consecrating you, the guests for coming, and sit down!"

"That's what I did," said Archbishop Henry. "I added one thing. I thanked Archbishop Cushing for all he had done for me and for the $10,000 check he had given me for our work in Korea."

Harold Henry was not a bishop for long when Rome asked him to build a major seminary in southwest Korea. Compared with this burden, all of the fund-raising that had gone before seemed simple. He was so aware of the enormity of the project that he came to the United States in 1959 with less than his usual enthusiasm. He bought a car and took to the road, covering 31,000 miles in eight months, criss-crossing the country, talking in churches and before groups, usually collecting about $25 a talk.

"Often I would get a successful businessman to ask six or seven other successful businessmen to lunch. I wouldn't eat. Just talk for forty-five minutes. I remember one day nine affluent men were at the table. I explained how they could decrease their tax burden. I said I realized they received many requests and that if they wanted to make a substantial donation I could wait a year or two. In most cases I left with at least $1,000, sometimes $2,000.

"In the first two months on the road I picked up $20,000. While that was a record compared with my past experience, I was on the verge of despair. It's just plain arithmetic: If I was to build a seminary to accommodate 220 students I'd need close to $400,000. At the rate I was going I would be traveling for years. I kept thinking of something Bishop Topel of Spokane said to me, 'If I have a project in mind I know that if God wants it I will get the money; if he doesn't want it, I won't get the money. So why fret?' I fretted anyway and prayed to God to let me know if he really thought that seminary was necessary.

"I was just about to write to the apostolic delegate to say that there are not enough golden apples on our trees, when a long distance call came from Marie Rowland. She told me to sit down because she had some news that would come as a shock. She said she had written of my predicament to a generous man. He sent a check for $100,000, but asked to remain anonymous. I took the princely gift as a sign that God really wanted me to keep plodding along."

With a resurgence of his old vitality, Bishop Henry headed for Boston. He phoned Cardinal Cushing to say he would like to see him.

"I don't want to see you," growled the cardinal. "I have nothing for you!"

"I won't ask for anything. I just want to visit you. After all I did receive the apostolic succession from you."

"I thought that would be the end of the line." After a long pause that was painful for Harold Henry, the cardinal snapped, "Come by at ten tomorrow morning."

When the bishop entered the room, he found the cardinal pacing back and forth with shoulders hunched and hands thrust into his cassock pockets. Even before he had a chance to sit down the cardinal lit into him.

"Harold Henry, I don't understand you! Out there in Korea working among the pagans! Why aren't you in South America? That's where you're needed."

"I'd go tomorrow if the Holy Father sent me."

"You've got the wrong end of the stick, Harold. What you should do is train Korean priests and nuns. Let them convert their own people. You get out and go to South America."

"Your Eminence," said the bishop, seeing an opening. "I have been commissioned by the Holy See to start a second major seminary in Korea. Your Eminence well knows that you must have Catholics before you can get candidates for a seminary or a convent."

The Cardinal stopped pacing, swung around and looked Harold Henry in the eye. "What do you want me to do about it?"

"Nothing. I said I would ask for nothing. I'll keep my promise."

The cardinal's ham-like hand slammed against the bishop's shoulder. "Let's call in the photographers. We need a picture of me handing you a check. I'm giving you $100,000."

Bishop Fulton Sheen also gave Harold Henry the encouragement he needed. On one occasion he raised $27,000 in an evening by speaking at a fund-raising dinner in Minneapolis.

"We returned to Annunciation parish around eleven that evening," Harold Henry wrote to friends. "I was in good shape but Bishop Sheen was completely bushed as this was his sixth day on the road giving four and five hours of talks each day. We raided the kitchen and had corn flakes, crackers and cheese, and milk. I got to know Bishop Sheen better than ever. I am extremely grateful to him for giving me a tremendous boost. He realized the responsibility I have in getting the seminary established and went all out to give me assistance and will continue to do so."

Self-made men were attracted to Harold Henry and he to them. Men who knew how it felt to have little or nothing were delighted with the way the archbishop did things. One of them said, "I know he gets full value for every dollar given him." Another was pleased to hear that the archbishop saved money by building a kiln to bake bricks out of the abundance of red clay on the seminary site. By baking over two million bricks for seminary, churches, and rectories he saves more than a cent a brick. He also saved money by setting up a buzz saw, tilt saw, and router, donated by A. J. Saxer of Cleveland, to develop a lumber yard in the front yard of his episcopal residence.

Another businessman was amused and pleased at the way Harold Henry lost his "no sweat" attitude when confronted by inefficiency, even in small matters. He saved a letter from the archbishop telling of getting a four dollar refund on his ticket because the plane he boarded was a prop instead of a jet: "So the agent had to spend twenty minutes issuing me a completely new ticket. I'm sure his salary cost United at least that much. Such inefficiency! I told the gent to give me a surcharge slip, but he said he couldn't do it."

Perhaps the thing self-made men most admired in Harold Henry was his strength of will and purpose. When he wanted something, he made sure exactly what it was he wanted and then went after it. He pursued his goal with the same vigor and spirit with which he played rugby in Ireland and Wales. And yet beneath all of this determination were an amenity of manner and a humility that came as a pleasant surprise.

One of the self-made men who admired Archbishop Henry was Thomas O'Ryan of Memphis, who came to this country early in the century and worked on the subway in New York, eventually establishing an advertising agency that handled the account of the New York Transit system. When O'Ryan heard that a seminary was being built in Korea, he established a permanent scholarship of $3,000. Then he came to Korea to ask what was the most urgent need of the moment. Harold Henry showed him a piece of property on which he would like to see a church, a rectory, and a doctrine hall. Even though the parishioners would perform the unskilled labor the total cost would be $40,000. Mr. O'Ryan took over the development of that parish, which became the most prestigious in Kwangju.

One special friend and benefactor, Gerald Rauenhorst, visited the archbishop in Kwangju in 1966. Impressed by what he saw and realizing all that still needed to be done, he became a generous patron to the Columban missions in Korea. Another close and enduring friendship of Harold Henry's was with Carl Kent and his wife Angela, an American couple who contributed generously to build churches and schools for the Korean missions.

The money to develop the Church in southwest Korea came from so many sources that to tell the complete story would be a book in itself. But here is an example of how varied were the helping hands: The archbishop wrote to the Kents in March of 1960: "I got a $25,000 interest-free loan (repayable in ten years) from Bentz foundation, Columbus, O. Also, they gave me two hot-water furnaces. Also got thirty-five sinks and twenty toilets gratis from Crane Co., Trenton, N.J., and three and one half tons of good radiators in Chicago. All will be shipped free by Catholic Relief Services."

Later he wrote of the generosity of the Raskob Foundation: $20,000 for Mokpo hospital, $30,000 for a boys' school, and two gifts of about $30,000 each to develop training in home economics in girls' schools.

The donations ranged from the "widow's mite" to the help of large organizations established for charitable purposes. The archbishop depended heavily on many donations of five, ten, and twenty-five dollars, and sent a letter of appreciation for each one. The large organizations of Oxfam, Corso, Misereor, and the Catholic Relief Services were also large contributors. All in all, these donors helped thaw the "financial frost" laying heavily across southern Korea after World War II, and especially after the Korean War.

Bishop Henry's momentum as a fund raiser was interrupted by Vatican Council II in the fall of 1962. In March of that year he had the first hint that he was to become an archbishop. By a wild coincidence the hint came while he was crossing the Delaware Memorial bridge, the same bridge on which he had learned that he had been named a monsignor. This time, however, no policeman stopped him. The news came over the car radio that the Holy See had instituted the hierarchy of Korea, which meant that every mission area would become a diocese or an archdiocese. Kwangju had been made an archdiocese, and Harold Henry became its first archbishop.

"A wag told me I ought to visit Wilmington more often and drive back and forth across the Delaware Memorial bridge, that maybe I'd get news I was made a cardinal. I tried it. Didn't work.

"The promotion gave me a better seat at the Vatican Council, right up next to the cardinals. As a junior bishop I would have had a place somewhere out near St. Peter's Square.

"During the Council I was thankful for what Father John Pak, my first pastor, had done. Since the proceedings were in Latin I could understand what was going on only because Father Pak had orated in Latin at breakfast, lunch, and dinner."

Several things came out of the Council that pleased Archbishop Henry. For one thing he was glad to see the vernacular adopted for the liturgy; the congregation could now participate in religious services with more understanding.

"I used to be embarrassed to use Latin at funerals when so many non-Catholics attended. They were at a loss. I noticed that in Korea non-Catholics avoided Mass; they couldn't follow it. But they used to come to Benediction because the hymns were sung in the vernacular."

Another change that pleased him was the reintroduction of the concelebrated Mass, meaning that the principal celebrant performs the actions while the rest of the priests join him in prayers. This has been a boon to priests who are elderly or ill.

"Take Father Paschal Kelly, for example. After being afflicted with multiple sclerosis, he was bed-ridden in St. Mary's Hospital in Minneapolis for eighteen years. Husky orderlies used to lift him into a specially constructed wheel chair so that he could sit up part of the day. People came to him from all over for advice. Movie stars and famous athletes visited him. He told me, not long before he died, that as far as he was concerned the finest thing the Council did was to make it possible for him to offer Mass again. He never dreamed that would happen."

Archbishop Henry felt that another good thing the Council did was to make orientals aware of the power of the Church in the world, especially in moral and social fields. He felt that orientals began to see that, resulting from the publicity given to the dialogue between the Christian and the non-Christian world, the Church had an interest in humanity as a whole.

He was pleased that the Decree on the Church's Mission Activity (*Ad Gentes*) took the missions out of the realm of charity and put them in the realm of obligation. He felt that, all in all, the Catholic hierarchy got a realization about the missions that it never had before. "About one-third of the bishops at the Council were from regions that would traditionally be called 'the missions.' I think they helped the rest realize that the Church shows most vitality in mission lands. There it's not tired or in a rut. The so-called developed Church can help with people and finances, but it's not a one-way street. The underdeveloped Church gives much in return. Spiritual values."

He was bemused by the rhetoric that came out of the Council. He wrote to the Rowlands, "I have been on the road for confirmations and assisting at 'Parish Days,' trying to build up the 'Community Spirit' and convince the people they are to 'give witness' to Christ. I am catching on to the new jargon!"

On another occasion he wrote, "To use the modern jargon, my life has been 'full' and I am meeting many 'challenges' these days; so I should really feel 'fulfilled'."

At the end of the second session of the Vatican Council, late in 1963, he decided to return to fund-raising, but his heart was not in it. He wrote to friends. "Frankly, I'm so tired of chasing the almighty dollars. I hate the sight of them now, but it is necessary."

CHAPTER
2 3

A New Start in Life

WHEN A MAN has lived sixty years he has completed one cycle of the lunar calendar. By now he should have accomplished all of his ambitions, say the Koreans, and should be free to spend his remaining years seeking serenity. This time of transition is marked by a ceremony, the *hwankap*, at which the honored guest, dressed in the white robes of a *yungkam*, sits behind a table loaded with delicacies. Each member of his family approaches, makes a profound bow, and offers a congratulatory cup of wine.

Since Archbishop Henry's "family" numbered in the thousands, his *hwankap* might well have been the largest ever held in southwestern Korea. More than 5,000 Korean Catholics came to the celebration in 1969. Some 200 priests attended, along with 17 bishops, Stephen Cardinal Kim, Korea's first cardinal, and Archbishop Ippolito Rotoli, papal delegate to Korea.

Not long after this celebration, Harold Henry started making plans to turn over the Archdiocese of Kwangju to a native bishop. He explained, "Missionaries are people who work to put themselves out of business. We develop a local clergy, turn the work over to them, and move on. A fisherman knows his own waters best."

This decision pleased his old commanding officer, Colonel Rowland, who said, "He's a real John the Baptist type of missionary. John the Baptist said, 'The Messiah must increase while I decrease.'"

On August 25, 1971, the archbishop wrote a farewell letter addressed to the "Dear Fathers, Brothers, Sisters, and Faithful of the Archdiocese of Kwangju." With an oriental ornateness he expressed his love: "It is always difficult to say goodbye to those who have been dear to one's heart. I love Kwangju as a father would his child. But even a father must give his grown daughter to another. That day is a sad one and a happy one at the same time. When he sees his daughter go to a fine home with a loving husband he rejoices. I rejoice that such a fine man as Archbishop Han takes from me now my beloved daughter, the Archdiocese of Kwangju. I know that he will be kind to her and spend his energies for her welfare. No father could ask for more. A bishop wears a ring to signify that his bride is his diocese."

At the end of the Korean War, when Harold Henry became a monsignor, Kwangju was a prefecture with 7,000 Catholics and eight parishes. When he left in 1971, the archdiocese had 76,000 Catholics, not counting the 45,000 who had migrated to Seoul and other cities, and the parishes numbered more than 50. At the end of the war there had been only one Korean priest in Kwangju, but now there were forty-one, thanks in large measure to the major seminary.

The stress of raising funds for the major seminary may have been responsible for the decline of the archbishop's health, a factor in his decision to leave the archdiocese at age sixty-two. Perhaps his illness was foreshadowed in a letter he sent from Rome as far back as November of 1963: "This Council is getting very tiring. My brain is about petrified now, and I believe I would vote for anything just to get away!"

He got away in time to reach Minneapolis for Christmas. When he arrived at Annunciation parish rectory, it was evident to Monsignor James Byrne and his assistants, Fathers Paul Dudley and Gilbert de Sutter, that the archbishop was exhausted. They suggested that instead of offering the Midnight Mass it might be better if he offered the Mass at 9:10 on Christmas morning.

While distributing Holy Communion the archbishop broke out in sweat, grew dizzy, and felt the pressure of deep, heavy chest pains. Not wanting to create any commotion, he summoned up all the will power he had and he kept hoping that after Mass a doctor friend would visit in the sacristy as was his custom. That Christmas morning, though, the doctor didn't come.

When the archbishop went to the rectory to rest, the pain subsided somewhat, but continued to return and subside intermittently. He recalled that a doctor had told him, "If you have chest pains and think it is a heart attack, it is very likely indigestion; if you think it is indigestion, it is very likely a heart attack. Take no chances."

He took a chance, though, and decided it was indigestion, for he wanted to keep a promise. He had promised Mary Zepp, a woman in her eighties, that he would drive her from Minneapolis to Alma to have Christmas dinner with her brother. He felt a special obligation to her because she had built St.

Five thousand Koreans attended the bishop's sixtieth birthday celebration, known as the *hwankap*. With him are Archbishop Ro and Bishops Choi, Han, Tji, Stewart and Chang.

Philip's Church, in Kwangju, in memory of her father. He kept his promise and drove the hundred miles over icy roads to Alma.

He stayed for dinner in Alma, and then returned to Minneapolis alone, suffering recurring chest pains all the way. When he reached Annunciation church at ten o'clock that night it was only with the greatest of effort that he could lower the garage door. He prayed that he would reach the front door of the rectory without collapsing. It was twenty-five below zero, and he didn't want to freeze to death on the steps. Fortunately, Father Dudley heard the car arrive and opened the front door; by now the archbishop could no longer summon that much effort. Father Dudley helped the archbishop inside, eased him onto a couch, and said he would call a doctor. The archbishop objected, saying he did not want to interfere with a family reunion, not on Christmas night. The young priest gave in but felt uneasy about it, so uneasy that he went to the archbishop's room at four o'clock in the morning only to find him sitting on the side of the bed doubled up with pain. Ignoring further objections, he called Dr. Robert Breitenbucher.

The doctor sent for an ambulance, and again there were objections, the archbishop saying that Father Dudley could drive him to the hospital at eight o'clock. The doctor said, "I'm not taking any chances. You're too much needed."

"Nobody's essential," said the archbishop. "Stick your finger in a glass of water. Notice the hole it leaves when you pull it out. That's how essential any of us are."

Archbishop Henry was taken to the intensive care unit at St. Mary's Hospital in Minneapolis, and spent the next six weeks in an oxygen tent. He liked the way Sister Josepha, the superintendent of the intensive care unit, pulled no punches in her dealings with him.

He said to her, "When I go, will I be doubled up in pain and gasping for breath the way they do in the movies?"

She answered, "No, you'll probably go so fast that the nurse on duty won't even know it right away."

After nine weeks in bed he was permitted to sit up for five minutes in a wheel chair, but his leg muscles were so atrophied that he could not stand, and after about two minutes he asked to be put back in bed. This came as a shock; he had never expected to hear himself asking to be put to bed. After hiking all those mountain trails in Korea, biking from village to village, and enduring the rigors of two wars, it had come to this, a plea to be put to bed.

After eleven weeks, Doctors Breitenbucher, James Mankey, and Charles Lindemann agreed that he could leave the hospital provided he stay with Bishop Leonard Cowley in Minneapolis.

As the archbishop remembered those days of confinement, "the restrictions were many. Don't climb stairs. Don't get excited. Bishop Cowley was an excellent policeman, working on *their* side. Even so I had a reputation for being an active fellow and so they put me on phenobarbital. That turned me into a Zombie. Couldn't even read. I fail to see how anyone could get a 'kick' out of that stuff. I begged the doctors to take me off it. After promising I would follow instructions, they did.

"But then I lost 'face.' One day near the end of April I got someone to take me to see the Minnesota Twins play. The game was so dull I almost went to sleep. No excitement. But apparently walking up one ramp was too much. More chest pains. At midnight Bishop Cowley called Dr. Mankey. Off again to the hospital in an ambulance for another month. To make me realize how childish I had acted, Doctor Mankey later showed me the EKG taken on my arrival at the hospital. It looked like a child had scribbled across the tape."

Archbishop Henry was not permitted to go to Rome for the third session of the Vatican Council II in September of 1964. He was, however, permitted to return to Korea in November.

During those eleven months of confinement in Minneapolis, the Catholics in southwest Korea were informed at regular intervals as to the state of their archbishop's health. Prayers were offered daily in every parish, school, and institution that he had been instrumental in starting.

At the Kwangju airport at least five hundred Koreans greeted him. They had erected a huge pine arch through which he would have to pass. The sight of their affection so touched him that he broke into tears.

After that first heart attack, on Christmas day in 1963, ill health became a cross the archbishop had to bear, but not always gracefully. He was an impatient patient. In 1968 he wrote to friends in the States: "I think I feel a lot better if I do not obey the doctors. They hamstring one so much. No use living forever and doing nothing."

At about that time, Sister Mary Clare wrote to some of his friends from the hospital in Mokpo: "We have had the archbishop here with us for a few days. He is a terrible man, really, since he works so hard no matter what we say to him. He was very tired this time and had a little chest pain which worried us not a little since he has not had pains now for a long time. He does not know how to take care of himself and the people are always pulling at him for something. He just does not know how to say no to anyone. There is no doubt about it he is one of the greatest missionary bishops of our time. May God spare him to us for a long time. If there were more people like him in this old world things would be very different."

Through his heart condition and high blood pressure Archbishop Henry learned once more that what seems a disadvantage can, in time, turn into an advantage. Through his frequent illnesses he learned to understand the health problems of others. During his vigorous youth and middle age, he admitted that he had no sympathy for illness in others. Especially difficult for him to understand were nervous disorders. His own disabilities taught him how severity for one's self should be accompanied by tenderness for others.

This new understanding shows in a letter he wrote in 1965 about a young priest who was working too hard: "Try to convince him that all is not labor! Too much or trying to do too much can actually be a hindrance to drawing close to Our Lord and doing an effective apostolate. A sick priest can only offer his sufferings; this sometimes has to be, but there is no use in trying to make oneself that way."

But through the years the archbishop must have had more feeling for the sick than he thought; certainly, this is indicated in a letter he wrote to friends in Tucson nearly three years before his first heart attack:

"I took one of my Korean priests down to the sisters' hospital in Mokpo right after Christmas. He wasn't at all good so I spent a week with him. It was touch and go for a few days but then he began to improve. He had an X-ray last Tuesday and was really making progress. On Wednesday a few of the priests visited him and he was feeling fine. I got a call about five o'clock on Tuesday morning that he had taken a very bad turn. I started out for Mokpo, but he was dead before I got there. God rest his soul. I escorted the corpse back to Kwangju that afternoon and from the time we laid him out in state until the funeral on Saturday the church wasn't empty day or night, with people praying for him. There were more than forty priests on hand for the funeral; plus Columban, Salesian, Seton Charity, Paul de Chartres, Blessed Sacrament, and Caritas Sisters; the Brothers of St. John of God; and Marianists. All of these plus some 2,000 Catholics marched from the church to the city limits behind the hearse. We will miss Father Pak; he was one of the councillors and a great priest, but I know he will be doing even more for us in heaven."

Up until age fifty-four Harold Henry knew he was mortal; knew it in his head but did not realize it in his heart. He knew how Joseph Conrad felt when he wrote, "I remember my youth and the feeling that will never come back any more—the feeling that I could last forever, outlast the sea, the earth, and all men."

After the heart attacks, the archbishop knew that his abundance of glorious vigor would never come back. He told that to the apostolic delegate in Korea when asking for assistance. As a result the Holy See appointed an auxiliary, Bishop James Michaels, a Columban, to help with the administration of the

Archdiocese of Kwangju. When the time came to turn over the archdiocese to a Korean, Bishop Michaels returned to the States to become the auxiliary bishop in the Diocese of Wheeling, West Virginia.

Although the vigor of youth was gone, Archbishop Henry felt that he could still make a contribution to the Church in Korea. Even after two heart attacks and a blood pressure characterized by ups and downs, he refused to coast. As he wrote to friends, "Once we get the idea we have done enough for the Lord we are finished."

He asked the Holy See to have Cheju province cut off from the Archdiocese of Kwangju and designated a diocese, one compact enough for an aging archbishop to administer and develop. The idea for this was implanted in his mind in 1968 when Governor Ku, of Cheju, asked why his province was the only one in Korea not raised to the rank of a diocese. The archbishop urged Governor Ku to write a letter to the apostolic delegate in Seoul pointing out that after World War II the Republic of Korea had recognized Cheju as a separate province, but that the Church had never given the island similar recognition. Many people in Cheju, he said, feel that the Church regards them as second-class citizens.

In June of 1971 the Holy See cut off Cheju Island from the Archdiocese of Kwangju and declared it an apostolic prefecture, a quasi-diocese. Since there are only 14,000 Christians in the province of nearly a half million population, Rome did not feel the area should as yet be declared a diocese.

"Some people wonder why I am called an administrator apostolic," said Archbishop Henry. "That's because Rome couldn't very well demote me to a monsignor or a bishop. So currently I am on the books as Titular Archbishop of Tubune in Numidia, a long defunct diocese in Africa, a place I've never seen. And that's the way it will be until there are enough Catholics on the island to have Cheju declared a diocese."

September 6, 1971, was the date of Archbishop Henry's installation, an event that the Cheju radio station called the biggest in the island's history. Thirty-one banners, strung across the road that encircles the island, bore such greetings as "Congratulations to Cheju" and "Welcome Archbishop Henry." Two obelisks erected in two of the city's squares bore similar inscriptions.

The Citizens' Hall was used for the ceremony so that at least 2,000 people could attend. Another thousand stood outside. Stephen Cardinal Kim and Rhee Hyo Sang, Speaker of the National Assembly, came down from Seoul. All the archbishops and bishops of Korea were present.

Right after the ceremony, the principal participants flew to the mainland because on September 8 Archbishop Henry would formally resign and Archbishop Han would be installed in Kwangju city. At least 5,000 persons attended these ceremonies held in the indoor sports arena. Another 2,000 stood outside.

Archbishop Henry received awards from the mayor of Kwangju City, the governor of the Province, the educational minister of the Province, and from the commanding general of the ROK Army stationed there. The Catholics of the archdiocese gave him a new Corona compact.

"I was ashamed to take it," admitted the archbishop. "I left my beat-up Datsun station wagon for Archbishop Han.

"For me that might have been the most difficult day in Korea. I had been in charge there for some twenty-one years. I was so overcome by the affection I felt that I broke down in the middle of my speech and couldn't finish it."

CHAPTER
24

Rocks, Wind, and Women

ON THE FLIGHT back to Cheju, Archbishop Henry told the passenger sitting next to him how haphazard travel to the island used to be. If all went well, and it seldom did, the ninety-mile boat trip from the mainland to Cheju used to take twelve hours.

"One time the open sea was so rough we anchored in the cove of an island for a week. Ran out of food and water. The captain asked the passengers if they preferred he return to Mokpo or wait out the storm. There was a split decision, with most preferring to wait out the storm so they wouldn't have to buy another ticket to Cheju. Both sides got impatient. The captain decided to chance the open sea. A few times the ship heaved so much that I thought this would be my last boatride. In the old days, Koreans so feared the sea that their favorite malediction was, 'To the sea with you!' On some of those trips from Mokpo to Cheju, I understood what a fierce curse that was."

The archbishop recalled his first visit to Cheju, about 1935, when he was a young pastor in Naju. He came to the island to visit his classmate, Father Thomas D. Ryan, known to his parishioners as Father T. D. Harold Henry had a warm spot in his heart for T. D. ever since their seminary days in Ireland. When the homesick American found the murky days depressing, T. D. Ryann sensed it, and out of his abundant good humor found a way to make the Minnesotan laugh.

The two of them had come to Korea together in 1933 and had suffered through the language course in Taegu. T. D. found the Korean language exceedingly difficult, saying "the devil invented it." He spent more time studying than any of the other young priests and somehow in the process kept up the courage of them all.

In recalling his first trip to Cheju, the archbishop said, "Father T. D. was a lonely man out there on the island, but never once did he complain. Out of charity I visited him from the mainland—one day by boat and nearly a day by bus to get to him. I never dreamed that the time would come when Korean Airlines would have thirty-six flights a day to the island and that the seven-hour bus ride would in time be reduced to one hour with a new short-cut road.

"I found T. D. kneeling in a flower bed planting flowers. He told me he was doing this to preserve his sanity as his flock was small, and under Japanese rule little could be accomplished."

When World War II broke out the Japanese threw T. D. Ryan in prison on trumped up charges of espionage. Fifteen of his parishioners were arrested and beaten every day until three of them "confessed" that their pastor had offered them money to steal the plans of the secret Japanese Naval Air Base located on Cheju. At the trial, however, they stated that they had been beaten into confessing a falsehood. The judge said, "You confessed and that's enough."

When put into prison at the time of Pearl Harbor, Father T. D. was a husky priest; when released he weighed only ninety pounds. Beri-beri, dysentery, and ulcers had taken their toll. After three months of treatment at a hospital in Ireland, he was his same strong self again.

The archbishop remembered when T. D. returned to Korea in 1947. His parish in Sugwipo township numbered seventy Catholics. Since then it has grown to 2,200. T. D.'s only complaint through those years of rapid growth was that he never had enough money to hire all the catechists he needed. From time to time, he would approach the archbishop and say, "What about a touch for a worthy cause?" The archbishop would ask, "What is the worthy cause?" and T. D. would answer, "Me."

As Harold Henry flew back to Cheju on September 9, 1971, to begin a new career, he knew that T. D.'s days were numbered. The Columban sister, Pauline Nagle, M.D., had recently told him he had incurable cancer. He accepted it as God's will and gave instructions that his personal goods be sold immediately and the proceeds plus any personal money he had be given to the Columban sisters' clinic in Hallim for treatment of the poor. All of his personal goods and cash amounted to about $700.

Harold Henry feared that one of his first official acts as prefect apostolic of Cheju would be to officiate at the funeral of the man whose friendship he had valued for forty-five years. And so it was. On November 23, the feast of St. Columban, Father T. D. Ryan was buried atop a high hill on the southernmost tip of Cheju Island looking out toward the Sea of Japan.

Archbishop Henry had always enjoyed his visits to Cheju and now he wondered how he would feel about living there. From the first day in his new assignment he sensed that life on the island would be pleasant. He especially liked the compactness of his prefecture—seventy-five miles long and forty miles wide. Now that the road around the island was paved and two roads across the mountain developed, he could travel at fifty miles an hour in his new Corona compact, compared with fifteen miles an hour by jeep in the days he visited as Archbishop of Kwangju.

The weather, while not the best in the world, is the best that Korea has to offer. It is good enough, and the scenery is beautiful enough, to attract a half million tourists a year. Since it is less than 200 miles from Japan, many Japanese come to Cheju for the pheasant hunting in the winter and for the beaches in the summer.

Among the Koreans, Cheju has become known as the island of rocks, winds, and women.

The rocks are volcanic in origin. For centuries Mount Halla, an extinct volcano, spewed lava which cooled to form the porous basalt that dominates the landscape. Large boulders, ranging from bluish-grey to black, dot the landscape and line the river beds and ravines. The beaches are covered with black sand. Rocks too heavy to lift remain in the field and are ploughed around; smaller rocks are piled on top of each other to make the walls that divide the island into a patchwork of irregularly shaped fields.

Cheju is situated at the center of a crossroads of the winds. Cold Siberian winds blow down from the north, pick up momentum across the open Yellow Sea, meet Mount Halla, and are deflected to the eastern and western side of the island. Warm, moist winds from the southeast also divide at Halla to add to the windsweptness of Cheju.

T. D. Ryan often described it as "a well-ventilated island." Stone walls are built with chinks in them so that the wind can pass through without toppling them. Sometimes snow blows so parallel to the ground it's a wonder it even lands. A nun observed that Chejuites are such loud talkers because they grow up shouting down the wind.

The women of Cheju attract attention because they are such a high proportion of the population. This dates back to the years right after World War II when trained North Korean agents were smuggled into Cheju to organize a guerrilla force among Communist sympathizers on the island. The guerrillas set up headquarters on Halla, which dominates the center of the island, and from this mountain attacked in all directions to burn, pillage, and slaughter. So many men lost their lives that for years to come villages were inhabited only by old people, women, and children.

To protect themselves from the raiders, the islanders built high stone walls around their villages and towns, walls that ranged from six to twelve feet in thickness and from ten to fifteen feet in height. The irony of this is that after the Korean War, when the missionaries needed churches for the rapidly growing Catholic population, they used the stones that the Communists had provoked the islanders into gathering. When Father P. J. McGlinchey wanted to build the Church of Christ the King in Kosan he was low on funds, as usual. The town elders told him not to fret; they organized a corps of hundreds of volunteer helpers to transport stone from the village wall to the building site. In one day the men, women, and children of Kosan transported enough stone to build the church and the wall that surrounds it.

Of all the women of Cheju, the most highly regarded are the divers. In the fishing villages that border the coastline, one out of every three households has a woman diver. When the tide begins to ebb she goes to work, even on a winter day when a Westerner might find an overcoat scant protection against the sharp wind. She changes into a cotton swimming suit, making sure she has a long scarf on her head, and carries a net bag with a gourd inside, a pair of underwater glasses, and an iron rake.

Sometimes she stays down as long as two minutes. With each surfacing she coos, making a soft, haunting, almost sexy sound that clears the lungs. After about fifteen dives, which she can normally take in an hour and a half, the diver comes out of the water to rest, and to empty her gourd which usually contains agar-agar, laver, shellfish, and abalone. Agar-agar is a seaweed used as a hardening agent in certain foods. Laver, a kind of sea cabbage, is a gourmet dish in the Far East. Each year Korea exports a half million dollars' worth of products gathered by the women divers of Cheju.

"This money is earned at a dear price," said Sister Ann Ward, a Columban nurse. "The divers age quickly and their life span is shorter than most women's.

"They are threatened by sharks, especially in early autumn. The scarf each diver wears on her head is used to fool the predators. When meeting sharks, the diver unties the scarf and lets it float on the water. The lead shark measures his length against that of the diver, plus the scarf; he decides that here is something bigger than he is. So he passes by and the rest follow."

Diving girls form the choir at Father Daniel O'Gorman's church, Sts. Peter and Paul, in Sing Chang. They sing with a breath control that would be the envy of an opera diva, but have one disadvantage: in the summer Father O'Gorman cannot plan on having a sung Mass because his singers are then diving off the mainland where they have the reputation of being able to go down deeper and stay longer than any of the other divers.

CHAPTER

2 5

Korea's Touchy Politics

Archbishop Henry agreed with his fellow Columban, Father Francis Herlihy, who wrote in *Now Welcome Summer*, "Politics are matters for a missioner to avoid. Unfortunately, he cannot always avoid things begotten by them."

Although Harold Henry tried to avoid politics, he was from time to time caught in the things begotten by them. After the Japanese Thought Control police, World War II, and the Korean War, he finally settled down in an uneasy peace, one that grew more uneasy all the time. Peace is probably not the correct word because a peace treaty has never been signed, and so North and South Korea are technically still at war. An armistice agreement, that stopped the shooting July 27, 1953, has since stretched out to one of the longest armistices in history.

A demilitarized zone 151 miles long and three miles wide separates the armies of North and South. In the North, Premier Kim Il-sung has 467,000 troops under arms, and in the South, President Park Chung-hee has 625,000.

Behind the ROK forces stand 42,000 United States troops. These, as Secretary of Defense James Schlesinger pointed out in the summer of 1975, would respond to an invasion from the North because the United States is tied to South Korea by treaty. At the time of this statement, Mr. Schlesinger caused worldwide concern by admitting that the United States has deployed nuclear weapons in Korea and keeps open the option as to whether or not to use them.

Most matters agreed upon at the time the armistice was signed have not worked out very well. For example it was agreed that a political conference should be held to discuss the unification of Korea. Nine months later, in April of 1954, such a conference was held in Geneva, but ended in failure.

The agreement to establish a Neutral Nations Supervisory Commission to monitor the strength of both sides also failed. The commission consists of four officers from nations that did not send troops to fight in the Korean War. The United Nations Command nominated Sweden and Switzerland to do its monitoring, and the Communists nominated Poland and Czechoslovakia. The Communists frustrated the work by denying the Swedes and Swiss the opportunity of observing the entry of war material at five ports in North Korea. So the United Nations Command, on May 31, 1956, suspended any further inspections by Czechs and Poles in the South.

The Swiss and Swedes are located in a camp on the southern side of the demilitarized zone, and the Poles and Czechs are on the north of it. The Swiss and Swedes established a camp astride the historic invasion route from Kaesong to Seoul, so as to be the first to know if the Communists again invade South Korea.

At least they thought they would be the first to know until a tunnel was discovered on November 15, 1974. A second tunnel was discovered on March 24, 1975. This brought about a series of meetings of the Military Armistice Commission, meetings that are as surrealistic in spirit as a Dali painting. The MAC consists of ten members, five appointed by each side. The conference building stands in a dreary landscape a few hundred yards south of the place where the armistice was signed in Panmunjom. It is so situated that the Military Demarcation Line, which bisects the demarcation zone, passes down the center of the conference table. The Communists sit on the northern side and the United Nations representatives sit on the southern side of the table. The United Nations and North Korean flags stand one at either end of the table. By agreement the flag staffs are of equal height.

"To a visitor seeing a MAC meeting for the first time there is a curious air of unreality about it," said Father Oliver Kennedy, a Columban missionary. "The two teams enter the room from opposite sides and take their places in silence without a word of greeting or sign of recognition. They might very well be men seeing one another for the first time, though in fact they all met frequently before. The meeting is conducted in an atmosphere of aloofness.

"The Communists usually ignore the opening statement by the United Nations and launch into a propaganda blast which has no relevance to the matter under discussion. The normal Communist line is that the United Nations were the aggressors in Korea, leading up to a variation of the theme, 'Yankee, go home.' After getting this out of their systems, the Communists may actually discuss the matter brought up by the United Nations Command. They may answer the questions asked or, as happens more often, may make counter charges or open up new subjects."

Major and minor violations of the truce terms occur on an average of one every forty-eight hours. They have varied in seriousness from spitting in the face of a United States military policeman at the conference site to digging tunnels beneath the Demilitarized Zone.

At the 362nd meeting of the Military Armistice Commission, on May 27, 1975, the UN Command demanded that the North Koreans cease their illegal tunneling. Major General William L. Webb, Jr., of the United States Army, said, "The illegal tunneling program represents the greatest threat to peace on the Korean peninsula since the Communist invasion of the south in 1950. The fact that you continue to tunnel in other areas in face of our protests and exposure of your illegal tunnels plainly shows you disregard the armistice agreement and persist in subterfuge.

"Your second tunnel was larger than the first. We are still exploring it. To cut such a vast tunnel through a bed of granite required time and resources that are staggering."

General Webb displayed photographs and sketches of the tunnels. One photograph was of a reinforced concrete wall with a steel gun port constructed in the middle of it.

The surrealistic spirit of Panmunjom came shining through when Major General Kim Pung-sop, North Korea's chief delegate, objected to everything General Webb had said. He claimed it was all a pack of lies, that the tunnels were blamed on the Communists as part of the United Nation Command's program of propaganda.

The tension inside that ugly corrugated steel shed in Panmunjom is felt all over Korea. It is felt even by the missionaries on Cheju Island, off the southern coast, who are as far from Panmunjom as they can get and still be in Korea. Since South Korea has the third largest army in the world, soldiers are seen at every turn and so there is the look of a country at war. At dusk the soldiers move toward the shoreline to guard against spies landing from the sea, a daily reminder that the peace is fragile.

The missionary is especially aware of the tension when he goes to the airport. In two hijackings the planes and passengers disappeared behind the Iron Curtain of the North and were never heard from again, and so security precautions are severe. Baggage is checked with thoroughness. No one is allowed to carry anything on board, not even the smallest piece of luggage. Everyone is frisked twice, once inside the airport building and once at the foot of the ramp leading to the plane. The security man frisks with thoroughness because he knows that if anyone hijacks that plane the security man will be executed. Every plane carries armed security guards dressed in civilian clothes. When the plane lands at any airport the first thing the passengers see are armed soldiers surrounding the airport building.

In spite of all precautions things still go awry. This was dramatized in the attempt on President Park's life by North Korean commandos. Time and again when missionaries come to their vacation retreat in Cheju, they tell of some tense situation that they experienced in some remote place.

Remote Huk San Do, which means the Black Island, is so barren and poor that it does not seem a likely place for the cross winds of political ideology to meet. And yet it was on Huk San Do that two Columbans, Fathers Joseph Cahill and Michael McCarthy spent a couple of exciting weeks taking care of the island's only secondary school.

"One night as we were preparing to go to bed," said Father Cahill, "we were startled by a rattling sound that echoed around the bay just below our house. Was it thunder? The sky was lit by countless flares. Machine guns . . . artillery fire . . . jet planes. It was like a scene from a war picture. We couldn't believe it was real. After all this was Huk San Do, miles from anywhere."

Soon the local police chief and an aide armed with a submachine gun came into the yard. He told the priests there was nothing to worry about. A North Korean gunboat that they had been expecting was being engaged a mile down the coast. A week earlier, in the mainland city of Kwangju, a brother and sister had met accidentally in the street. This was their first meeting in the seventeen years since the end of the Korean War. He had gone to the North and was now returning home as a Communist spy.

"His sister brought him home and persuaded him to surrender to the police," said Father Cahill. "He was to be picked up by a North Korean espionage boat the following week in Huk San Do. But with his cooperation the South Korean army and navy had prepared a surprise reception for it."

The North Korean boat was sunk, but a number of the crew managed to get ashore. Since these had to be tracked down and captured, Huk San ceased being a quiet, peaceful island.

When the search included combing out a coastal cave, a small rowboat was commandeered in which a party of police and soldiers entered the cave. Six Communists were hiding there. They threw a grenade which killed the fisherman rowing the boat. In the ensuing fight all of the North Koreans were killed.

More fugitives were in the hills. The thick foliage and dense fog on the mountains helped the North Koreans evade their pursuers. After two weeks the search was called off and the soldiers and police surrounded the village waiting for the Communists to come down from the mountain for food.

After six weeks they came down. Four of them were shot and seven police and soldiers were killed in the fight. Archbishop Henry assisted at their state funeral in Mokpo.

Another spy story came out of a remote mountain district where Father Oliver M. Kennedy had a parish at Changsong. It began when North Korean agents succeeded in evading the South's coastal patrols to land spies who quickly moved inland and hid in the mountains.

"As the days went by, I began to sense a watchfulness in the people around me," said Father Kennedy. "The local reserve forces were armed. All the young men around here carried rifles and the talk was always about the spies. Everyone seemed to agree that 'they will come to Changsong.' When I asked why, I was told that when the spies ran out of food they would have to approach some built-up area, and Changsong was the biggest town in this remote mountain district.

"Every day brought reports of the capture of more spies. Twenty-five had been killed or captured. Now the people were really on the alert.

"My cook had been away in hospital and sent word that she would arrive by train at 9:30 in the evening. I went to meet her in the jeep and wondered how anybody could come near our town with all those roadblocks. To get to our railway station I had to leave the old town and cross a bridge to the new town. On the half-mile trip I went through four checkpoints and had to state my name, address, and purpose at each, as well as show a special stamp. I had no paper so the first guard stamped the back of my hand. Another stamp, put on my hand at the station, was necessary for the return trip.

"A week later I was on the way to the post office when I noticed more soldiers than usual. All were hurrying toward one end of the town. Coming out of the post office I heard gunfire, and I knew that the spies had arrived."

The battle took place on the lower slopes of a hill about a mile out of town. With grenades exploding and rifles firing all around, Father Kennedy watched the action that went on and off for the next two days. Eventually, the number of spies killed or captured in the area reached 115.

In time the curfew was lifted, rifles disappeared, and roadblocks vanished. Little by little, Father Kennedy's parishioners began to relax. From then on the troops assigned to guard the remote coastline grew in number.

During his forty-two years in poor, troubled Korea, Harold Henry was wary of political involvement. He feared that the Church would be captured by particular interest groups. Whether such groups were revolutionary or reactionary made no difference; they put their own partisan interests above all else.

His stance was not easy to maintain, especially since he agreed with the Latin American bishop who said there are two kinds of missionaries who can do real harm: the first ignores social realities, and preaches as though we live in a world apart from everyday human problems; the second presents the Gospel as chiefly a social message, with Marx taking precedence over Christ.

Archbishop Henry knew that balance was the answer. The extremist is always destructive. Yet he realized that balance was the hardest thing in life to maintain, and that extremism was a magnet that draws many people.

Time and again Harold Henry had to be firm in making clear that he did not wish to be politically involved. For example, when President Park took over the South Korean government in a coup, some of his officials began to haunt the archbishop urging him to fly to Washington to assure President Kennedy that the coup was not Communist-inspired. At the time, the seminary was in the planning stage and the archbishop needed permission to begin building; the officials assured him that if he carried the message to Washington, the approval for the seminary would, without doubt, be granted immediately.

"I know the coup wasn't Communist-inspired," said the archbishop. "But if I do this for you, you will never trust me again. If I get involved on your side, I may, in time, get involved on another side. I don't feel I should be in politics."

He took this stand in spite of his approval of President Park. His approval is expressed in a letter to friends, even though in his vast correspondence he rarely said anything political. In May of 1967 he wrote to Carl and Angela Kent: "Elections are today, I sure hope President Park gets reelected. It seems quite sure he will. The Church has fared well under him and he has done much for the economy of the country. Personally he is above reproach and is merciless when he discovers corruption. Under his regime was the first time Catholics could get into high office on their merit. Religion is not considered in their appointments. During the Rhee regime, Catholics were discriminated against because they were loyal to John Chang. During Dr. Chang's time he put in many Catholics or persons recommended by priests feeling they were trustworthy. That was dangerous for the Church, of course. So the situation is ideal now."

The archbishop always had a warm spot in his heart for John Chang: "He was a dedicated Catholic. His greatest success was the number of converts he won because of his integrity, especially among the intellectuals. They, in turn, influenced others."

Syngman Rhee once used Harold Henry's name during a campaign and the archbishop still resented it. The incident began in New York at Cardinal Spellman's birthday party. During the dinner the cardinal turned to Ben Limb, the Korean observer at the United Nations, and said, "I have a chalice that I would like to send to my good friend Bishop Henry. Could you see that he gets it?"

Shortly afterward, Syngman Rhee, who was running for reelection for a fourth term, sent word through the apostolic delegate in Seoul that he would like to see Bishop Henry right away. Although the bishop was in the midst of an arduous confirmation schedule, he went from Kwangju to Seoul on the Wednesday night train and returned on the Thursday night train. At the ceremony Rhee said, "I would have sent this to the governor of the province, but since it has come from such a dear friend as Cardinal Spellman, I felt I must personally present this to you."

Coming from an anti-Catholic these words sounded strange to Harold Henry. Soon he saw the political gesture behind them. Rhee called in the photographers and the picture appeared in all Korean newspapers; Korean radio repeated the story each hour for thirty-six hours before the election. The archbishop recalled that four months later Rhee was overthrown.

Harold Henry was never so apolitical that he did not care whether the North took over the South. He realized the Church would not fare well under the North. He knew that above the 38th parallel organized religion was practically extinct. Up there the cult of Premier Kim Il-sung surpassed China's cult of Chairman Mao Tse-Tung in intensity and extravagance. Even so the archbishop was confident that invaders from the North could only destroy church buildings; they could not destroy the faith in the hearts of a million people.

As Harold Henry saw it, North Korea was an oriental despotic state of an extreme communistic type. No other Communist country, with the exception of Albania, was so shielded from contact with the outside world. Even contact with other Communist countries was limited.

The archbishop felt some security knowing that North Korea walked a tightrope, made uneasy by the ideological dispute of the two Communist superpowers. In case of war it would need weapons from Russia and manpower from China, and so it had adopted a vacillating policy of staying in the good graces of both sides. Perhaps such divided loyalty gave pause to Premier Kim Il-sung.

"The North will never attack as long as the South is strong," said the archbishop. "And it certainly is strong now. The ROK soldier is excellent. Any GI who fought in Vietnam will tell you what fighters the Koreans were.

"I had several ROK generals to dinner one night. One of them later became chief of the Joint Chiefs of Staff. There were seventeen stars at the table. Quite a constellation. To a man, those generals said they don't want United States troops to fight on the ground. They'll do the dying themselves. They need to be supplied with plenty of 'hardware'. They need the United States Air Force to provide cover and the navy to protect the flanks since Korea is a peninsula, like Florida. The ROK government is now doing all in its power to convince the United States that the South Koreans will defend themselves, unlike the South Vietnamese. At dinner that night the generals said that even Russia wants the United States to stay in South Korea, feeling that the American presence is a deterrent to China."

In justifying his nonpolitical alignment, the archbishop pointed out that the Columbans work in a wide spectrum of political coloration. At the time, of all their missionary locations only Japan and Fiji could be described as democratic in anything like the American or European sense of the word. In Korea and the Philippines the governments are paternalistic. In Peru and Burma the governments have swung to the left; in Chile to the right.

He agreed with his confrere, Father Bernard Smyth, who observed that the Columbans have worked in democracies, quasipdemocracies and antidemocracies and have found it possible to carry on missionary work under almost any form of government, except one, atheistic Communism. It drove them out of mainland China and out of North Korea. In any country except a Communistic one, if a missionary keeps clear of politics, he is respected and suffers no repression.

"It is hard to escape the conclusion," wrote Father Smyth in the magazine, *Worldmission*, "that Communism is afraid to coexist with a competing idea of what life is about. Perhaps we shall have to wait a decade or two for the emergence of a Chinese Solzhenitsyn, deeply loving China, but loving truth and human freedom more, who will corroborate, with compassion and sadness, much of what expelled missionaries have said about the Communism which drove them out of China and which still brooks no seriously competing voice."

It is more difficult each year, Archbishop Henry observed, to remain apolitical in a world becoming more and more saturated with ideology. The best he could say for the situation was that it kept life fairly lively. In seeking the balance between the Word of God and the world of man, missionary work will never get monotonous.

CHAPTER
26

The Flight from
Loneliness

ARCHBISHOP HENRY knew what his old friend Father Gerard Marinan meant when he wrote, "I remember the past so well that what is actual seems less real than what is gone. And I search with a certain poignancy for what can never be again."

The poignancy was there for Harold Henry, too, even when he reminded himself that those days long past were less than sunny. He remembered how lonely he felt walking the muddy streets of Noan and Naju. In passing between rows of small Korean shops and an occasional larger Japanese store, he ran the gauntlet of curious eyes. White-robed, stately Korean men in their black stove-pipe hats stared at him. Women, in their easy fitting skirts and trousers, seemed in a hurry; with so much to do, they paid scant attention to the stranger. Groups of children followed him keeping a safe distance, and turning attention to something else when he returned their gaze. How alone he had felt.

Father Marinan described the homesick feeling when writing of his early days in Kwangju: "With a city this size sprawling at my doorstep I had small excuse, it might seem, for being lonely. But I was. In the crowds that swarmed around me I hadn't a single friend or acquaintance. My knowledge of Korean, barely sufficient for the most pressing business of the day, was totally inadequate for any kind of sustained conversation. Thus, I was a stranger for some time even to the few families that comprised my congregation. The silence of the desert is noisy compared with the silence of unintelligible speech, and no solitude is like that of the stranger in an alien crowd."

Although he came to feel at home in Korea, the archbishop was still concerned about the loneliness among his priests, especially the young ones. He recalled that in the early days the only place a missionary could go to "get away" would be to the rectory of another priest. This was not much of a change, and besides it put a busy pastor in the embarrassing position of having to entertain.

Aware of this problem, Harold Henry decided to do something about it at the time he moved from Mokpo to Kwangju. Adjacent to his residence he built fourteen small rooms where priests could come to rest and relax. All they had to do was sign their names to a chart and move into any room that seemed vacant.

"Sometimes as many as twelve priests arrived while the meal was in progress," the archbishop recalled. "The kitchen staff never once complained. This tells something about the Korean temperament. In any other country we couldn't have kept a staff for a week."

Because of his concern for all 128 Columbans in Korea, he welcomed the idea of using Cheju as a vacation spot. He willingly agreed to have the Columban Fathers build a modest house high above the Sea of Japan about a mile outside of Cheju City. His old friend Father Frank McGann was appointed the director, a happy choice because of his gift for hospitality.

Each Monday night the island missionaries came together at the Columban House. At the time when it was crowded with priests from the mainland, they went to the archbishop's residence where appointments were never necessary. This was a crowd that laughed easily and took pleasure in small things. The missionaries showered each other with friendly abuse, their humor running to jibes, put-downs and unkind remarks, the kind used only when friendship is secure.

Archbishop Henry usually attended the Monday night gatherings. He ate sparingly, and then went directly to the bridge table. Most of the missionaries gathered in the lounge where Father McGlinchey tacked up a bed sheet to show movies borrowed or rented from various sources. When the movies failed to arrive, the non-bridge players tried their hands at 500 or a card game called 110. By midnight the priests were going back across the dark, rutted road to their lonely parishes. If the weather was severe, and it can be on Cheju, those from the far side usually spent the night at the house or at the archbishop's residence.

In search of companionship, and to escape the summer heat of the mainland, Columbans came from all over Korea south of the 38th parallel to stay at this spot. They used the beach, played golf, and, of course exchanged anecdotes. This was where the archbishop resupplied his treasury of stories, those he would use on his next fund-raising expedition in the United States.

Most of the stories the missionaries told were humorous. Every so often, though, they allowed themselves to get serious with their confreres and told of serious events—the surprise conversions, the boy without hands, the apostle who lived on death row.

One of the surprise conversions centered around Mark, who helped Father Matthew Reilly with his parish paper work. Mark became a Catholic while in the army but dreaded to tell his parents because they were always so anti-Catholic.

Upon returning from military service he delayed making the announcement as long as possible. When Sunday came he got up enough nerve to say, "I'm going to eight o'clock Mass. I'm a Catholic now." His mother and his father looked at him with amazement.

His mother blessed herself. So did his father. His brothers and sisters hugged him. They explained that they, too had joined the Church. When the excitement died down, Mark said he had been baptized on April 10. There was a gasp of surprise and the family chorused, "That is the day *we* were baptized!"

The boy without hands, Michael Ja, lived in Father James Buckley's parish. When he was throwing dynamite into the river to stun fish and send them floating to the surface one stick exploded prematurely. From that day, life became more and more of a burden for Michael. Children made fun of him; his friends went off to the army; and when his father died he realized he could do little to help his mother. The climax came one night in church when he was cradling his hymn book in his arms in choir. The book tumbled from his grasp, and Michael ran crying from the church. That night he failed in his attempt at suicide.

"That night I did some hard thinking myself," said Father Buckley. "Something decisive had to be done for Michael immediately. The next day I went to see General Philbin and Sergeant Carberry at Camp Long. They got in touch with the National Rehabilitation Center in Pusan, and were told that within a few weeks Michael would be an expert at using artificial hands.

"How to pay for his artificial hands and his stay at the rehabilitation center? Captain Deitz and Sergeant Carberry took charge of that. Presently, a check from the men at Camp Long was on its way to Pusan. And two weeks later we had our first report from the center. Michael could already write, type, and serve tea."

After four weeks of treatment Michael returned home. The change in him was remarkable. Not only could he dress and perform all the normal actions of the day, his whole approach to life was different.

Captain Deitz made arrangements for Michael to set up a shoe repair shop at Camp Long. Michael hired a man to do the manual work while he himself received orders and kept books. A little advertising, a little propaganda among the officers and men, and presently Michael was earning enough to help his mother and younger brother.

Next, romance entered Michael's life. While in Pusan he had met a girl who was visiting her cousin at the rehabilitation center. After his return home they corresponded. Finally, contrary to all Eastern custom, she offered herself to him in marriage.

"Michael couldn't figure this one out at all," said Father Buckley. "One evening he came to see me, blushing and fidgeting. He said he had reconciled himself to the fact that no girl could possibly interest herself in a man with artificial hands. Well, anyway, at Camp Long, in the presence of the men who had helped him, Michael was joined in wedlock to Josephine Soh."

Another anecdote told at the Columban House also speaks of the possibilities of the human spirit. It began when Father Francis Holecek met John Pak in a Seoul prison. John had been on death row for four years waiting to be hanged for murder.

In Korea the prisoner is never told the date of his execution. Each morning he awakens wondering if this is his last day on earth. He finds out only an hour beforehand when the guards come to take him to the gallows.

John became a Catholic while in prison. Soon he began making converts. He talked about religion during the brief periods the convicts were allowed out of their cells for exercise. He talked of it to his cell mates; usually there are six men to each six-by-nine-foot cell and all prisoners are moved every two months or so.

All in all, John Pak made seventy-five converts. And then one morning in the summer of 1974 the guards came for him.

Almost every anecdote prompted Harold Henry to haul up from his vast treasury one that was similar. That story about John Pak caused him to recall the afternoon Father John Ra, a newly ordained Korean priest, came to the episcopal residence in Kwangju showing signs of shock.

"I just saw a man hanged," he said.

"You'd better have a drink," suggested the archbishop.

"I already had one."

Father Ra explained that he had converted a Communist spy who was awaiting execution in the local prison. Early that afternoon he received a phone call from the chief warden, saying, "Don't ask any questions, but come right away. Bring whatever is necessary for a dying man of the Catholic faith."

Upon arrival, Father Ra learned that his convert Joseph was to be hanged at 3:30 that afternoon. He heard Joseph's confession, gave him Holy Communion, and prayed with him.

"On his way to the gallows," said Father Ra, "he asked not to be tied up. He wouldn't cause any trouble. With the rope around his neck he was asked for his last words. He said that having been caught as a spy was a great grace. Had he not been caught he would never have known that there is a merciful God whom he would soon see face-to-face. The warden said there must be something in the Catholic Faith to help a man face death that way."

As Archbishop Henry listened to these stories, he marveled more and more each year at the kind of life missionaries chose for themselves. Here were men educated well enough to enjoy the pleasures of the privileged, but who chose to suffer with the underprivileged. If they were living for themselves alone they would find an easier way. Judging from the anecdotes it is evident that anyone looking for "a good deal" would be silly to join a mission band.

CHAPTER
27

Watching the Sunset

GUESTS at the archbishop's table could be a mixed lot, especially on Cheju. A typical guest list might include an officer from the United States Army, a Korean bishop from the mainland, an American schoolteacher from Seoul, and a Columban from across the island.

It was well that Maria, the maid, was trained in Western ways by the wives of two veterinarians, Doctors Bell and Fogerty, who came as volunteers to the Columban farm on Cheju Island. This training in both oriental and occidental courtesy was an advantage in a house where East and West met daily.

Because of the variety of the visitors, Sister Marina, the cook, catered to a variety of tastes. Although herself a Korean, she cooked American dishes and even prepared spaghetti and lasagna in the Italian manner. In learning the latter art from the apostolic delegate's cook, she was such an apt pupil that the archbishop feared the apostolic delegate might try to attract her to his staff in Seoul.

The meal was always eaten leisurely. The archbishop set a slow, deliberate pace, a far cry from the days in Noan and Naju where he bolted his food and paid for it with a rebellious stomach. Since conversation at the table was usually highly anecdotal, it was another way for him to collect stories for future travels abroad.

At the end of the meal everyone stood for an expression of thanksgiving. With a twinkle in his eye, the archbishop sometimes made a bow toward Father Devine, while saying a prayer that included, "May the divine assistance remain always with us. . . ."

Father Donald Devine came to Korea eighteen years earlier as a young Columban from Buffalo, New York, to serve as episcopal secretary. When the archbishop moved from Kwangju to Cheju, in the fall of 1971, he came along, bringing Carlos Yu, a Korean orphan the archbishop had sent to high school. Later Carlos taught himself to type in both English and Korean; he also handled legal affairs with government offices and drove the car for the archbishop, an unusual but useful combination of skills.

Father Devine's assistance went beyond correspondence and reports. He became a companion and a friend. Of him the archbishop said; "He deserves credit for sticking with me for this long. He is a wonderful man to have around. So gracious to guests. So even-tempered. As a seminarian he worked in the Buffalo chancery every vacation, so he got to know more protocol than I ever will."

As Archbishop Henry's right-hand man, Father Devine saw that all went well around the place. Along with Father Joseph Crofts, pastor and treasurer, he designed the two-story red-brick residence. Although an inexpensive house, it is an admirable piece of architecture, characterized by wide, running balconies and plenty of sliding glass doors that frame the eminence of Mount Halla. Father Devine planned the interior decoration so that Korean paintings, bonzai trees, and oriental screens live in harmony with the Western furniture bought at an auction at the American Embassy in Seoul. The landscaping, though, is not his handiwork but that of Korean Catholics who came inside the walled garden one morning to spend the day setting out nearly 2,000 bushes, flower plants, and trees.

After dinner, the archbishop's favorite recreation was a game of bridge. Quite often Father McGann came over from the vacation house, and Father John Quinn from his parish across town, to challenge the archbishop and Father Devine.

The game was usually interrupted by the arrival of a Korean Caritas Sister who took the archbishop's blood pressure each evening. To assess Harold Henry's health, Sister Scholastica, a high-school teacher, walked the four blocks from her convent to the episcopal residence. Because of the archbishop's medical record of heart attacks and high blood pressure, the Columban sisters in the hospital at Mokpo on the mainland wanted somebody to keep them informed as to how things were going on Cheju Island. Sister Scholastica did that with dedication.

When the evening promised a brilliant sunset, and there was no bridge game, Harold Henry sat on the balcony outside of his bedroom enjoying the way pinks and mauves played across Mount Halla just before dusk. If a visitor shared the balcony, chances are the conversation turned to mountains, for

Fifteen thousand Koreans marched in the Archbishop's funeral procession in March of 1976.

Mount Halla refuses to be ignored. It demands attention if for no other reason than that it is the second highest in a country of many mountains. If all those mountains were flattened out, the Koreans say, this country would be bigger than the United States.

The talk about mountains might cause the archbishop to recall the role of mountains in mission work in Korea. As a young priest he faced up to them in visiting his mission stations. Because of the mountains, it took all the self-discipline he could muster when awakened in the night to arise and take the last rites to a dying parishioner in some remote mountain village. This often meant climbing faint trails while lashed by torrents of rain in summer and by blizzards in winter.

On such dark nights the young Columban used to recall an article his friend Gerry Marinan had written about mountains having a special place in Scripture—Sinai, Lebanon, Nebo, the Sermon on the Mount, the ark atop Ararat, the transfiguration on the mountain, Mount Olivet, and, finally, Calvary. Harold Henry decided that if God speaks to man through mountains it is only fitting that a missionary learn to live with mountains, and soon he came to like them.

Off to the right of the archbishop's balcony, an orange sun sinks into the Yellow Sea whose waters wash the shores of the China that Harold Henry never reached. In time he was glad that he hadn't. He said: "The providence of God is remarkable. Had I gone to China I doubt that I would have stuck it out. Bandits, floods, Communists spitting in your face . . ."

He could never have endured the aloneness of those missionaries in the remote sections of China. He shuddered to think that Father Hugh Sands had spent three years in China without seeing a fellow priest. Eventually, he met a Chinese priest disguised as a vegetable peddler and went to confess to him while walking in a crowded market place.

The archbishop recalled another Columban, critically ill in a remote part of China, freezing one minute and burning the next. Finally, the sick man told his cathechist to go for a priest. The nearest one was thirty miles away. The trip, through deep snow and severe cold, would take at least a day each way. During the long wait, the missionary, too sick to keep a fire or prepare food, stared into space, seeking to separate reality from delirium. When at last the visiting priest stood in the door, the first thing the sick missionary said was, "I've been lying here thinking: If there is no Heaven, aren't we a bunch of damned fools?"

While waiting on his balcony for the end of the day, the archbishop had on his left the unchanging Halla and on his right the unchanging sea. But directly in front was a scene forever changing. The old Korea is giving way to the new. Stone cottages covered by thatch are being crowded out by Western houses enlivened by pink, green, and blue tile roofs. In the streets are more taxis than bullock carts. Mongolian ponies are still much in use, though; ponies whose ancestors were brought to Cheju when Genghis Khan wintered there. The mogul warriors were using tough shaggy beasts, and their leader boasted, "Where we ride, the grass will never grow again!" Out beyond the cluster of houses and the taxis and the ponies stretches the airport that serves some thirty planes daily. Beyond the airport are miles of fairly good road, for the twentieth century came to Cheju in the past ten years.

So many changes had come to the island in Harold Henry's time, but even more came to his area of special interest, the Catholic Church in Korea. When he arrived in 1933, there were less than one hundred thousand Catholics in all Korea, and now there are over a million in South Korea alone. There were few Koreans among the clergy in those days, but now of the seventeen bishops in South Korea, thirteen are Korean. Of the 900 priests, 2,800 sisters, and 180 brothers, the majority are Korean. This majority should increase because nearly 600 young men are preparing for the priesthood in Korea's two major seminaries.

Another change could be found in his own mission society. The Columbans now numbered a thousand priests. Their work had spread to twelve countries: Ireland, Great Britain, the United States, Australia, New Zealand, Korea, Burma, Japan, Fiji, Peru, Chile and the Philippines.

Something else that had changed since Harold Henry came to the missions was the relationship between Catholic and Protestant. Perhaps a telling anecdote will serve best to recall how the relationship used to be: During World War II, when Bishop Galvin and his priests were homeless in China, they were offered hospitality in a Baptist compound. At that time the director of the compound wrote in his journal: "I can just hazard a guess as to what our people at home would say if they ever suspected that there was a Catholic bishop and his priests living in our mission here, and that one of the rooms in his residence has been converted into a Catholic chapel where Mass is celebrated every morning." Although the journal entry is only thirty-three years old, the attitude it reveals seems more dated.

Sitting and watching the sunset was a change, too, for Harold Henry. In his youth he had little time for that. He so preferred the life of action that few of his days could be described as routine. If any day threatened to be ordinary, he did something about it, usually he set out on a journey.

After illness had narrowed his horizon, he still managed to live larger than life. As the possibilities for the vivid life decreased, he came to know a touch of the sadness, not uncommon among aging missionaries, the sadness that comes with the need to substitute convenience for adventure. A retired Columban, in recalling how one of his friends was dragged to death behind wild horses, sighed: "Ah yes, he was a martyr. And here I am shoveling snow."

Harold Henry wanted to die in harness. He never wanted to retire in his native United States. He feared he might feel like the Columban who, having spent thirty years in Burma, could not overcome the uneasiness he felt in the States and wrote: "I go to give a talk at a school and I see how students take food for their trays in the cafeteria and don't eat it. I see stacks and stacks of food in the supermarket for dogs and cats. In the coldest weather a waitress puts ice in your glass of water. I used to choke up every Christmas in Burma to see how pleased children were with the slightest gift, say a pencil or a tablet. Here nieces and nephews complain in the midst of abundance. There's so much waste."

The secret of retirement, Harold Henry felt, can be learned at a horse race. At the finish line the horses never stop short, but ease off with a graceful canter. That's the secret: look around for the canter most graceful for you. To pull up too fast is damaging.

Life on Cheju was a canter compared with the mad race in Kwangju. That it was a graceful canter was due in large part to the quiet efficiency that Father Devine and the staff brought to life in the episcopal residence. The very compactness of the island helped, too. It was easier to administer than the sprawling Archdiocese of Kwangju. The statistics suggest a more manageable situation: Nine churches, twenty-two mission stations, a high school, a middle school, and two kindergartens; nineteen priests, twenty sisters, three brothers, seven seminarians, and 4,377 Catholic families.

Cheju island isn't just compact in acreage, it is compact in spirit too. It is something of a big family; everybody seems to know everybody else, and word about anything gets around fast.

Archbishop Henry hoped to use this small town "grapevine" to develop Cheju into the province with the highest percentage of Catholics. He hoped to reach an ever-widening audience by training more catechists and developing his school system. Since the average salary for a catechist is $120 a month, and since teachers' salaries and the cost of construction have risen, a lack of money hindered growth in recent years.

A change came when the archbishop reached the shady side of sixty; he saw some things in a different way than when he was on the sunny side. He said that anyone who didn't change just wasn't paying attention while the lessons were being taught. For example, he realized more and more each year what his old friend Father McCarthy meant when, in discouraging times, he wrote to Bishop Galvin giving his thoughts on what a missionary should be:

"I don't think it matters much whether a man is a monk or a scholar, externally. The successful missionary must always be a contemplative at heart. The names do not matter. Our lives can only be reduced to a few fundamental laws: humiliation, suffering, prayer. They are, as it were, pegs on which we hang our work, and if it does not hang on some one of these three, we are wasting our time. If it is mean and servile it conforms with the law of humiliation; if it is hard and painful, it conforms to suffering; if it is done for God, to promote his work, then it is prayer. At least, Ned, that's how I look at the thing."

Such thoughts always brought the archbishop around to the word "vocation." He believed it was his sense of vocation that made loneliness, suffering, and humiliation more or less bearable. He remembered that in the seminary Father Harris used to repeat that a missionary's vocation boils down to one admonition: "Going therefore teach ye all nations."

Some time in 1922 Harold Henry had said yes, and from that hour his life began to fall into place. His vocation started to take shape when he admired the courage of the Columbans as revealed in the pages of *The Far East*. Of that he felt sure. He also remembered his father showing him an advertisement which said that a bright boy may start studying for the priesthood after completing the seventh grade, and he remembered thinking: "O boy, here is a chance to skip the eighth grade!" He also recalled holding the highly uninformed opinion, since modified, that priests and nuns are incapable of sinning, and seeing this sure route to salvation as a good deal.

When Harold Henry arrived in Omaha, Father Paul Waldron asked him why he wanted to become a priest. Harold stood mute, something unusual for him. He was ashamed to give such prosaic reasons. As he grew sensitive to the way God uses natural means to bring about a supernatural plan, he was no longer ashamed of prosaic reasons. Living an improbable life had made him realize that God really did write straight with crooked lines, and that his ways were not our ways.

On his balcony in Cheju, he sometimes felt the poignancy and awe that he must have felt, more than half a century earlier, when from a summer cottage at Clear Lake, Iowa, he wrote to the superior general: "The sunset shows much glory to God." In the evening of his own life, he was determined not to miss the glory of the sunset. Toward death he took his old attitude of "no sweat!" He awaited its coming as he awaited the coming of winter, or the coming of each night, as one more aspect of God's plan.

He spoke often of something his brother Bob said on his death bed. In recalling the many heartaches and headaches suffered in the Philippines, he said, "Sometimes I had so many troubles I thought the world was falling in on me. But now that is all past. All of those difficulties seem as nothing. When you reach this point you see things in a new way."

Harold Henry began seeing things in a new way following his severe heart attacks. That's when he began to learn that it is better to respond than to react. After that he approached life a little more relaxed, working to improve things but never expecting to make them perfect. He no longer acted as though perfection was a possibility. He became resigned to repeating daily, "Let there be light," and then groped as best he could with the amount of illumination allotted for that hour.

He never attained all of the serenity a *yungkam* seeks. Old aggressions and determinations would not go away, but persisted in breaking through. This gives credence to Plutarch's observation that, "Dispositions mold lives in their own fashion."

The biggest change in Harold Henry in the last year of his life was that he became more aware of mystery. He said that reexamining his life for this biography was the greatest spiritual retreat he ever made. It made him aware of how many ordinary men do extraordinary things. Some power must be working through them! He retold the story of the Columbans with fascination, for the first time seeing their work as a conspiracy between God and man to get something done. He was thankful he had been given a role to play in the mystery. He could think of no other life he would rather have lived.

Death came to Archbishop Henry at prayer on the morning of Monday, March 1, 1976 at age sixty-six. He was in his tiny chapel beneath the balcony when the end came quite suddenly. Had he been given a choice of where and how he would die, this would have been the place and the manner of his choosing. Such a death was strangely calm for a man who had feared execution at the hands of the Japanese, had shown heroism in Patton's attack in Germany, had outwitted guerrilla fighters in Korea—and had survived mishaps in the air, typhoons at sea, and blizzards on the mountains.

On the night before his death he had played bridge with Fathers McGann, Quinn, and Crofts. All agreed he was in good form throughout the evening. When the visitors left, he said to Father Crofts that he would say Mass for the Caritas Sisters in the chapel at 8:30 in the morning.

"The next morning I awoke as he let his dog out of his room at 7:30," said Father Crofts. "I said to myself: He is well. Then at very close to 8:30 I heard him going downstairs to the chapel to get ready for Mass. A short time later I heard the dog barking and the girl, Mary, who works in the kitchen, came running up the stairs and rushed into my room saying, 'The Archbishop has falled down!' "

The wild barking of the dog at the chapel door had attracted Mary's attention. She found the archbishop slumped forward on the prie-dieu in front of his chair. He was stretched out on his side before the Blessed Sacrament altar by the time Father Crofts had hurried to the chapel with a tank of oxygen from the archbishop's bedroom. As he lifted him to an upright position, the archbishop gave a gasp and died. Father Crofts gave him absolution and anointed him.

Sister Scholastica arrived and took his blood pressure. It was zero. Paul the janitor carried the archbishop on his back upstairs to the bedroom. The doctor arrived at nine o'clock only to verify what the others already knew.

At 9:20 Father Crofts and three Korean priests concelebrated Mass. Shortly afterward Archbishop Henry, dressed in white vestments, was laid out in the parlor of his house. From that moment forward there was a continual flow of mourners who came to say the prayers for the dead. Everyone was free to come quickly because March 1 is Revolution Day, a state holiday. As one Korean said: "He was considerate even in his dying."

At about midnight the body was placed in a coffin made by John Kim who had built all of the churches on the island. Some women of the city draped the coffin with black and padded the inside with white.

On Tuesday noon the body was brought in procession to his church in Cheju City where Mass was concelebrated by all of his priests with Archbishop Youn from Kwangju as the chief celebrant. From that moment, even through the night vigils, there were always at least thirty or forty Catholics and two priests in the church.

At noon on March 4 the priests of Cheju Island carried the body of Archbishop Harold Henry from Jung Ang Cathedral to Sin Seong schoolyard where Mass was concelebrated by more than a hundred priests including Cardinal Kim, two archbishops, six bishops. The papal Internuncio, the Most Reverend Luigi Dossena, presided.

In the funeral oration Cardinal Kim said: "His life was his sermon. The way he lived was a message to all of us to live a life immersed in love for our fellow man." Several thousand people stood in the schoolyard on the bright sunny afternoon listening to the cardinal tell of some of the things Harold Henry had done for the needy and the lepers. The mourners, from all over the island and the mainland, represented all walks of life. The president of Korea had sent a representative and a floral arrangement.

The funeral cortege began moving toward the east up a hill near the edge of town. It was led by a band and followed by a group of nurses and hundreds of students. Then came the hearse; it was actually an ambulance, and the Columban Sisters had covered it with white flowers before bringing it in from their clinic in Hallim. Behind it walked Cardinal Kim, the apostolic nuncio, and the bishops and priests.

Then came the mourners who by their very number proved that Harold Henry had achieved the *adaptation totale* that the French missionary had recommended to him forty-two years earlier. The procession of 15,000 Koreans, so vast that it brought all traffic to a standstill, stretched for more than a mile with men and women walking six abreast. They proceeded up the hill reciting the rosary and singing hymns all the way to the cemetery three miles outside the city. Again Harold Henry became a pioneer, for he is the first religious to be buried inside those grounds.

When it was over, Father Crofts said: "They buried him as if he were a king, with a mound of earth higher and bigger than the rest. And with a large area in front for the people to gather. Everybody cooperated to make this a fitting tribute to his excellency's forty-two years in Korea. That's because all who met him loved him. All of these honors were given to him not because he was a Catholic archbishop, but because he was himself."